The
Alcoholic
Man

The
Alcoholic
Man

What You Can Learn From The Heroic Journeys of Recovering Alcoholics

Second Edition

Sylvia Cary, M.A., M.F.T.

LOWELL HOUSE

LOS ANGELES

NTC/Contemporary Publishing Group

Library of Congress Cataloging-in-Publication Data

Cary, Sylvia.
   The alcoholic man : what you can learn from the heroic journeys of
recoving alcoholics / Sylvia Cary.
         p.   cm.
   Includes bibliographical references and index.
   ISBN 0-7373-0089-2
   1. Alcoholics—Rehabilitation—United States—Case studies.
2. Alcoholism—United States—Psychological aspects—Case studies. 3.
Self-actualization (Psychology)—Case studies I. Title.
HV5279.C38   1999
362.29'28—dc20   99-5441
                                                         CIP

Published by Lowell House.
A division of NTC/Contemporary Publishing Group, Inc.
4255 West Touhy Avenue, Lincolnwood (Chicago), Illinois 60646-
1975 U.S.A.

Printed in the United States of America
International Standard Book Number: 0-7373-0089-2
99 00 01 02 03 04 RRD 18 17 16 15 14 13 12 11 10 9 8 7 6 5 4 3 2 1

FOR THE HEROES IN MY LIFE

For These Twenty-One Brave Interviewees
With Admiration

For Sponsor Jack
With Appreciation

For The Late Bill W.
With Gratitude

For My Husband, Lance
With Love

CONTENTS

Contents

Contents

FOREWORD

Ten years ago, when I wrote the original Foreword to psychotherapist Sylvia Cary's *The Alcoholic Man*, I was struck by three things: That she was writing about long-term recovery (which others weren't writing about); that she referred to the recovering alcoholic man as a "hero" (certainly not a name anybody else was calling him, especially when he was drinking); and that she was able to look right into the hearts of eighteen recovering alcoholic men and describe from their point of view—based on her interviews with them—what the recovery experience is really like, and how it feels to get sober and stay sober year after year.

Many times, since the first edition of *The Alcoholic Man* came out, I have found myself using it as a tool in my practice as a physician treating addiction. When I have to confront an alcoholic man still in denial, or a man who is making those tentative first steps into sobriety, or the family member who has a stake in the alcoholic's fate, I often give them a copy of *The Alcoholic Man* and say, "Here, this may help you understand what I'm talking about. It explains a lot." Anyone who deals with substance abuse knows that tools like this can be a lifesaver. I'm grateful that Sylvia Cary has written a book that provides me with something that makes my job easier.

The physician's role in working with alcoholics is a tricky one. When you tell a patient he has a heart condition, he hears it as a diagnosis. But, when you tell a patient he has alcoholism or any other drug addiction, he hears it as a put-down or insult. I find I'm always asking myself how I can help this man or woman see the truth. But for alcoholics, especially men between eighteen and forty, it's particularly difficult to ask for help. A guy can be running a company of 5,000 employees and have twelve vice presidents, but it's still hard for him to say, "I can't handle this beer." Usually, he has no idea that *that* is what's behind the fact that his marriage is falling apart, or his job is on the line, or that he is starting to manifest troubling physical symptoms. When I tell him he has to quit whatever is biting him, he's more likely to tell me, "I'm still fine. I go to work every day. I'm healthy. I'm having a good time. It's not hurting anybody else. Why stop?" He's still into blaming: "It's not my fault. *They* are giving me stress—my boss, my wife, my kids, the governor, the president." We laugh at this, but the blaming is always there. As a very wise man in the addiction field, Father John Powell—a learned writer on addiction—once said, "Growing up starts when blaming stops." If the man keeps drinking, the bad things that are already happening will turn into worse things. If an alcoholic becomes a thief and gets shot dead, you can say that it was the bullet that stopped his breathing, but it was the alcohol that ended his life.

The old stigma about being an alcoholic or addict has lessened, which is good, because people seek treatment sooner if they don't feel ashamed. Today, more people seem to know more about alcoholism and drug addiction than ever before. Books, movies, articles, and television shows about the subject have helped the public shed their dated stereotypes about these illnesses. That's encouraging. What is *dis*couraging, however, is the possibility that this lessening of stigma has encouraged more women (hardest hit by stigma) to drink. Statistics show that women have been doing a prodigious job of narrowing the gap between themselves and their male counterparts. What is also *dis*couraging is the fact that there are still too many physicians who are in the dark ages when it comes to recognizing addiction. Many have the mindset that drinking or drug use is merely a *symptom* of another illness, not an illness itself. I find this a shame. If I could have my way, I'd recommend that all physicians go to at least thirty meetings of Alcoholics Anonymous, or one of its offshoots, so they can learn what addiction looks like in all its diverse forms and thereby do a better job of diagnosing and treating it.

I am delighted that Sylvia Cary has added three new recovery stories to this updated version of her book. Short of going to a real AA meeting and hearing recovering alcoholic men share their stories in person, at least by reading these stories, readers can get a sense of what alcoholics go through when they leave their addictive behavior behind and enter the new world of twenty-four hours-a-day sobriety.

We still don't know what causes alcoholism and we still don't have a cure. These facts haven't changed in the ten years since this book first came out. But we're slowly closing the gap from cause to cure. Some remarkable studies are being done in the areas of brain chemistry and genetic involvement in addiction. And there are some promising new medications to cut down on the phenomenon of craving. However, until the day comes when we can give a man an addiction-busting pill, or science can find a way to manipulate his genes and chromosomes and make him immune to addiction, we're stuck with the same old ways of diagnosing and treating addiction that we've been using for years.

When people ask me what the cure rate is for the addicted population, or for a specific treatment or twelve-step group, I have to admit I haven't the foggiest idea. To date, nobody knows for sure just how many of the estimated 11 million alcoholics, 1.5 million cocaine and crack users, 810,000 heroin addicts (and this number is fast growing), 800,000 amphetamine users, and 10 million marijuana users that try to stop using each year and how many make it.* We only have "guesstimates." The National Institute of Alcohol Abuse and Alcoholism (NIAAA) states that roughly 50 percent of the people who try to get well relapse within the first few months. By the end of one year the figure is even higher. The Betty Ford Center, which strongly emphasizes the importance of following in-patient treatment with aftercare and AA, considers it impressive that even one-third of their many thousands of alumni stay active and in touch. This doesn't necessarily prove that they are sober, but it's a good indication. In AA, a 90 percent dropout rate by the end of the first year is a figure that's been floating around for years. This isn't as dismal as it sounds, because many who drop out try again and make it the next time.

When it comes to comparing AA with other kinds of treatment, I have been pleased to see that studies such as the NIAAA's *Match Study*, which compared AA with two other major treatment approaches (cognitive behavioral therapy and motivational enhancement therapy), concluded that twelve-step programs are just as effective as other excellent treatments, even those that cost money. (AA, of course, is free.) So, all those academic types out there who still like to dismiss AA because it doesn't have a scientific base, should pay attention to what physicians like myself have known for years: Overall, AA—even though it doesn't work for everybody—is still the best deal in town. That's why we keep referring our patients to AA. And, when AA is combined with other treatments, it's even better. That makes the recovery statistics go way up.

As readers will see, a number of the recovering men interviewed in Cary's book consider AA their main treatment, but

*Statistics from NIAAA, the National Clearinghouse for Alcohol and Drug Information, SAMHAS, and Time magazine, May 5, 1997.

augment it with other things—counseling, group therapy, exercise, special diets, and meditation. On the other hand, there are studies that show AA participation is critical to the mix. One such study by Lt. General Barry McCaffrey, head of the office on National Drug Control Policy, involved at least one thousand subjects, and that reported in the *Journal of the American Medical Association* (*JAMA*) in August of 1998. It pointed out that if recovering alcoholics *don't* keep up with their 12-step work, they can end up in trouble. AA is for life.

Currently, I think the biggest threat to the treatment of alcoholics and addicts is the health care delivery system. Health Maintenance Organizations (HMOs) and the like often don't allow people to get the help they need. Many chemical dependency units have closed. Alcoholic and addiction patients are only in the hospital for a one to three day detox, and then they're out—basically left to fend for themselves. There's none of that bonding with other alcoholics that goes on in the longer term treatment centers that is so important.

Other chemical dependency treatment centers have been combined with psychiatric ("dual diagnosis") units, but instead of being run by recovering alcoholics with the credential of having "been there" themselves, they are run by psychiatrists with their pens blazing, writing out unnecessary prescriptions. I think psychiatrists should keep their hands *off* newly sober alcoholics, and not rush to give them pills until the alcoholics have been clean and sober for at least four to eight weeks or more so that the physician can see what the man is really like without any chemicals. After the guy has been sober a while and good histories have been taken, if his depression or his mood swings still won't quit, *then* medication can be considered. But first you need to see what you've got.

One of my ongoing complaints about *some* (not all) AA members is that they are not educating themselves about the kinds of medications being used today. A man who has been taking a tranquilizer, like Xanax or Valium, cannot safely stop cold turkey without some medical help. Even stopping alcohol can be dangerous for some individuals. They can have convulsions. But sometimes newly sober men speak in AA meetings about being weaned off their medications. Even though the physician has carefully instructed them on how to cut down step-by-step, they are sometimes told to "just stop" by an AA member who doesn't realize that this advice could do great harm.

It's hard for me to believe that I've put in yet another decade of working in the addiction field since the first edition of *The Alcoholic Man*. I look at all the changes—and there have been many—but what I'm most struck by is the fact that there are two areas in which I haven't changed my views one iota. I am still confident: 1) that alcoholism truly *is* a disease; and 2) that for effective treatment to take place total abstinence is an essential requirement.

I know there are people walking around who want to fight the disease concept. I'm afraid this debate will still be raging in the year 3,000. But, after having spent over thirty-five years of my life treating or dealing with alcoholics and addicts of every stripe, I see chemical dependency as a disease like any other. It has a beginning, a middle, and an end. It has a diagnosis and a prognosis. It has symptoms; it can be replicated; it is chronic; it progresses over time; patients can relapse; there's the withdrawal phenomenon; and if it is not treated, it ends in death. *That's* a disease.

So, I find myself impatient with those who not only say alcoholism isn't a disease, but offer *controlled abstinence* or *harm reduction* instead of abstinence as a solution. This is another reason why I appreciate Sylvia Cary's book; she has chosen only those men who define sobriety as "total abstinence from mood-altering chemicals." Therefore, when a man states that he has sixty days of sobriety or seven years of sobriety, he means *continuous total abstinence* from chemicals. This way, readers will know that when the word *sobriety* is used, everybody is on the same page. The only exceptions to this are people who have legitimate reasons to take medications—schizophrenics, people with bipolar disorders, biochemical depression, and the like.

This is so cliché that I'm almost apologetic about saying it, but it's still true: The earlier a man faces the truth about his addiction, the less it will cost him in every area of his life (including financially), and the better his chances will be of having a rewarding recovery.

If every alcoholic and addict would just be willing to say, "I've got a problem. Where can I get help?" they'd be doing a lot to put addiction professionals like me out of business. Just think how much money (not to mention time) could be saved in this country if we didn't need all those MDs, all those anticraving medications, all those hospital detox units, all those treatment centers, all those surgeries on bad livers, and all those divorce courts or jails.

If we can judge anything by the twenty-one recovery-under-fire stories in this book, then it's safe to say that as we head into the new millennium, the candle of hope is burning a little more brightly for *The Alcoholic Man.*

Who knows, with all the research going on, maybe one of these days there *will* be a pill that a man can take to knock out his alcoholism.

But then another interesting question arises, a question which AA members really enjoy asking each other as a kind of philosophical exercise: "If science came up with a pill to cure alcoholism right now, would you take it?"

For Sylvia Cary, that will have to be the subject of another book.

–JOKICHI TAKAMINE, M.D.
Past Chairman, American Medical Association Task Force on Alcoholism;
Member, American Medical Association
Task Force on Drugs

PREFACE

Who hath woe?
Who hath sorrow?
Who hath contentions?
Who hath babbling?
Who hath wounds without cause?
Who had redness of eyes?
They that tarry at the wine;
They that go to seek mixed wine . . .
At the last it biteth like a serpent,
And stingeth like an adder.

—*The Holy Bible, Proverbs Chapter 23: 29–32*

A lot of booze has passed under the bridge since the first edition of *The Alcoholic Man* nearly a decade ago. They keep on making the stuff, and men keep on drinking the stuff.

Looking at the figures, you'd think little has changed in ten years. There are as many alcoholics now as there were ten years ago; there are as many alcohol-related deaths now as there were then (100,000 a year); and, of the 10 percent of alcoholics who attempt to quit each year, still only one in ten of *those* succeed. The rest slip and have to try again later—or not at all. So many alcoholics; so little success at treating them.

Does it mean we should throw our hands up and forget about trying to get alcoholics to stop? No, because that one person in ten who tries to get sober and makes it has an impact on the rest of us. Like the proverbial pebble in the pond, when Jake Jones cleans up his act, his sobriety spreads out to dozens of others in his sphere, and they are all the better for it. At any given time, there are over two million sober people in Alcoholics Anonymous (AA), the oldest and largest self-help group in the world—meaning that millions of *other* people are being touched by it—people in every profession, in every town, in over 160 other countries. This is a very good thing.

The "Hero" Word Revisited

After the first edition of *The Alcoholic Man: What You Can Learn From the Heroic Journeys of Recovering Alcoholics* was published, some critics were uncomfortable about the idea of calling sober drunks "heroes." After all, when they're out there drinking, they are anything *but*. They are maddening. They are horrific, not heroic. But my point then (and now) is that once such men get sober and start cleaning up their acts, amazing things begin to happen. Many actually become men of *character*.

A decade ago, words like *character, integrity, honesty, responsibility, reliability, courage,* and *dependability* weren't being bandied about much. This kind of vocabulary was considered archaic and somewhat embarrassing. But, thanks to a national resurgence of interest in spirituality in the 1990s (resulting in mega best-sellers for the publishing industry), and thanks to the phenomenon of the Clinton scandal (which dominated the media during the waning days of the decade), public discussion about these "archaic" concepts was suddenly heard on every TV talk show: What makes up character? What is virtue? What is a hero? Why are heroes important?

Now, the notion that recovering alcoholic men can transform themselves into "heroes"—can actually learn to acquire the skills and do what it takes to become men of character—no longer seems like a stretch. Now I feel somewhat vindicated; I think my decision to use the "hero" word in this book was the right one. In truth, if the recovering alcoholic man *doesn't* learn how to become a hero, his chances of staying sober are slim to none. Dishonesty, irresponsibility, lack of integrity, and resentment are all those other *un*heroic traits that will make him drink again.

Recovery Over Time

One reason I wrote *The Alcoholic Man* was because I saw a need for a book that dealt with *long-term* sobriety. I noticed that most of the books published focused on how to *get* sober and how to survive those first few years, but none talked about how to deal with being sober *over time*. It's as if people assume that once a man is sober, that's it; nothing else changes; let's move on to the next case. However, as I point out in the *Introduction*, that's not true. The process of recovery, of transformation from jerk to hero, is ever-evolving. Each year of sobriety is different from the year before, often (as we'll see here) in predictable ways.

In preparation for this revision, I logged on to an Internet bookstore (something I couldn't have done a decade ago), input the search term "alcoholism," and came up with a list of 1,500 books on the subject—a staggering number compared to the mere handful of books available when I entered the addiction field more than twenty-five years ago. However, a quick perusal of many of the titles on this long list showed me that there *still* isn't much available on sobriety over the long haul. So, once again, answering the old question: *"I'm clean and sober, now what?"* is what this book is all about.

What's Different in the Addiction Field?

While many things (like the statistics about abuse and recovery) have stayed the same, there is also a lot that has changed in the addiction field. Here's a list of just some of these changes. I haven't listed them according to importance, nor have I commented on which of these items is "good" and which is "bad." I've just jotted down the items for your interest. If you're trying to quit drinking, or if you're already sober and trying to stay that way, here are some of the things you're going to run into. You can judge for yourself which might help your progress, and which might hinder it:

- huge increase in the availability of information on addiction, especially on-line.
- less stigma about being an alcoholic or addict.
- shorter "denial" phase.
- earlier diagnosis of addiction (raising the alcoholic's "bottom").
- earlier willingness to accept the diagnosis of addiction.
- more research into the genetics of addiction.
- more research into brain chemistry and addiction.
- more medical and mental health professionals specializing in addiction.
- less focus on psychological causes ("stress," "unhappy childhood," etc.).
- more focus on *action* therapy—i.e., what to *do* about it.

- fewer long-term (three weeks plus) in-patient treatment programs.
- more short-term or out-patient treatment resources.
- impact of HMOs on addiction treatment.
- impact of insurance companies who refuse to pay for addiction treatment.
- more detox-only hospital stays.
- world-wide growth of twelve-step recovery groups.
- growth of other treatment approaches.
- new medications to lessen craving.
- new medications to lessen the discomfort of withdrawal.
- fewer deaths during withdrawal stage.
- ongoing debate over whether or not alcoholism is a "disease."
- ongoing debate over whether or not "total abstinence" is the "cure."
- ongoing debate over the use of medication in sobriety.
- ongoing debate over the very definition of "sobriety."
- stricter laws (drunk driving, drug sales, etc.).
- increased tabloidization of addiction treatment (e.g., celebrities going to Betty Ford Center and AA and speaking out).
- ongoing impact of the relationship between addiction and HIV/AIDS.
- increased awareness of dual addictions (e.g., alcoholism *and* gambling, sex).
- increased awareness of dual diagnoses (e.g., alcoholism *and* depression, bipolar).
- decreased availability of structured intervention programs.
- less loyalty to AA; more loyalty to treatment program.
- tendency of those in recovery to augment AA with other treatment.

What's Different in This Edition?

Happily, I was once again able to get my colleague, Jokichi Takamine, M.D., physician and past chairman of the AMA's Task Force on Alcoholism, to update the Foreword he wrote for this book ten years ago. He has kept up with the latest happenings in all the important areas, such as addiction research, medications, and treatment, so his input is especially valuable.

I also re-interviewed Sponsor Jack, a man who now has twenty-eight years of AA sobriety under his belt, and still sponsors (mentors) dozens of AA men at a time, not just those who are newly sober, but those with long-term sobriety as well. Once again, Sponsor Jack's comments are a great asset. Since I'm a woman, I felt it was important to check out my material with a man, a recovering alcoholic man, who really knows this subject from personal experience.

In addition to a new Foreword, and this new Preface, there's another new chapter, the Introduction: Toward a New Kind of Hero. Here's where I handle the basics. I use a lot of terms in this book (hero, addiction, alcoholism, abstinence, sobriety), and you may assume that you know what these words mean, but don't count on it. I define many of them in specific ways. "Alcoholism," for example, means drinking and/or drugging—not *just* drinking. That's important to know. So I strongly recommend that you read this chapter. Here's where I'll also tell you a little about the twenty-one recovering (three new ones are included) men I interviewed, explain why all twenty-one of them are from Alcoholics Anonymous, give you a little AA history, throw in some tips to the wives, lovers, and others on how to deal with a man in recovery, and talk about a topic dear to my heart—*Spontaneous Remission*. There really *is* such a thing as spontaneous remission from addiction, and I want to tell you about it—because it's an important subject that you rarely hear discussed.

The new Chapter 1: Can An Alcoholic Change His Spots? is now devoted to three brand-new interviews with recovering alcoholic men (Jim, Jason, and Brian) who were still out there drinking or using when the first edition of this book came out. Now *they* are sober. Each of these three men illustrates some important points. The first man, Jim, is a good example of what we still think of as the classic "pure" alcoholic—a man who drank alcohol but didn't take drugs, then hit bottom, and finally dragged himself into AA without stopping off at a treatment center first. The second man, Jason, is more typical of the late 90s-going-into-2000 entry into AA, a man who did drugs more than he drank alcohol, got sober while still young and functional, and walked into AA after a month at an expensive treatment center. The third man, Brian, is a man who found AA the hard way—in prison.

In addition to introducing you to these three new men in Chapter 1, I'll also discuss two topics of great interest to men in early sobriety: Sex and Work. Lots of men have had their sex lives wrecked by drinking or using. Now they want to know: Is there sex after sobriety? Work is especially worrisome for men whose livelihood is dependent upon their ability to be "creative." Men who write or paint or compose or sculpt for a living fear their creative muse will evaporate if they stop drinking or using. We'll take a look at this, too.

I've also revised the Epilogue. It now contains some thoughts on AA's survivability, some additional thoughts on AA as a tribe or herd, a discussion of the alcoholic man after 2000, and an expanded discussion of what AA men need to know about character in order to help insure their sobriety.

In addition, I've added an Appendix A which includes a 15-question Generic Addiction Quiz for those who still aren't sure if they're addicted to alcohol or drugs, or if they suspect some other addiction and want to check it out. Appendix B a list of Seven

Steps to Trigger a Spontaneous Remission. Appendix C is a list of tips on How To Upgrade Your Character.

Failed Follow-Ups

Even though *The Alcoholic Man* was never supposed to be a scientific study of recovery, merely an anecdotal one, when I set out to do this revision I still thought it might be interesting to contact the eighteen original interviewees to see what's been going on with them over the last ten years. I did learn that three of the eighteen men had died. I went to the funeral of one of them (Arthur) who died of a heart attack. He died sober. That's very important to AA people, by the way—dying sober. It's the first question you hear: *Did he die sober?* Via the AA grapevine I also found out that Phil (the second to last interview in the book) had died—sober. The third death is one I haven't been able to confirm, so I'm not going to pinpoint who it is.

Following up on the remaining fifteen men turned out to be trickier than I had anticipated. Even though I knew where to find many of those who'd been sober a long time, I couldn't track down the men who were in early sobriety at the time I interviewed them. I tried local phone books, local contacts, even tried the Internet, but these searches proved fruitless. I gave up. However, *statistically* I know that chances are that half to two-thirds of them drank or used again. Numbers like that just go with the territory.

Finally, to make this revised edition of *The Alcoholic Man* even more user-friendly, I've added a brief summary of each man's story in the Table of Contents. There's a reason for this. In twelve-step recovery groups, it is said that sooner or later you'll "hear your own story" from somebody else at a meeting. When that happens, it often helps the new man commit to his recovery. Identification can do wonders. So if you are picking up this book for yourself, or for someone else, scan the summaries first to see which one is most like your own. Then, if that story doesn't do it for you, move on to the others. Now let's move on to the Introduction: Toward a New Kind of Hero for some of those all-important basics.

INTRODUCTION

TOWARD A NEW KIND OF HERO

I count him braver who overcomes his desires than him who
conquers his enemies; for the hardest victory is over self.
                                        —*Aristotle* (B.C. *384–322*)

He is sensitive, yet strong. He is sexy, yet faithful. He is serious, yet playful. He is courageous, yet gentle. He is responsible, honest, loyal, nonjudgmental, and creative. He knows who he is, and he is comfortable with all kinds of people of all ages. He exemplifies the work ethic.

He persists where others give up. He is a man of his word, he keeps his commitments and promises. He doesn't drink or take drugs. On top of all this, he knows how to love. Who is this hero I'm describing?

He's the recovering alcoholic man.

At first glance, the terms "alcoholic" and "hero" don't seem to go together. How can an alcoholic be a hero? The hero, in myth and legend at least, is a man of great strength and courage; a man we admire not only for his heroic sentiments, but for his heroic actions. The practicing alcoholic is hardly that. He is more anti-hero

1

than hero. He is the kind of scoundrel you hide your daughters from, the man who lies, who steals things, who bashes up cars, who cheats on his woman, who beats up on his kids, who avoids responsibility, who shatters trust and destroys relationships, who ends up being despised. Obviously, no man who is still out there doing any of these things is likely to be thought of as a hero. He starts looking like a hero only when he stops.

This book is about twenty-one alcoholic men, anti-heroes all, who became, or are in the process of becoming, heroic. They are men who have stopped practicing their destructive drinking and drugging, and have *stayed* stopped. One of the men we'll be meeting has been sober for over forty-three years.

Clean and Sober and *Then* What?

Because there are so many people who still need to get sober, we tend to pay more attention to them than we do to the two million people who already *are* sober, and have so much to teach us about what it's really like. It's as though once the afflicted man is out of the woods, we breathe a sigh of relief and go on to the next case. Maybe that's one of the reasons why so little is written about *recovery over time*. It's simply not dealt with. Most of the existing literature only deals with the early stages of recovery—just the first few years—the assumption is that after this phase, all recovery looks alike.

But all recovery *doesn't* look alike. The ongoing process of transforming a drunk into a hero goes on over a long period of time. Based on the examples of the millions of men who've gone on before him, different phases occur at fairly unpredictable times.

The age at which a man starts drinking or using drugs is important. Whenever mood-altering chemicals (and alcohol is one of them) enter the picture, it throws the normal maturation process out of whack, and pushes the man into a kind of developmental time warp from which, like Rip Van Winkle, he may not awaken until he finds sobriety. Then, he's got to play catch-up. That's why, during the first ten years of a man's sobriety, his sobriety age is more important than his chronological age. If he started drinking young, he's got to learn how to grow up, how to talk to girls, how to be responsible on the job, how to be honest—how to stop being a child. It takes him awhile to be on a par with other men his own age who have never been sidetracked by addiction.

However, as we'll see in the cases of the twenty-one recovering alcoholic men we're about to meet, once they get clean and sober, they not only catch up, but start pulling ahead of their non-alcoholic contemporaries. Some even become heroes.

In normal development, the most dramatic changes happen in infancy and early childhood. It's the same in the early stages of sobriety. Somebody with six months of sobriety is light years away from where he was at just thirty days. On the other hand, a man who has been sober for twenty years isn't all that different from a person who's been sober for twenty-five years, and more like other men his own age. He's caught up.

In the beginning, it's easy to generalize: "All newcomers are crazy." Later on, it's impossible because the man has become uniquely "himself." He has become the man he was on his way to becoming when his journey was so rudely interrupted by his addiction.

The Long Haul

So, what *is* the recovering alcoholic's journey really like over the long haul? What has he gotten himself into? Can a man *really* change? (Many remain skeptical.) What stages will he go through? What will happen in those two most important areas that Freud called "love and work?" Will his finances get straightened out? Will he regain his kids respect? Will "broken fences" be mended? What are the stumbling blocks, booby traps, and pitfalls along the way to achieving one's "long-term" status? Is it okay to go to bars? What are the signs of an impending relapse or "slip"? How will the recovering man ever learn to handle the crises of every-day life—the fears, losses, illnesses, and deaths—without resorting to his old ways of handling such events: Drinking or using? And the wives, lovers, and others want to know: Is he worth waiting for? Or is he a lost cause?

For those who have a stake in an alcoholic's sobriety, getting good answers to these questions may help them decide whether or not they want to hang in and wait for him to become more herolike. For the alcoholic himself, getting good answers to these questions may mean the difference between deciding to stay sober or going back to chemical addiction.

Hopefully, the answers in this book will encourage all to hang in.

Gentlemen, Choose Your Definitions

One of my favorite descriptions of addiction (because it really nails what it *feels* like to be addicted) comes from a book called *The Craving Brain: The BioBalance Approach to Controlling Addiction* by Ronald A. Ruden, M.D., Ph.D., with Marcia Byalick. (HarperCollins Publishers, 1997). The book begins: "'*Gotta have it*' *is the driving thought of an addict. 'Gotta have it.' A drink, a drag, a hit, a line, a pill, another piece of chocolate. 'Gotta have it.' Getting it is all that matters."*

I don't know anybody who's addicted to anything who can't identify with this!

And it's only one of many definitions of addiction. There are probably hundreds. Take your pick. In the end, you have to choose the one or two that are the easiest for you to identify with and remember. When I'm seeing patients who are still on the cusp of denial (saying, in effect, "I don't want to know"), I toss out three or four favorite definitions just to see if one of them rings a bell. Here's a run-down of the most common ones.

The American Medical Association's (AMA) definition

Even though a famous surgeon general, Dr. Benjamin Rush, referred to alcoholism as a disease way back in the 1700s, no one really listened. Most hung onto the notion that it's a moral or willpower issue. Then, in 1956, the American Medical Association became the first official group to label alcoholism a "disease" (meaning it has symptoms, a progressive course, and will end in death if not treated). It does *not* mean that there's an alcoholism "germ," or that alcoholism can be seen under a microscope. While today the disease theory is widely accepted, it's still something people like to fight about—and do.

The Alcoholics Anonymous (AA) definition

Back in 1935, AA described alcoholism as "an allergy of the body combined with an obsession of the mind." Judging by the recent genetic and brain chemistry studies, there's an amazing amount of truth in this.

Umbrella definition of Alcoholism

When laymen say "alcoholic," they usually mean somebody who drinks too much alcohol. When people in the addiction field say "alcoholic," they usually mean somebody who either drinks too much alcohol or uses too many mood-altering chemicals. Or both. It's an umbrella term that covers it all.

Standard definition of addiction

Here's a three-fold, more formal-sounding definition of addiction: Addiction is characterized by *a) an obsession with, and a craving for, a specific substance or behavior; b) a loss of control over that substance or behavior, and c) the continued use/abuse of that substance or behavior, despite outside circumstances and negative consequences.* According to Jokichi Takamine, M.D., the physician who wrote the Foreword to this book, "It's as if you had an allergic reaction to penicillin, and then couldn't wait to go take it again!"

A handy little formula: "Alcohol + Problems = Alcoholism"

Here's what it means: If drinking alcohol or taking a drug is interfering in any negative way with *any* life area (work, family, emotional, social, legal, health, financial, creative, spiritual), and yet the person keeps on drinking or using even after he's aware of this, then it's alcoholism. For example, if a man loses a job, gets a divorce, feels depressed, loses friends, gets a drunk driving arrest, has financial problems, lets his talents slide, feels cynical about his life's purpose, and so on, and it's related either directly or indirectly to the use of alcohol or drugs, it's addiction.

The Diagnostic and Statistical Manual, Version IV definition (DSM-IV)

In the updated version of the *Diagnostic and Statistical Manual of Mental Disorders (DSM-IV)*, published by the American Psychiatric Association, and used by all the mental health professions, the term "alcoholism" isn't even listed. Instead, the DSM-IV lists differences between "alcohol abuse" and "alcohol dependence." *Abuse* isn't considered as serious as *dependence*. You have to have more of the criteria to be "dependent" than you do for an "abuse" diagnosis.

The "Is somebody else complaining" definition

If somebody (a spouse, parent, child, lover, friend, neighbor, boss, or cop) is complaining about a man's drinking or drug use, it's probably alcoholism. People don't complain about things that aren't problems.

Most people think that once the alcoholic stops drinking alcohol, no more alcoholism. Not so. In recovery circles, you're still labeled an alcoholic even if you haven't had a drink or any other mind-altering chemical for fifty years. An alcoholic is an alcoholic for life, just as the diabetic is a diabetic for life. Abstinence from alcohol or drugs, like abstinence from sugar, halts the progression but doesn't cure the disease. To date, there *is* no cure for addiction, nothing that takes it away and enables a man to drink again normally.

In alcoholism treatment, when you remove the alcohol, some like to say that what you're left with is the "ism," the psychological part of the illness. It's this part that's healed by the man's active participation in an ongoing (for life) treatment situation.

What's "Sobriety"?

Just as the definition of alcoholism has expanded, so, too, has the definition of sobriety expanded—from "freedom from alcohol" (which is still AA's official definition) to freedom from alcohol *and* all mood-altering chemicals. In some sections of the country and in some other countries, the definition of sobriety is looser; mood-altering drugs like marijuana and tranquilizers aren't included.

But this is changing as people understand that a drug is a drug is a drug, whether it's alcohol or something else. If it's mood-altering, it has got to go.

Many newly sober men don't like this expanded definition of sobriety and argue with it. But experience in the recovery field has taught us that most alcoholics and addicts cannot handle chemicals. If they stop taking one, they'll just pick up another and get hooked on that. Quitting all of it is what works the best. It's getting rid of all the potential triggers.

In this book, when I speak of an alcoholic, I'm talking about somebody who is addicted to *any* mind-altering chemical. And when I speak of sobriety, I'm speaking of somebody who doesn't put any mood-altering substances into his body for any reason— "no matter what" (as AA puts it). The only exceptions to this are cases where people need medications for operations, dental procedures, legitimate pain, or for serious psychological disorders, such as genetic depression, bipolar disorders, or psychosis.

Length of Sobriety

This is a status symbol in Alcoholics Anonymous. People are proud of how much time they have, and are given respect for it. Sober time, of course, means *continuous* abstinence, not abstinence interrupted by a few slips here and there. If a man takes even one swallow or pill or puff on purpose, it's a "slip," and he loses his time and has to start all over again.

Sobriety is like a marathon race: Many start off, but only a handful finish. Even among those who make it, most didn't make it on the first try. Even after years of sobriety, slips can happen.

For example, we'll meet a man, Chuck, who drank after he'd been sober for *thirty* years. As awful as slips are, sometimes they can serve a cleansing function. With Chuck, it forced him to deal with the grief-work over the death of his wife, something he'd been avoiding. Chuck was lucky. He managed to get back to the program and start again. After once having thirty years, he now has ninety days.

Who Are The Men?

This is not a scientific study. This book is based on twenty-one interviews with recovering alcoholic men who are at different stages of their sobriety, from thirty *days* up to forty-three *years*. In addition, I interviewed Los Angeles psychiatrist, Paul Grossman, M.D., a man who works with alcoholics, but is not one himself, and an AA "sponsor" (a kind of mentor or guide), Sponsor Jack; as mentioned in the Preface, Sponsor Jack had been sober for eighteen years at the time of the initial interview, and is now twenty-eight years sober. I picked Sponsor Jack because, over the years, he has sponsored many men at many different stages of sobriety, so I thought he'd have some good input. He did. At the beginning of each chapter, I'll begin talking about a particular stage of sobriety, and then we'll go on to meet the man (or men) who represents that stage, keeping in mind that not every man is a perfect "fit" for the stage he's in.

Local Talent

Because I live in Los Angeles, I interviewed local talent, all men (with the exception of one from Seattle) who are currently living in the Southern California area. Ironically, it turned out that most of the men I interviewed were born and brought up someplace else, which tells you something about the transient nature of Southern California. It's actually a very good cross section of

America. The men represent California, Colorado, Virginia, Nebraska, New Jersey, New York, Massachusetts, Texas, Maryland, Washington, Kansas, Canada, and Scotland. Some of the men were first introduced to Alcoholics Anonymous someplace else. For example, our seven-year man, John, began his AA life back in Scotland and continued in AA when he arrived in America.

The lengths of sobriety represented here are thirty days, sixty days, ninety days, four months, one year, two years, three years, four years, five years, seven years, ten years, fifteen years, twenty years, twenty-two years, thirty years, thirty-five years, forty-one years, and, finally, forty-three years of sobriety. The age-range of the men is seventeen to seventy-seven years. The seventeen year old, Tim, has four years of sobriety, which means he got sober at the tender age of thirteen. This is happening more and more. AA is exploding with youth, women, and minorities. And even though, at only seventeen, Tim's immaturity is still obvious, now that he has been in the AA "greenhouse" for four years, in some ways he has shot way past many of his non-alcoholic peers.

The twenty-one men include one black (Walter, with twenty-two years), and two men with twin brothers who also have joined AA. (Dean, twenty-two years sober is an identical twin; while Mark, sixty days sober, is a fraternal twin.)

Different religions are represented: Catholic, Protestant, Greek Orthodox, Jewish, Baptist, and even a convert to Buddhism. Various marital and socioeconomic states are also represented (often in the life of just one recovering alcoholic man). Finally, some men choose to use their real first names, and some, like "Charlie Brown" in Chapter 5, felt it might be uncomfortable or even dangerous to be identified in any way. No last names were used to honor AA's tradition of anonymity at a public level. This is not so much to protect the man from exposure as a member of

AA as it is to protect AA from the individual member who may prematurely announce his "cure" to the world and then go and fall on his face. This kind of thing isn't very inspiring to others.

History of AA 101

Alcoholics Anonymous has had a tremendous impact around the world. Many call AA one of the great social influences of the twentieth century. It all started in 1935 in Akron, Ohio, when two hopeless drunks—a New York stockbroker named Bill Wilson, and an Ohio surgeon named Dr. Bob Smith—eyeballed each other over a kitchen table and talked about their mutual problem. In so doing, they accidentally stumbled upon the secret of recovery—the phenomenon of "one drunk talking to another." These two men, now sober, turned around and talked to others—and those men talked to others. And at the end of a year, there were one hundred alcoholics who no longer drank. And then these men talked to others—and so it went. Today, there are two million sober AA members in 162 countries.

Before AA, there was pitifully little treatment for alcoholism, other than evangelical groups, drying out hospitals, sanitoriums, and funny farms. The diagnosis of alcoholism was like a death sentence. Over the centuries, all kinds of theories have been put forth to explain it. A man became an alcoholic because he was immoral; he had no willpower; he was psychologically sick; he grew up in a poor neighborhood; he was stressed out; he was genetically impaired; he was biochemically imbalanced; and so on. Some of the so-called cures for alcoholism have been horrendous: Flogging, the pillory, boiling in oil, drunk tanks, shunning, four-point restraints, and mental hospitals. And since alcoholism has always had a ferocious stigma attached to it, anyone who *was* one was an outcast. It hasn't been called "the disease of loneliness" for nothing.

Because some of the older men interviewed in this book actually knew AA's cofounders (Dr. Bob Smith died in 1952 and Bill Wilson in 1971), they have found themselves in the unique role of being cast as disciples of these two remarkable men, and encouraged to share their memories of them with others. As it turns out, four of our twenty-one interviewees knew the cofounders personally, so some of their recollections are included here—not just for their pertinence to our topic of long-term recovery, but also for their historical value.

Why Only AA?

All twenty-one men interviewed for this book are involved in Alcoholics Anonymous or one of its many spin-offs.

Of course, Alcoholics Anonymous isn't the only way to get sober and stay sober. Nor is it the only training ground for heroes. The truth is, anybody who stops drinking has a chance to turn his life around. But men who are involved with a twelve-step program seem to have more fun, get more done, and get it done faster. That's because, for alcoholics, AA functions like a *greenhouse* for plants. The structure of AA, its twelve-steps, its traditions, and the fact that much of the treatment happens in a group setting utilizing the support of other people, all seem to speed things up. Great changes happen quickly. Here, a man can become a hero in record time.

One example of a *non*-AA recovery is the alcoholic psychiatrist I wrote about in the first edition (and have also included here) who's been sober for eleven years. He told me, almost proudly: "I haven't changed one bit since I got sober. The only two changes in my life are: I don't drink alcohol, and I don't go to places where alcohol is served." That's all well and good, but when you read about the psychologist, Barry, in Chapter 10, a man who's been sober ten years, you'll see all the positive changes he has made in the same amount of time. He makes it look as though maybe the psychiatrist is missing something. AA calls this kind of sobriety "white-knuckle sobriety" or "biting the bullet sobriety." It's not considered much fun. And it's really hard to keep up one's motivation day after month after year.

There are two other reasons for picking men out of the AA greenhouse for this book:

1. They are easy to find, and most are eager to talk and pass on what they know.
2. Their definitions of important terms like "alcoholic," "sobriety," and "relapse" are consistent, so there's not much chance of confusion. "Sober" means the same thing to all of them.

So, while *The Alcoholic Man* isn't a book *about* AA, it definitely is a book that's set against an AA backdrop, and it's obvious that I make a case for AA. It's my view that for any man who wants to get sober and stay that way, and wants to become a hero in the process, AA is his best bet. It's available all over the world. It's free. And there are no strings attached.

For Wives, Lovers, and Others

Alcoholics who are still drinking are maddening. In some cases, they are frightening. And each one of them has somebody, somewhere, who has a stake in his fate—a wife, a girlfriend, a lover, a neighbor, a boss, an employer, a child, a best friend, a doctor, a parent. And they all have questions of their own: Will he make it?

If he does, will I still care? How will his sobriety affect our relationship? Do I want to hang around long enough to find out?

Sobriety isn't always good news for relationships, especially in the beginning. (See more about this in chapter 2). For those who assume that everything is going to be great once that man gets sober, this is a shock. Maybe a little advance warning can help to soften the blow.

Jealousy is one problem. A guy sobers up. Now, instead of being conked out on the couch, he's at AA meetings every night. He's never home. He's got new friends, new influences. Pretty women at meetings are giving him hugs, unaware of what a jerk he's been for the last decade. Worse, AA strangers start calling him up, asking him for his opinion about things, and he's actually giving it to them—*he* who had his face in a bowl of chili only a month ago. This is not how it was supposed to be.

Sooner or later, however, if the wife/lover/other is patient, that toad may actually begin turning into that prince she's been hoping for. But there's no guarantee, and it won't be overnight. *Five years* is the ballpark figure, the length of time it usually takes for the toad-to-prince thing to happen. *Five years* for a druggie or a drunk to finally grow up and start thinking of somebody other than himself for a change; *five years* for him to start getting his act together and begin using those communication skills he's supposed to be learning. Are you willing to wait five years?

Addiction is progressive and catching. It gets worse over time, and hurts everybody. Recovery is also progressive and catching. It gets better over time, and helps everybody. Anyone choosing to stick it out with a recovering alcoholic man is probably in for some nice surprises, as well as some disappointments. Good things can begin happening right off the bat, even though the journey itself still takes years. Sponsor Jack's wife tells the story of how the two of them went to a party only weeks after Jack got sober. She was astounded to see what a nice, funny guy he was when he wasn't drunk and insulting people. The other party guests really liked him. She hadn't seen *that* side of Jack in years. She'd forgotten all about it. But obviously, under his alcoholic disguise, there had been a hero screaming to get out. Sobriety was his chance.

The Treatment Mystique

People who have alcoholics in their lives feel they should *do* something about it, and often the only solution they can think of is, "Get him into *treatment*."

There's a mystique about this word, as if there's some kind of special magic that goes on during treatment that happens nowhere else. But the truth is, after detoxification (which is primarily a medical issue), there's no such thing as "treatment" for addiction—there's only *talking*. Most so-called "treatments" for addiction are just variations on this theme. Talking is what goes on behind the walls of treatment centers; talking is what goes on in out-patient addiction counseling; talking is what goes on in group and individual therapy; and, of course, talking is what goes on at Alcoholics Anonymous meetings—"one drunk talking to another." Whether it's for money or for free, the magic that seems to work best is talking, talking, and more talking. And that can happen anywhere.

So it's an excuse when an alcoholic or addict claims, "I can't get sober because I can't afford 'treatment'." Once detoxed, any man can afford treatment. All he has to do is show up at an anonymous group meeting and sit down—and he's in *treatment*. And not only is the AA meeting itself treatment, but so is the conversation that takes place on the front steps before the meeting or in the coffee shop afterward. It is still "one drunk talking to another," and it still works.

Once the talking begins, the recovery begins.

Spontaneous Remission from Addiction

"In medicine, as in life, until the mind has been prepared to see something, it will pass unnoticed, as invisible as though it did not exist." — Ovid, ancient Roman poet

Before we move on to Chapter 1, I want to talk to you about one of my favorite topics, the phenomenon of *spontaneous remission from addiction*.

Now, everybody has heard of spontaneous remission. We usually think of it as an unexplained recovery from a physical illness. Somebody gets cancer; then it goes away, and nobody knows why. In the medical field, the concept of spontaneous remission goes back to ancient times. Hippocrates, the Greek father of modern medicine, believed that in each patient's case there is a "favorable moment" during which time healing is most likely to happen.

The place where we're not used to hearing about spontaneous remission is in the area of addictions. Hark! I've got some encouraging news for you: Spontaneous remission happens to the addicted, too. Just step inside the twelve-step world and ask any recovering alcoholic, addict, gambler, smoker, or compulsive overeater to tell you about the *exact instant* when his addiction stopped, and chances are he'll tell you it happened right after he'd had some kind of *Aha!* thought or *moment of clarity*—when he saw things honestly for the first time. This is the psychological equivalent of a spontaneous remission.

A spontaneous remission from addiction is usually triggered by some internal or external event, often one so minor that it goes unnoticed. It can be anything. The person hears something, sees something, feels something, thinks something, smells something, dreams something, reads something, remembers something, and in that instant, in *that* person, it resonates. There's a click inside, a psychological—perhaps even chemical—shift, and the next thing the man knows, his addiction problem doesn't seem so overwhelming anymore because now he knows at a gut level that he's *got* what it takes to *do* what it takes to fix it—no matter what. *Zap!*

After more than twenty-five years in the addiction field, I've heard thousands of these spontaneous remission stories, each one unique, yet the process is always the same. Like a scientist getting that light bulb turned on, there's the input of information, there's the period of time during which things are mulled over inside, then finally there's some additional stimuli or input, sometimes a seemingly very insignificant one—and kaboom, it all falls into place. Eureka!

It catapults the alcoholic into sobriety. But he doesn't get to ride this into the sunset. He's got to maintain this marvelous state by doing a whole lot of work.

While nobody can make a spontaneous remission happen (that's why it's called spontaneous), there *are* specific actions that anyone can take to *increase the chances* of one occurring. You can make the field so fertile that when one more seed is dropped in, it takes root and blooms.

Remember, it's never one specific action that does the trick, but an accumulation of actions, one piled on top of the other, that brings a spontaneous remission about. Same thing happens with slot machines. It's not any one specific silver dollar, but an accumulation of silver dollars that triggers a jackpot. You'd never go to

17

Las Vegas, put just one silver dollar in a slot machine, not win, and then complain that the machine didn't *work*. But people will go to just one AA meeting, not get sober, and then say that AA doesn't *work*. The thing is, in AA, just as in Vegas, timing is everything.

It may take three meetings (or silver dollars), or it may take fifty meetings (or silver dollars) before you hit paydirt. Failure comes from giving up one silver dollar or one meeting too soon. (Author's Note: If you're a compulsive gambler, please ignore this little analogy!)

This sounds simple. So simple, in fact, that it's almost too hard to get. When a man is primed for his spontaneous remission, anything works. When a man is not primed for his spontaneous remission, nothing works.

If you are interested in more details about what specific actions you can take to prime the pump for your spontaneous remission, flip to the end of this book to Appendix B, "Seven Steps to Trigger A Spontaneous Remission."

Now let's meet the three new additions to this book, Jim (one year sober), Jason (four months sober), and Brian (five years sober).

1

CAN AN ALCOHOLIC CHANGE HIS SPOTS?

"All that we ask of the newly sober alcoholic man is that he change absolutely everything."

— An Alcoholics Anonymous sponsor

Getting sober is easy. Most alcoholics and addicts have done it dozens of times. It's staying sober over the long haul, living life one day at a time—for *years*—that's hard. That's the part that takes courage. It's not for weaklings.

Men who have gone through the pain of getting sober want to know what they're in for. That's the purpose of this book—to answer questions: What is day-to-day life as a sober man really like? Is it possible to change one's spots after so many years of drinking or drugging? How will getting sober affect my work? My sex life? My creativity? My family? My soul?

The guy who thinks that sobriety won't change anything in his life is in for a shock—the first of many. Just as chemicals affected every area of his life, so, too, will sobriety. Before he's through, no stone in his universe will go unturned. It's part of what makes the journey rough, and what drives the lesser men back to the bars. It's also what makes it exciting.

In this chapter we'll meet three new additions to this book, Jim, fifty-two, a year sober; Jason, thirty-five, four months sober—both still "newcomers" in AA's eyes; and Brian, forty-three, five years sober. As I said earlier, what's interesting about Jim and Jason is that they represent two ends of the AA spectrum: Jim is one of the last of that rare breed of alcoholic, called the "pure" alcoholic. He drank alcohol (but didn't use other chemicals), lost everything in the process, came into AA without benefit of a treatment center, had a bad slip, and is now back in AA again as a "retread." And he did it all the old-fashioned way.

Jason, on the other hand, is more typical of the newer breed of AA member, getting there by way of the Betty Ford (Treatment) Center in Rancho Mirage, California. He used pills, cocaine, pot— but *very little alcohol*. Still, he "embraces" (his term) the label "alcoholic" because he goes along with the umbrella definition (described in the *Introduction*) that says an alcoholic is someone who is hooked on alcohol *and/or* some other mood-altering substance. In the old days of AA, Jason would have been called a "high bottom" or "silk sheet" drunk, a man who gets sober while he still owns something, like a wrist watch. Jason, however, like so many others these days, got to AA younger, richer, and healthier than his counterparts in the past.

The third new interviewee, Brian, is interesting because of *where* he got sober—in prison (Lompoc in California). That's not an easy thing to do. Brian states (and the statistics back him up) that drugs and alcohol are a snap to come by in prison. In fact, he made his own brew and sold it to get money to buy drugs. According to a 1999 White House press release, the vast majority of all prisoners report drug use—up to 83 percent of state prisoners and 73 percent of federal prisoners. Brian says that based on

his own personal experience, it's much higher, maybe nintey percent. Yet he managed to get more than three years of sobriety
under his belt before he was released from Lompoc. He now has
over five years.

We'll start off with Jim.

JIM

I'm a classic alcoholic. For years I drank only beer. I didn't even
touch the hard stuff until later on, so my arc was very slow. It
took me a dozen years to have my first blackout. I've never done
hallucinogenics or narcotics or pills. I'm just not wired that way.
I did try marijuana, but I don't like to smoke. That method of
ingesting anything into my body doesn't appeal to me. I just like
to drink. I prefer drinking things to eating things. I even like
drinking out of the blender.

Jim, fifty-two, was born in a small Kansas town. He and his
younger brother were reared by a mother with manic-depression.
"By the age of five she was coming unglued, and I knew just one
thing: I had to save her. But I wasn't able to save her. She ended
up having electroshock treatment and getting divorced. What that
taught me is that people don't change. The mean get meaner, and
the crazy get crazier."

Jim's drinking picked up when he came to Los Angeles to go
to film school. "I found myself in with a whole different breed of
cat. Most of my classmates were from Brentwood and Beverly
Hills, and I saw early on that in the movie business it was going to
be a case of *who* you know, not *what* you know, and if I wanted to
make it I was going to have to make friends."

What helped Jim "make it" was alcohol. Alcohol helped him
overcome his small-town shyness. He made friends, did well in
school, wrote and produced a movie, sold another screenplay, and
married a connected classmate. "Her family knew people in the

21

movie industry. She grew up across the street from the John Wayne estate, and I was wowed by that. And she was crazy about me."

Things began to get off track with the birth of their first child in 1988. "Suddenly the game changed. Until then my wife and I had had an unspoken contract: I was allowed to be the child in the family, so long as she *treated* me as an adult. But when our child was born, she expected me to grow up and start bringing in money (which I wasn't doing). Instead, I got involved with the production of my new screenplay (meaning there was still no money coming in), and drinking. As a result, right after our second child was born two years later, she asked me to leave."

Jim reacted in typical alcoholic fashion—relief. "Now I could drink to oblivion—the way I *wanted* to drink." He went down fast. At first he lived with friends, then ended up in a low-rent apartment in Pasadena. Jobs came and went. Waiter jobs. Word-processing jobs. The whole cycle. He drank himself into emergency rooms five times. "I had no medical insurance, so it was all on me."

Eventually, Jim found AA. He got sober and stayed sober for over a year. But staying sober proved too hard when a family drama triggered a massive slip. He'd gone back to Kansas to be with his dying mother and learned that she'd left him and his brother $2,000 each.

> Within hours of the funeral, my brother told me he thought I should give him my share. This was the first inkling I had that something was wrong. I asked him why he felt I should give him my money, and he told me it was because *he* was the one who'd been running back and forth to see Mother—"while you've been out there in California doing whatever it is you've been doing out there, so you owe me that." I told him that maybe I owed him something, but I didn't think I owed him all of it, that I didn't think it was a reasonable request. At that moment, I turned around and started to walk away from him—and suddenly he hit me with his fist on the side of my head. He hit me so hard that it

knocked me off my feet, broke my glasses, and cut my eye. I was shocked. I got up and went at him; we had a fistfight. My stepfather, whose own health had deteriorated to the point where he could only walk with the aid of a walker, got us apart—*how* I'll never know! Then my step-father kind of flipped out and started ragging on me, calling me a drunk—even though he'd never even seen me drunk. I was furious at everyone in the world. I left town, checked into a motel, got a bottle, and drank continuously over the next week until I collapsed and ended up in an emergency room in Fayetteville, Arkansas, vomiting blood, with blood gushing out of my bowels.

It was in this hospital, flat on his back with tubes running in and out, that Jim had a life-changing "moment of clarity" or spontaneous remission (discussed in the Introduction), similar to the one Bill Wilson, AA's cofounder, had when he was hospitalized. Wilson's moment resulted in his getting sober, and later cofounding AA. Jim's moment allowed him to transcend his turmoil and finally see the light.

I was laying there, and I heard a voice in my head, but the voice seemed to come from someplace deeper in my gut, and it said, "If you don't leave this hospital right now and go back to L.A. you're going to die." That was it. I understood what 'right now' meant. It meant, "You're not going to die today, but sooner or later you're going to die in some small town here in Arkansas." I was still drunk, but I managed to talk the doctors into releasing me AMA (against medical advice). I got myself to the airport. I got lost at the airport. I missed a bunch of flights. My luggage got lost. But I finally got back to Los Angeles, rushed back to AA, and began, once again, to pick up the pieces of my life.

Jim has accomplished a lot in the year he's been sober—sobriety itself being his main accomplishment. He even wrote a new screenplay. "I'd kept that money my mother left me. I didn't give it to my brother. I decided to use it to pay myself a salary and write the script."

After that was done, he got a job unrelated to the movie industry. "I now work as a litigation secretary for a lawyer and it's great. I'm grateful just to be there."

Daily life is like a minefield for the newly recovering alcoholic. Anything that so much as ripples his emotional surface can trigger a slip. And every newcomer responds to ripples differently. "I got *crazier* sober," says Jim. "I'd look at each new problem I was facing and say to myself, 'How are you going to deal with *this* one? This one is surely going to make you drink!' But I kept squeaking through."

Jim has managed to deal with resentments (the so-called killers of alcoholics), both his own and those of people in his life. His ex-wife stayed furious at him well into his sobriety because of all those years he flaked out on his kids, when he'd call her up at the last minute and tell her he couldn't pick up the children because he was too drunk. Ultimately, she'd told him, "You're never going to see them again."

This kind of threat can really get a guy's gut grinding, even if he's not newly sober. Not being allowed to see his kids drove Jim wild.

> I wanted to drag her into court, but my AA sponsor advised me to leave it alone and let it play itself out. I fought with him over this, but his better judgment won out. One day my ex-wife just called me up, and I've been seeing my kids ever since. We picked up where we left off. I've told them I'm an alcoholic. They seem to be taking it in stride.

Jim's relationship with his brother is slowly improving.

> At my sponsor's request, I made amends to my brother for my part in our little family drama. I think he's still feeling resentful that I'm in Southern California and he's "stuck" in Kansas City—but that's for him to work out. It's up to *him* to make his own dreams come true.

Not surprisingly, a big issue for Jim has been the concept of change, and AA's warning that if the alcoholic doesn't overhaul his personality he'll drink again. Jim's mother's failure to change had made him cynical, had convinced him that he, too, was incapable of change.

> So when I got to AA and I heard people talk all that happy *change talk*, saying things like, "Thank God, I used to be this and now I'm that," I'd think, "Yeah, yeah!" But the longer I stay sober the more I start noticing that my thinking is actually changing, that my demon of anger just isn't there as much, that my mind no longer races and wakes me up at three in the morning. I feel a peace and calmness and self-assurance I've never felt before. At first, I thought it was just momentary, that it would go away, but it hasn't.

Therein, of course, lies a danger for recovering men. If they don't keep doing the work, they won't keep getting the results. So far, Jim has been doing both.

JASON

I loved pills. They took my pain away. I became a prisoner of pills. And they started me down that slippery slope.

Jason, thirty-five, who says that he knew by the age of fourteen that he was going to become a musician and songwriter, did just that—and has hundreds of records to his credit. He was born in New York City and is included here because he's a good example of a nineties mixed bag "alcoholic" whose "drug of choice" wasn't even alcohol.

> I did get drunk once at thirteen at a friend's New Years' Eve party, but I didn't get drunk again for four years. I just wasn't interested in alcohol. It wasn't physiologically addicting to me. It wasn't my pitfall. But marijuana was another story. I really liked it. I smoked on the weekends all through high school.

In college, Jason developed a cocaine problem. Then it was morphine and codeine and heroin. When he hurt his back, his doctor prescribed the painkiller, Vicadin, and he got hooked on that. When his first doctor wouldn't allow him to have more than six pills a day, he found other doctors who aided his cry for help, thereby managing to score up to fifteen pills a day.

Jason is a good example of how alcoholics can so easily switch from one drug to another, and get hooked on all of them—and why sobriety *has* to mean freedom from all such chemicals—whether it's a martini in a fancy restaurant, heroin in an alley, or a prescription from a licensed physician. Sponsor Jack, who has been sober for twenty-eight years and has sponsored many men just like Jason, has said,

> A drug is a drug is a drug. All I know is that my body doesn't know the difference between a prescription and a score. My body doesn't care if I get it from a diplomat in surgery, or from a guy named Snake on skid row. My body responds to both the same way: I get hooked.

As with so many other contemporary recoveries, Jason's denial stage was relatively short. "I realized I definitely have the disease," he says simply.

Maybe this shorter denial phase stems from the fact that there is less stigma these days about alcoholism. Fewer people seem to get hung up on that demeaning skid row bum image. Therefore, younger people have less shame about addiction, are less likely to keep it a secret, and are less likely to look for the causes. Jason echoes this attitude. "I think a lot of addiction is genetic. But the causes really don't matter. The bottom line is, what's the present situation? If the present situation is addiction, admit it and do something about it."

Initially, what Jason did about his addiction didn't work: He checked himself into a local detox center,

> But I didn't want to know anything about AA or their groups or any of it, so I left and went home, finished making a new record, got my internist to put me on Ambien (like Valium), and got hooked on that. When I tried to get off of Ambien I ended back on Vicadin.

After taking thirty or forty Vicadin, he was sent to the Betty Ford Center. He suffered through a miserable withdrawal:

> They wanted me to experience the full pain of withdrawal, to brave the monster, so to speak. I didn't sleep for fourteen days and I couldn't walk. I looked through the yellow pages for gun shops because I wanted to shoot myself. I was so angry at them for not giving me anything to make the withdrawal easier. Yet I knew that if I left the Betty Ford Center, I'd cop pills right away, and all it would take would be *three* pills for me to get right back into it. Then I'd have to go through the same thing all over again. So I stayed. Basically it took me twenty-one out of the thirty-three days that I was there to withdraw from Vicadin.

Jason has been sober ever since.

Another way Jason is typical of more recent AA recoveries is the fact that he doesn't make AA his only recovery program. Once upon a time, AA discouraged members from getting outside treatment. It was felt that AA alone should be enough. No more. Most younger members try a cornucopia of things before they settle on some combination of treatment elements that works for them. For Jason, AA is mixed with a regular exercise routine. "Exercise is an important part of my recovery program. At least two hours. I swim every day. I'm uncomfortable if I don't. I go to an AA meeting a day, sometimes two. I go to group therapy in Malibu three times a week, and I see a therapist three times a week."

Busy guy. Busy *sober* guy.

BRIAN

I had a pessimistic outlook on life and wanted to escape reality from the start, even though I had great parents, and I grew up in a nice neighborhood.

Brian, forty-three, an only child, is convinced that his alcoholism is genetic, that he was born with it in him. He started using drugs and alcohol at the tender age of ten, graduated to heroin by sixteen ("Heroin put me out of the world the fastest and the longest."), started robbing stores and pharmacies to get money for heroin, and by age twenty-two was in prison. There, he hooked up with a prison gang so he could get drugs and alcohol, "and stay alive."

Brian goes on, "The gangs pretty much run the maximum security prisons. We made our own wine. It's like Vodka. They call it *pruno*. I had all I wanted. Plus, I'd shoot heroin about every day." When he got out, he started robbing banks—again to support his heroin habit—and ended up back inside prison for bank robbery at Lompoc, USP (United States Penitentiary) in California.

Brian is another case of *spontaneous remission*. The trigger for him—and it was indeed a dramatic one—was the murder of his friend and fellow inmate in a fight over drugs and alcohol.

I can remember the exact moment. I was standing there as they were wheeling my friend out after he'd been stabbed through the heart. We'd just done shooting some heroin, and they nailed him. There was blood everywhere, it was a mess. I knew in that moment that it had come to the end of the road for me, that I was either going to kill myself, or I was going to get clean and sober. The day after it happened, I decided to kill myself. But then they announced over the loudspeaker that some AA people were bringing in a panel and having a meeting, so I walked down to the AA meeting instead. I've been sober ever since. I became secretary of that meeting. AA became the most important thing in my life.

Sylvia: What was the reaction of the other inmates when you went to AA?

Brian: I was always a very feared person in State Federal Prison. I'd spent most of my life in there, so people knew who I was, and knew I wasn't hiding out by going to AA. So I was a real role model, for the guards as well as the inmates. It was like, "Will you look at that! Blond boy's got a thirty day chip!" (AA hands out chips, like poker chips, for thirty, sixty, and ninety days, and for six and nine months of sobriety. After that, it's a cake for every year's birthday or anniversary.) I got congratulated because they knew I was a drug addict and a real hard-core convict. They were happy for me. AA is becoming more popular in prison. Even if a man is doing life, he wants a *better* life in prison, so he starts going to meetings. I got a lot of my friends to go.

Sylvia: What were your impressions of that first AA meeting?

Brian: I remember I was really scared. The panel came in. They were very nice. I listened to what they had to say and I started taking their advice. I read the section in the *AA Big Book* called *"How It Works,"* and I heard them say that if you were willing to *go to any lengths* you could stay sober, and I knew I was ready to go to any lengths. My whole life had been based on anger and rage—which is fear, really—and I knew I couldn't go on like that. I got a sponsor inside prison, and I wrote my Fourth Step inventory (drinking and using story), and after I read my inventory to my sponsor, I went back to my cell, and for the first time in my life I started crying—and then I prayed to God for hours, and I asked God to take over my life. I've been praying ever since. I don't miss a night.

Sylvia: What's been the hardest thing to handle since you've been out?

Brian: Relationships. I got involved in a relationship after I got out of prison. The girl was here—and then she just up and left. That was a painful thing. There were nights I couldn't sleep. But I just kept calling my AA friends, and I prayed a lot, and I got through it. I never even thought about drinking or using.

Sylvia: What's your advice to newcomers, especially people still in prison?

Brian: No matter what you're going through—the car breaks, the girl leaves—just don't *react*. Try to relax. Calm down. Focus your thoughts upward, to God, pray to God, try to let a higher power take over. Because for a guy like me, my whole life has been reacting to different situations with disastrous results. So now, anytime I start getting into anger or fear or pain, I know I have the choice to either focus my thoughts to God's goodness and pray for him to take over my life, or just react.

Sylvia: The future?

Brian: I'm really looking forward to going back into prison—not as an inmate, but as an AA member taking panels into prison, carrying the AA message to other guys like me who can't make it on the street. I can tell them I've had a change of heart, a spiritual change, that it's possible to change. I can honestly tell them that I no longer have the desire to use or take a drink. I don't even think about it anymore. I haven't in years. That change really took place.

Nagging Issues in Early Sobriety

Along with the concerns you'd expect a newly sober man to have, like, "How do you stay sober and get through the day—and night?," there are other issues that bug men in early sobriety.

Two of the main topics of worry are sex and work, especially if it's creative work.

So the new questions that arise are: Is there sex after sobriety? Is there creativity after sobriety?

Let's start with sex:

Sex

Drink provokes the desire but it takes away the performance.
—William Shakespeare

When they are still drinking or using, few men escape without having their sexuality impacted in some way—usually negatively. In talking about his own sex life, Brian said, "When you're a heroin addict, you don't care about sex. You just care about heroin."

Alcohol and drugs can do a number on a man's sexual functioning. It can interfere with his desire and mess with his erection (which he can lose at the drop of a hat, or not get at all). It can retard ejaculation, decrease arousal, decrease orgasmic pleasure and intensity, and can inflame the prostate gland which, in turn, can interfere with erection and climax. It can also atrophy the testicles and decrease sperm output.

Different drugs (other than alcohol) have their own different effects. Jason's experience is typical.

> I was the classic cocaine addict. I associated cocaine with sex for years. I found it arousing and stimulating. It made me nuts. But I know lots of guys who found coke inhibiting. I'd hear them say things like, "Oh, man, every time I did coke it was a joke. I couldn't get it up—blah, blah, blah." It was when I used pills that I found I didn't even care about sex. I worked. I did my music projects. I functioned in the world. But after work, I just lay on my couch in the den with my dog and the phone. I didn't give a shit about sex. Anytime I wanted to have sex, I'd have to go back to cocaine.

Typically, it takes six months to a year of sobriety to get all this ironed out, maybe longer if the man has been on drugs. Early sobriety impotence makes men nervous that they'll never get it on again, so their sponsors have to keep reminding them to be patient—a newly acquired virtue.

A lot of guys have to learn how to *talk* to women first, have to learn from scratch how to have a relationship, have to learn how (and here's a word that makes many a man cringe!) to *"communicate."*

Jason says that in these last four months since his release from the Betty Ford Center, his sex drive has been minimal. But he's not concerned about it. "Right now I'm enjoying being by myself, getting my work done, and following through on my responsibilities. That's really where I'm at right now. The other can wait."

Meanwhile, there are other perks of sobriety to enjoy—as Brian discovered.

> I'm finding that people gravitate to me more because I'm sober. It's like there's been an energy shift inside, and I've finally become committed to taking care of my life day by day—which is really how a true metamorphosis occurs, a step at a time. I have embraced this way of looking at things.

Creativity

Work is the other big worrisome issue in early sobriety, especially for men (like Jason) whose livelihood depends upon the ability to be creative on a regular basis. One frequently asked question is "Will being sober take my creativity away? If I had to use coke or booze to create before, can I do it now stone cold sober?"

This concern about one's creative powers being stripped away by sobriety is reminiscent of the early days of psychoanalysis when patients worried that getting rid of their neuroses would mess with their creative muses. Jason found these worries to be unfounded.

I know a lot of creative people who think, "Oh, shit, man, I'm not going to be able to write anymore. I'm going to have The Block." For myself, I know that's not true. I had a lot of success when I was using—I was one of the top producers in the country and I had two top ten records as a writer. But I've also had a lot of success sober.

The good news sent back from those up at the front is that work and creativity are better sober. Basically, chemicals wreck creativity. It's only a man's perception that he's more creative under the influence, just as it's only his perception that he sings better in the shower. It ain't necessarily so. After all, "creativity" doesn't live in that bottle of booze or hide out in that white cocaine powder. Creativity is *within the man himself*. It's only fear that keeps it trapped inside, and there are other ways to remove fear. Jason learned that drowning it in chemicals doesn't work for very long.

> Now that I've had a lot of songs recorded that I wrote straight, I'm finding that in sobriety I'm quicker, my sense of recall is even better, and my bullshit barometer is more finely tuned. It used to take me a couple of days after I'd written a song to see where it could be improved. Now it takes me only one day. I no longer need to put myself in a bunch of emotional pain to write music. Nor do I need to put chemicals into my body anymore to write music. I can draw from my life experience while I'm in a sober state. I've been completely in *The Zone* during the last sixty days recording my new record, and I haven't taken a thing. It has given me new hope that my life and my music will only continue to get better.

Now let's back up and look at Lewis, a man with only thirty (actually, only eighteen) days of sobriety. We'll see why it is that all newcomers are affectionately called "crazy".

2

ALL NEWCOMERS ARE CRAZY:
Louis, Sober Thirty Days

I like the idea of being a "crazy newcomer." I was a litle crazy before I started drinking, so why not now that I've stopped?

What Everybody Knows

In the addiction-recovery field, there are certain things that "everybody knows."

"Everybody knows," for example, that all newcomers are crazy. They are also dishonest, immature, irresponsible, unreliable, and flaky. Newcomers are so much alike, it's easy to generalize about them. On top of everything else, they are thoroughly self-centered. A Los Angeles AA old-timer tells the story of how he was awakened early one morning by an earthquake. As he was in the process of seeking cover, his phone rang. From under a desk, he managed to answer it and recognized the voice of a newcomer who lived only a few blocks away.

"I'm in an earthquake!" the newcomer wailed.

"I know you'll find this hard to believe," the AA old-timer said, "but *I'm* in an earthquake, too!" and he hung up on him.

But in the beginning, the newcomer is like a puppy and finds that most people are pretty good-natured about the messes he makes. "Well, what can you expect from a crazy newcomer," they'll say with a shrug and a smile.

It's no coincidence that AA newcomers, at least in some parts of the country, are called "babies." (On the East Coast they're referred to as "pigeons.") Even if the newcomer is fifty years old, weighs 245 pounds, and is senior vice president of a bank, he's still considered a "baby" in Alcoholics Anonymous. It's a mistake to be fooled by the fact that newcomers look like grown-ups. They need to be told to "sit down, shut up, and listen" so that they can learn what they need to learn to survive.

The newcomer is on an emotional rollercoaster, flying high one minute and feeling depressed the next. Sometimes his feelings have nothing to do with what's going on. Part of this can be biochemical. He hasn't finished detoxing yet, and everything is out of whack. From his point of view, he's so accustomed to drama that it's only when he levels off that he realizes something is wrong! He may even try a little mischief to pump himself up again so he feels "right."

Basically, the newcomer hasn't a clue as to what he actually feels. That's why he's such a bad judge of character. He thinks opinions and feelings are the same thing. He listens to people's words but is often oblivious to their actions. When asked "Are you happy, sad, mad, or glad?" the newcomer doesn't know.

This business of not knowing himself is one of the recovering alcoholic's main problems. AA will begin to teach him how to uncover who he is.

Detox Without Tears

Reproductions of a classic AA painting are hanging in AA meeting halls and clubhouses all around the world. The painting depicts the "twelve-step call"—when one alcoholic helps another. A sick alcoholic, who has taken to his bed, is being visited by two AA members who have brought with them the best detox medication known at the time, a bottle of whiskey. It sits on the nightstand. They'll give it to him over the next few days, in decreasing doses (to prevent the possibility of a convulsion from too rapid withdrawal), until he is detoxed. Even so, the man will still most likely have to suffer through the dreaded shakes and jangles, heebie–jeebies, sweats, and sleepless nights.

But today, detox is a whole new ball game. In-patient chemical dependency treatment centers and detox units give the alcoholic medication instead of whiskey to "bring him down slowly," making the shakes and jangles largely a thing of the past. Detoxification from alcohol and from certain other drugs simply isn't the rough ride it used to be.

A medically supervised detox, as opposed to doing it cold turkey, has both its good and bad points. On the plus side, not only is it more comfortable, but it's safer because it reduces the risk of medical complications. The bad part is the fact that the detoxee doesn't get the full "benefit" of his suffering. Remembering just how miserable his first thirty days were has kept many an alcoholic sober for life!

One of our consultant-interviewees for this book, a man who has now been sober in AA for over eighteen years and has supervised hundreds of AA men through their own detox days, is Sponsor Jack.

In the old days, when a newcomer dragged himself into AA, shaking and sweating, he was immediately surrounded by AA members wanting to twelve-step him. Today, the man who comes into AA fresh out of a treatment center looks so well put together, he hardly gets noticed. He's clean-shaven, well-rested, well-fed, and under his arm he's carrying his copy of the AA Big Book, "signed by my therapist," he says proudly!

The upshot of this is that the recovering alcoholic doesn't always get what he needs to survive, which is lots of attention, lots of love, and the immediate opportunity to share "experience, strength, and hope" with another recovering alcoholic.

Some think this might be why so many newcomers these days go right back "out there" again, why the recovering statistics aren't particularly impressive, even from the best treatment centers. Typically, only one out of every ten treatment center "graduates" will still be clean and sober a year later.

Newcomers don't like to hear about these odds: "You're trying to bum us out!" They don't understand why AA old-timers worry so much about them in the beginning. But the old-timers worry because they know how very fragile and vulnerable newcomers are and how likely they are to get into dangerous situations they can't handle. These situations are everywhere: seeing old friends, going into a bar, being at the wrong party, or with the wrong girlfriend, going into the "old" neighborhood, getting a phone call from a former dealer, having a minor crisis. Newcomerthink is: "If I *desire* it, I have to *do* it." It's called being impulsive. "If I desire it, I *don't* have to do it" comes later.

Even cars driven by newcomers can't be trusted. All by themselves they've been known to turn down streets where cocaine dealers just "happen" to live. (*Happen* is a popular word with newcomers. For example, "She just happened to be sitting next to me, and we just happened to go out for coffee together after the meeting, and I just happened to go home with her, and go to bed with her." And probably later, his wife will just "happen" to sue him for divorce!)

More Will Be Revealed

"More will be revealed" is an AA expression frequently directed to newcomers. What this means is that it's okay to go ahead and interpret your life any way you want to, but when you're sober longer, when you start to remember things, when your frozen feelings begin to thaw out, that's when you'll begin to see things differently. The truth about your life will be revealed to you.

Psychology students are often taught a good rule of thumb: Whatever the patient says, consider the opposite. If a patient says "I have no anger," look for anger. If a patient says "I have no sadness," look for sadness. The same applies to newcomers. If a newcomer says he feels one thing, consider the opposite, because "everybody knows" that newcomers don't know what they feel. They're not lying; they simply don't know. Neither is it true that they haven't been getting any bodily clues about how they feel, like the gut-churning sensation that so often means "No!" It's just that they haven't been paying attention to their feelings, or they've been drowning them out with chemicals. In sobriety, most alcoholics are astounded to discover that they have pretty good gut instincts after all, and that they can learn to unbury them. "There will be a time," promises AA's "Big Book," when the sober man will "intuitively know how to handle situations" that used to "baffle" him.

Even during his first thirty days, "more is revealed" to the recovering alcoholic man about the very nature of his addiction, about the power of obsession, about the importance of rigorous honesty, and about who's really responsible for his condition: He is. No more blaming.

He will also discover that he's a sitting duck for other addictions. No sooner does he stop one than another pops up. I know a woman who gives a very funny "podium pitch" (that's when an AA member tells his or her "story" at an AA meeting) about her first-year addiction to chocolate chip cookies. The hope is that each new addiction will be less destructive than the last. Obviously, being addicted to cookies is better than being addicted to crack, and being addicted to jogging is better than being addicted to cookies, and so on.

Love and Work

The two big themes in a man's life that Freud called "Love and Work" begin to be dealt with early on in sobriety.

Before the recovering alcoholic man can have a deep, committed relationship, he's got to learn the basics of communication, honesty, and integrity. The man who gets sober only to discover he's with a partner who isn't good for him, who may even have a neurotic need for him to stay an alcoholic, asks, "How did this happen?" Well, it happened because he didn't heed his "gut feelings" about the relationship right from the gate. As one newcomer sadly concluded, "I felt from the beginning that getting married to her was a mistake. In fact, as I was driving to the church I had this knot in my stomach, this churning inside, but I just tried to push it aside and ignore it. The champagne helped."

However, in sobriety, ignoring these inner warnings is a no-no. A stitch in time saves nine.

In the work area, before the recovering man can unearth his life's mission (or as one of our interviewees put it, before he can look for "a game worth playing"), he's got to learn how to show up at his job, on time, and not resign every time something displeases him. If he's lucky enough to be sitting on a talent of some kind, he'll have a chance to discover what it is and develop it—as long as he stays sober. His main mission, of course, will always be his sobriety.

Throughout his first year, if possible, the recovering alcoholic will be encouraged to avoid making any major decisions. This is so that he can concentrate on survival. He shouldn't get married, separated, or divorced; he shouldn't quit a job, or get a job. He shouldn't move. And he definitely shouldn't commit suicide! "If you kill yourself in your first year, you'll be killing the wrong person," AA says. Major decisions made too soon are usually regretted.

The Wrath of Women

Most newcomers fail to appreciate just how frustrating they were to live with when they were out there "practicing their disease," as the expression goes. When they sober up and discover that their wives, girlfriends, employers, and children are still mad at them, they are usually astounded. Most had been sure that once they were sober everything would be fine, "So why is she on my case now?" But codependents just don't forget that fast. And they're cautious, too, wondering if the alcoholic will fall on his face again.

Even in sobriety, the alcoholic gets cause and effect all mixed up. He says, "I drank because my wife was irritable," forgetting what it was he did in the first place that made her that way. Could it possibly have been his—drinking? And "irritable" is putting it mildly. Most women who have been putting up with an alcoholic for any length of time are enraged. And this anger usually starts to spill out during the recovering man's critical first thirty days, especially if he's in a chemical dependency treatment center. Our

41

psychiatric consultant, Dr. Paul Grossman, who has worked with so many of these codependents, puts it this way:

> The wife probably hasn't dared vent her spleen until the guy's safely in the hospital, but once he's there she lets her anger out, which of course is very disconcerting to him. He says, "Gee, here I am, doing what I'm supposed to be doing, what *she* wanted me to do, and now she's angrier at me than ever. Women!"

I Liked You Better Drunk

From her point of view, having been involved with an alcoholic or addict means she's probably pretty burned out on the relationship. Once she hoped he'd care about how *she* feels and be sorry for *her* pain, but he was too self-absorbed for that. When he continues to be equally self-absorbed in sobriety, it's the last straw. The changes he does make, she doesn't always like. If he gets weekend passes or day passes from the hospital, where does he go! To an AA meeting—instead of staying home with her. Suddenly he has new friends and a new attitude. "What *is* this?" she says. She starts to have nostalgia for the good old days when he was drinking and she knew where he was and what he'd do next. She may be astounded to hear words coming out of her mouth she swore she'd never say: "I liked you better when you were drunk!"

And for the newly sober man who may be struggling with his own ambivalence, these are just the words he's been waiting for.

"You liked me better when I was drunk, did you? Well, just for that I'm going to give you what you want." Then he grabs the car keys, and before he can say Jack Daniels he's on his way down the road to the Whiskey Gulch Café.

It's amazing that newcomers survive their first thirty days. Not as many do as we'd like, perhaps, but some do, especially the ones who remember the simple secret of success: one drunk talking to another. Newcomers who insist that it just *has* to be more complicated than this, so they don't even bother trying, are doomed to drink again.

With all these things that "everybody knows" about newcomers in mind, let's talk to our first recovering alcoholic man, Louis.

LOUIS

The hardest part about getting in recovery is the feelings *part, the getting in touch with those feelings that have been lying dormant for years.*

Louis, thirty-four, is a tall, brown-haired, pleasant looking man with an open, friendly manner. Interviewed while still in a recovery house for alcoholics, this is his first official attempt at sobriety. He has eighteen days.

Louis, like Jim in chapter 1, is another one of those rare "pure" alcoholics who never took any drugs other than alcohol. "I was never an experimenter," he says. His detoxification process was swift and uneventful, and he seems not to be suffering from any physical consequences of his thirteen years of addiction. "Aside from being a little chubby from the drinking, and feeling a few twinges in my liver, which have gone away now, I think I'm in pretty good physical shape."

Because Louis is exceptionally bright, a quick study, and articulate, he appears to have more of a grasp of the "recovery game" than he may actually have. As "more is revealed," it will become increasingly clear to him that when it comes to staying sober, intelligence is handy, but "intellectualizing" can be deadly. Survival will depend on coping not with ideas, but with feelings.

Louis states that alcoholism "runs rampant" on both sides of his family, mostly among the males. Both of his grandfathers died

43

of alcoholism. His father is an alcoholic (now apparently in permanent recovery) who suffered numerous serious relapses during the time Louis was growing up. And only weeks before Louis's admission into treatment, his brother was found dead of an overdose in a park with needle marks on his arm. It was his thirty-second birthday. Louis's sister, who is six years younger, didn't develop alcoholism but did develop a severe eating disorder.

Louis was born in Michigan. His father was in the service, so the family moved a lot—first to Georgia, then to San Francisco. It was there that the first tragedy struck the family. Louis's parents were passengers in a car that was struck by a drunk driver going 100 mph the wrong way on the Nimitz Freeway. His father was thrown out into a field and lived. His mother was killed. Louis was only seven years old.

Soon afterward, the three children were shipped to Grandma's house in Michigan, and there began a two-year period during which life was so idyllic that Louis's grief was put aside and never dealt with. "During those two years at Grandma's there was a lot of denial going on," Louis says. "We just never talked about our mother's death, not with anyone, not with our father or our grandmother or anyone." Instead, they enjoyed a Utopian existence.

> My grandmother owned a lake. She was like a female Ben Cartwright on the *Bonanza* TV series. I lived there with my brother, my sister, my grandmother, my aunt, my uncle, and three girl cousins, and it was such fun there that we basically forgot that we ever had a mother or a father. We'd wake up in the morning, put on our suits, and run down into the lake and splash around all day long. Everything was fun, fun, fun. My anguish was obliterated.

While Louis was frolicking at the lake in Michigan, his father's addiction was progressing rapidly in San Francisco. At one point, he was living on Market Street and sleeping under the Bay Bridge. But after awhile, as was his pattern, his father got cleaned up and pulled himself together. This time he even got married. Next, he decided to go to Michigan and "rescue" his children and bring them back to California.

> We hated him for doing that. We didn't remember him. We wanted him to go away. But he took us anyway. And in no time, he was back to drinking and using again. For the next few years life was torment and hell. At one point my father burned down the house because he fell asleep with a cigarette. My brother and I had our bedroom in the basement, and we literally had to run through fire at three o'clock in the morning to get out of the house, and then we had to stand there and watch this pathetic man who was our father try to put out a raging inferno with a garden hose.
>
> The house-torching was the last straw for our stepmother. She took the daughter they'd had together and left. The next time my father cleaned up, he moved us kids to a new city and went to work as a counselor in an alcohol and drug rehabilitation facility. This reprieve lasted a few years, but then he relapsed again, and was fired again—and so it went.

While many young men in this kind of family situation might have made an early escape into alcohol and drugs, Louis did not. He had other obsessions to attend to—namely chess and portrait painting. That's what probably saved him from an even worse alcoholic career.

> I was introverted, so instead of hanging out with my peers I sat in my room all day and painted and played chess. By the tenth grade I'd beat everybody in school, so I started entering tournaments. From there I went to the U.S. high school championships and did well. I was a Master when I was still a teenager, and today I rank in the top thirty.

Louis states that he didn't begin drinking alcohol until he was twenty-one, which means that he had a chance to have a chemical-free adolescence and develop a little more maturity than many alcoholic men whose addictions began earlier. As a result, Louis comes across as perhaps less flaky than many under-thirty-day newcomers.

In fact, in Louis's case, as in the cases of many alcoholic men who also happen to be adult children of alcoholics (ACAs), he developed into the opposite of "flaky." He became the responsible one, the "rescuer." Initially, it showed up at home.

> In the beginning, I thought that my brother and sister and I were all so strong that we'd make it just fine, in spite of our mother's death, and in spite of our father's alcoholism. But one by one we started to drop. First my brother developed schizophrenia in his late teens, and after that it seemed as though insanity of one kind or another just took over the whole household. I kept trying to fix my brother, to "snap" him out of it, and when it didn't work, I became cynical and disenchanted. The next thing that happened was my sister's anorexia, plus she got into other weird stuff, like she fixated on this older man and camped out on his doorstep until the cops had to come and take her away. At that point I was convinced that *I* was the only sane one, the only strong one, the only survivor. I decided that it was my job to somehow fix everybody, so what I did was quit school (I'd been going to college for a math degree) so I'd have time to fix everybody, and also so I could "explore the world of alcohol" was how I put it. I decided this— even though I *knew* that alcoholism ran amuck in the family. Obviously, I was just as insane as the rest of them!
>
> Anyway, after setting out to "explore the world of alcohol," I ended up drinking alcoholically for thirteen years. In that time, the longest I was sober was two weeks.

Having quit school, Louis supported himself with chess tournament earnings, occasional portrait sales and by being a part-time knife-sharpener so he could still play chess on weekends. He also did a three-year stint as a mailman, often getting drunk on the job.

> I could case my mail quickly, so I'd go out and run my route in three hours and get done by noon, and I didn't have to be back

on the job until three, so I'd spend three hours at the bar. Nearly every day I drove that postal jeep, drunk. I never got caught. People don't really watch postal vehicles too closely because they assume they're on the ball!

In the relationship area, Louis appears to have perfected the ability to avoid confrontation, sidestep intimacy and steer clear of decision-making.

> I never told my father I was a drinker. I'd drop by the house and he'd say, "How are you doing?" and I'd say, "Oh, fine! I'm doing well in chess and my painting is going well." I'd always keep it vague. He'd say, "Have you seen your brother lately?" and I'd say, "Oh, I saw him a while back," whereas in truth I hadn't seen him for a year and a half because it was too painful.

In his relationship with his girlfriend, Louis was also a classic non-committer and avoider. And in his words, she herself was a "classic enabler from a dysfunctional, alcoholic family." Translation: For ten years she was willing to live with him and put up with him. Asked why they never married, Louis said:

> She has enough good qualities to fill a scroll, but because she's seven years older than I am and because she'd already had her kids and had her tubes tied, I spent ten years being tormented about whether or not I wanted kids. So my solution to this dilemma was to drink, to obliterate myself. I ended up forcing her to kick me out, so that solved *that* problem!

Louis also avoided making the decision to get treatment. It was made for him in the form of an informal "intervention" process, which is when other people step in on purpose and force the issue.

Louis: After my brother died, I was living at my father's house and I guess he took a very critical look at me and decided that what happened to my brother wasn't going to happen to me. So one day when I came home there were a bunch of cars out front, and I thought, "Gee, party!" I walked in and my father was there with some of his AA compatriots, and my girlfriend was there with this somber look on her face, and I looked around and everybody was looking at me and I realized quite quickly that I was the object of their attention.

Sylvia: Sure sounds like intervention-time to me!

Louis: Yeah! They all had these "poor Louis" looks on their faces, and my father said, "Sit down, *son*," and I thought, "Oh-oh!" I sat down and they started in on me. It was like a firing line. My girl-friend started telling about all the insane things I'd done to her over the years, and then the others took their turns, and when it was all over my father gave me the ultimatum.

Now, I didn't want treatment. I had the classic feeling that I could do it myself. I didn't think I had a problem, even though when I was drinking I did crazy, dangerous things, like giving rides to strange people and ending up in bad areas. Once I plowed into a parked car and woke up to find my wallet gone. Later a guy with a rifle chased me in his car. I was going 65 mph when I turned into a cul de sac, so I just ditched my car and ran. But still, I didn't think I was *that* bad! But when my father said: "Get treatment or get out!" I said, "Well, if you put it that way, then all right. Maybe there's something I *don't* know about all this that I need to learn after all."

Sylvia: What's the best and the worst parts about being in recovery for you?

Louis: The best part is being able to talk to and relate to people who are in my boat. I've never done that before. That's quite an exhilarating feeling. The worst part is the feeling part, trying to look at the feelings that I've buried, like that two-year period in my life just after my mother died and we were at my grandmother's. I can remember all the events, but I just can't dredge up the emotions associated with the events. It's like a two-year block.

Louis also has the job ahead of him of dealing with his current grief over the so very recent death of his brother.

> My brother was a good chess player, too. We were competitors. Once he even beat a player who is now number one in the country, so he had his moment in the sun. Seeing someone like that go down the drain, first from schizophrenia and then from alcoholism, has been very difficult. In a way he died twice for me, and I think the first time was the hardest. Sometimes I feel a sense of relief that he died because all his torment is ended now. And I feel guilty for that. I've got all *kinds* of feelings.

Because Louis has "all kinds of feelings," he doesn't identify as a "true stuffer." He says: "At my brother's memorial service I cried and was a quivering blob of Jello™. I don't think if I was a true feeling-stuffer I'd have been able to do that."

Another task Louis will be tackling is learning to curb his "ACA" need to rescue people. He is only starting to become aware of the extent to which he does this. In the recovery house, he has already started catching himself in the act of saving souls.

> Probably one of the biggest problems I have right now is my tendency to get overly involved with other people's problems. This morning I was depressed because a woman here at the recovery house—somebody I've been able to relate to—is not happy here and wants to leave, is *going* to leave, and I know that if she leaves, it will upset me. And all my life, once I'm depressed about one thing, I start thinking about everything else that has ever depressed me and it's like a snowball effect. It all comes crashing down on me.

A good guess in Louis's case is that somebody leaving stirs up memories of his mother's death. That may partly explain his depression over his housemate's pending departure. But if he's going to get depressed, at least he's in a safe place for it. It's at times like this that being in a treatment setting can be a lifesaver. Were he "outside" on his own, his depression might lead to a "slip."

At eighteen days, this incident is Louis's first major test of his sobriety. In the past, he admits that he'd probably have handled his pain by "running to the bar and getting drunk." But Louis says that he believes something has changed inside of him: "I noticed both last night and this morning that even though I was upset about this person leaving, I still didn't have the desire to drink over it."

That shift alone is both critical and encouraging. Apparently, Louis is beginning to see that there are other ways of handling pain and stress besides drinking—and that his *primary* responsibility is to stay clean and sober. He can't "save" his housemate, but he *can* save himself.

Sylvia: What are your plans for after you're discharged from the recovery house?

Louis: They say that alcoholics and addicts never complete anything, so I'm going back to school to get my math degree. It will be good for me to finish that unfinished business. I don't know what I'm going to do with it. One thing I do know is that I'm always going to be a chess player. I'm a lifer in that respect. Now that I'm sober, I'm amazed that I was able to rank as high in the country as I did seeing as how I was drinking so prolifically. Drinking got in the way of chess big time. Maybe in sobriety I can move up the ranks. And I'll always be a portrait painter, too. And maybe someday I'll get into some other, spontaneous areas of art like cartooning and sketching.

My father is getting remarried again, only this time it's a good thing. He's sober and she's a wonderful lady. They're going to be traveling, so I'll have his house to stay in. I don't have any alcoholic or addict friends. I do have people who love me. I have direction. It almost seems like it's *too* good to be true.

The fact that Louis has good aftercare plans and a safe environment to return to with few drinking temptations is a definite plus.

One area where Louis will probably have some surprises ahead is in the relationship area. For example, his girlfriend is apparently still in the picture. *He* thinks everything about the relationship is just fine: "My girlfriend and I are friends and we'll stay friends, even if we don't live together again. There's no hostility or animosity between us." However, while he's been in the recovery house, his girlfriend has been going to Al-Anon meetings and reading books and seeing videos on the subject of "dysfunctional families" and she's no doubt learning a lot. In no time flat she's likely to "get in touch" with a few buried feelings of her own as the result of being with Louis for ten years, and she may very well decide to "share" them with him! If she does (and most enlightened codependents do this), it may surprise him to know what emotions she's been sitting on!

More will be revealed!

And there are dangers ahead for Louis as well as surprises. But Louis, like most newcomers, underestimates the power of his own addiction, and *over*-estimates his strength at fighting it. "I have no trepidations about leaving the recovery house. I know there will be problems and times of stress in the future, but I think I'll be able to handle them now because I realize that there are people who care for me. It's really quite neat for me and I'm pretty lucky."

And then, casually, Louis throws out the kind of comment that can send chills up the spines of seasoned old-timers in recovery who know what he's up against—who know that the odds of Louis or *any*body staying sober are stacked against him: "The only thing I'll ever wonder is—Could I have done this sobriety thing on my *own*, without the program?"

Perhaps Louis noticed the look of horror on my face at the very idea that somebody with his alcoholic track record could even *think* about trying to go it alone, because he quickly added: "But that's a moot point now, isn't it? Because here I am!"

3

THOSE FRIGHTENING FIRSTS:
Mark, Sober Sixty Days

Last week I went to this nice restaurant with my brother and his girlfriend. It was a situation where I'd normally drink, and all of a sudden I started having an anxiety attack, with sweaty palms and everything. I started smoking one cigarette after another, and I kept telling myself, "This will pass. This will pass." I don't know if other people go through this. It's all so new. What worries me is thinking maybe it's not going to get any easier.

Welcome to Sixty Days of Sobriety!

For men who have spent their first thirty days in the protective atmosphere of a treatment center, their second thirty days is quite a shock. It begins with getting discharged into the "Real World" and having to face the "frightening firsts"—the first day home from the hospital, the first day back at work, the first business trip, the first social occasion, the first sexual encounter, the first football game on TV with all those beer commercials, the first craving attack, the first crisis. There's also getting through that first time a man tells somebody outside the family that he's an alcoholic. Once he does it, he usually experiences a sense of relief, as this man discovered after his discharge from a chemical dependency treatment center:

I had to phone a woman at my job about my hospital insurance claim. This was a woman I knew and liked. I figured she probably knew I'd been in a CD unit, and I was afraid she'd judge me for it. When she heard it was me on the phone, she said, "Oh, hi, how're you doing?" and I said, "Fine." Then there was this pause, and she said, using AA terminology, "One day at a time?" I got kind of quiet for a minute. Then I answered, "Yeah, one day at a time." And she said, "That's great! Keep coming back!" which is also something they say in AA. That's when I screwed up my courage and asked, "How do you know about the AA program?" and she said, very discreetly because other people were around, "Because my son was sick with the same thing you had, and he has two years now, so keep coming back. It worked for him." I had chills! I couldn't even say anything. It blew me away.

Getting through a disclosure like this is a tremendous hurdle for the newcomer, especially for men, who tend to be more secretive than women about such things.

Other sixty-day shocks include the fact that not everyone out there in the Real World is as understanding and supportive as they were in the treatment center; the fact that right after discharge, one's peers in treatment begin to relapse; the fact that cravings for chemicals don't go away and stay away; the fact that wives, girlfriends, and old drinking buddies sometimes try to sabotage the newcomer's sobriety; the fact that not all women find nondrinkers sexy; the fact that feelings, once they thaw out in sobriety, can hurt; the fact that it's harder to walk into an AA meeting alone than it is to be driven there in a van with your fellow patients; the fact that "working the program," "using the phone," and "living one day at a time" are easier said than done.

Here's what Sponsor Jack says about this sixty-day stage:

If the first thirty days were spent in the wonderfully controlled environment of this hospital—with beautiful women counselors listening intently to the man's every word—then being discharged is a rude awakening. The man goes home and the paint is still peeling, his wife hasn't liked him in years, his kid is still picking his nose, and his boss looks at him funny. The magical glow wears off very quickly.

The next shock is going to be the first AA meeting he attends on his own.

He doesn't always find AA to be the warm and wonderful place it seemed to be when he went there with his group. Usually he's ignored. People who are forty or fifty days sober out of hospitals may get *no* attention, whereas the obvious newcomer, who didn't go to a hospital, gets an enormous amount. People push one another out of the way to give him their phone numbers.

As was pointed out in the last chapter, the hospital graduate looks so "together" that nobody knows he's fragile and hurting. *He* doesn't even know it. Says Sponsor Jack:

When they come into AA physically sober this way, they don't have the advantage of being at a *dis*advantage, by which I mean, because they look so good they miss out on getting the help they need from others to survive. The older AA member feels he has no leverage with such a newcomer. He can't say, "Who cares what you think! Look how your hands are shaking!" All he can say is "Hur-rumph! Hur-rumph! I've been sober longer than you, so shut up and do as I tell you!" The old-timer may well turn around and go look for a *real* newcomer who needs him enough to genuinely listen, somebody who's still shaking and still smells like an alcoholic. So there's a lot of stress involved when a new man walks into an AA meeting where they're not overanxious to see him.

Some AA members believe that as a result of such things, AA's recovery rate has gotten worse, not better—that maybe, in some ways, hospital programs do some harm.

There seems to be more recidivism than there used to be. These days, earlier diagnosis and painless detoxification mean that the alcoholic may not have suffered enough to be willing to "go to any lengths" to stay sober. If he doesn't like something, he leaves. Of course, being in a hospital is certainly better than being left lying on the street—so in that way a CD unit is obviously a good thing. But in other ways, it may present a few problems.

Green-Eyed Monsters

According to Dr. Paul Grossman, the sixty-day stage of sobriety can be particularly stressful for the family man (or the man with an ongoing relationship with a woman) because of jealousy. Once he's home, *her* insecurity surfaces.

> Family members, especially wives, begin to think, "Gee, he loved me when he was drunk, but what about now that he's sober? Now he has this marvelous life ahead of him, all these new people in his life; maybe he won't need me anymore. Maybe he'll realize that he never loved me, that he only picked me because he was sick." The recovering alcoholic comes home feeling great and finds this depressed woman waiting for him. That's bad enough. When she starts getting jealous, it's worse. She wonders, "Who will he meet at these AA or CA [Cocaine Anonymous] meetings? Why is he sharing all these intimate secrets with them and not with me?" Hopefully, couples will learn to communicate well enough to get through these tricky times.

Dragon Slaying

In some ways, the sixty-day man has a rougher time than the sixty-day woman. There's more social pressure on the man to drink and be a "real man." The macho factor. If a man orders a soft drink, people assume he's a wimp. Or he *thinks* that's what they assume, which ends up being the same thing. A woman, on the other hand, can be at a bar and order a diet soda and people assume she's on a diet.

As Sponsor Jack says, "In the treatment center, the recovering alcoholic man's 'classmates' were supportive; after discharge, he finds that some of his old friends are not: 'We're going to have a beer, Charlie, what are *you* going to do?'"

So the recovering alcoholic man—to prove to himself and to others that he's strong—does something dumb, like this man did: "the first week I was out of the hospital, I marched myself right down to my old bar, and I sat there with my buddies for seven straight hours—just to test myself and see if I could do it." As if life wasn't going to offer him enough "tests" without his having to go looking for them! Women, however, rarely feel the need to do this.

AA warns that "if you don't want to slip, don't go where it's slippery," but the macho man won't listen. He's seen a dragon, and he has to slay it before he can rest easy. Crazy newcomers! If one of these dragon slayers has a sponsor, he's probably giving the poor man sleepless nights. Sponsors know only too well the usual outcomes of such tests. Any jerk can sit in a bar and order tomato juice once, maybe more than once, but sooner or later, if he keeps it up, he'll cave in.

Meetings-Meetings-Meetings

No matter how many times it's stressed that the three most important things in AA recovery are meetings-meetings-meetings, the newcomer doesn't believe it. As he gets to feel better, as he puts more distance between himself and his pain, he forgets how bad it was; how much he hurt. The danger in this is that he starts to cut down on his AA or CA or NA [Narcotics Anonymous] meetings, especially if he hasn't been welcomed there with open arms.

Sponsor Jack: A lot of people come in and hang around AA for sixty days, and then they become irritated with AA and begin to regard it as castor oil, something they're supposed to do but don't like. They make comments like, "AA didn't work for me. Nobody paid much attention. I couldn't find a sponsor. It's a closed clique." They stop going, and if they stay away for more than a few weeks, they're drunk or loaded again. Sometimes, if they go out and then come back to AA, the *next* time they're ready for it. It takes persistence, being willing to try again and again, to make it.

What the newcomer doesn't understand is that AA should be regarded as a treatment program for the disease of alcoholism in the same way you'd regard dialysis treatment for kidney disease. It's critical. And if only a few hours a week of treatment is required in order to live a normal life, it seems a small price to pay.

Sponsorship

It's not an AA "law" (there aren't any), but it certainly is highly recommended that every AA member—no matter how long he's been sober—gets a sponsor. By sixty days of sobriety, the new man should have done this.

A sponsor is an AA teacher or "mentor," someone who has been sober in AA (or CA, NA, and so on) for at least a year, so he's had a chance to go through (and survive) "the frightening first" plus a crisis or two. A sponsor is a working role model, someone who not only will be a good example for the newcomer but will also work one-on-one with that newcomer to help him learn the ropes without hanging himself.

In picking a sponsor (a "temporary" one can be selected first), the newcomer should look for someone he can relate to, someone he can easily communicate with.

It is recommended (again, it's not a law, and there are exceptions) that men sponsor men and women sponsor women. The reason for this is obvious: When the recovering alcoholic is dealing with an addiction that could kill him, sexual chemistry might only serve to interfere with his primary goal—saving his life.

Newcomers are usually nervous when the time comes to ask somebody to be their sponsor. You hear, "I don't want to bother him," or, "What if he says no?" The newly sober are afraid of that rejection. They have to be reminded that if the sponsor says yes, he isn't just doing the "baby" or "pigeon" or "sponsee" a favor. He's working a "selfish" program in the best sense of the word, since sponsoring somebody else keeps the sponsor sober, too. Remember that the AA secret of success is "one drunk talking to another," which is the essence of sponsorship.

MARK

I keep thinking getting better means accomplishing things, but that's not it. Getting better means just staying sober one day at a time and not getting sidetracked.

Mark, twenty, a slender young man with a long, thin face, is a fraternal twin. He is currently stationed at an Air Force base in California. The night before our interview, he had gone to an AA meeting and received his "chip" (token) for sixty days of sobriety.

Mark and his brother have two sisters, ages twenty-two and fourteen. The older sister has been diagnosed as schizophrenic.

Of the four kids, I was the "good" one, the responsible one. I got good grades. I made my bed. I cleaned up my room. I made dinner. My parents had all kinds of problems, including drinking. My older sister was crazy; my brother was a total jerk. So at thirteen, when I started to get depressed, I figured it was nothing compared to everybody else's problems, and I never told anybody about it. They didn't need my problems. They needed me to take care of things.

Once I asked my father straight out, "Why do you guys drink so much?" and he said, "It's because of your older sister." So from then on I had a big resentment toward her. I didn't realize she was so sick.

Mark's mother now has two years of sobriety in Alcoholics Anonymous (she went through a treatment center), and his father has six years of sobriety, but *not* in AA. "I can see the difference between my mother and my father," Mark says. "My father hasn't changed much, but by going to AA my mother has changed a lot. All I have to do is compare them, and it's easy to decide which way I want to go."

Mark began drinking on a daily basis in high school where he had two sets of friends: his regular friends and his partytime friends. He and his partytime friends all had the combination to a special locker where booze was hidden.

> People think you have to put away a certain amount a day to be an alcoholic, more beers than anybody else, but that's not true. It's what those beers you drink *do* to you that counts. They made me volatile. I'd go to clubs with my friends, and we'd go into the bathrooms and bust up mirrors, break toilets, and then we'd go out into the parking lot and smash up people's cars, people we didn't even know.

At the base Mark hit his "bottom." After three drunken fights in one week, including one with his supervisor ("I got beaten up all three times!") he knew he was in trouble. As a result, he was hospitalized in a chemical dependency treatment center. Mark talks with a kind of nostalgia about those first thirty days:

> When I was admitted to the hospital, I didn't want to talk to anybody about my past or be honest about how I felt, so the first couple of days I kept a low profile. But then I realized that if I was ever going to get help, here it was, so I'd better start opening up and try to be as honest as I could—and right away I began to

feel better. Basically, the whole day was like therapy because all you did was talk about your problems. There were ten of us going through the program together, and you really learn to care about one another because you're all there for the same reason. I learned a whole lot about myself. It turned out to be the best thirty days of my life.

AA teaches that the number one killer of alcoholics is resentment—for obvious reasons. Resentment is uncomfortable, and when an alcoholic is uncomfortable he might drink, which could kill him. So alcoholics don't have the luxury of nursing resentments.

I had many resentments and they became my excuses for drinking. I resented my parents for being alcoholics and I blamed my problems on them. I was the victim. I was the child of alcoholics. I thought I'd never give those resentments up, but I've had to. At least I'm trying to. If I catch myself being resentful, I'll let myself feel the resentment, briefly, and then I make myself let it go.

Mark, in typical fashion, went through a whole slew of frightening firsts between thirty and sixty days of sobriety. For him, dealing with friends was one of the most difficult.

"The norm for someone my age is you drink beer, so when I stopped drinking, I lost nearly all my friends."

What made it worse was the fact that all his "classmates" from the treatment center slipped.

The guys from the base that I went through the CD unit with are all back to drinking now. It started with the two guys I was closest to. They just wouldn't go to AA. They both started drinking. First they'd just drink once a week, then twice a week, and now they're back where they were before. Then the other seven slipped, and I'm the only one still sober. On the base, when they get drunk it's like they're determined to get me to slip too. They go out of their way to come right up to me and say, "Here, Mark, you want a beer?" and they'll shove it in my face. It really got to me the first couple of times this happened. When you're twenty years old, that's the *worst* kind of situation to be in, where a whole bunch of people are taunting you. I'd feel like I was trapped in a damned cage. I swear, if I'd been drinking I'd probably have torn them limb from limb. I wanted to tell them "f — off" but I just walked away. I had to. I guess they were just testing me to see if I was strong enough to refuse.

Mark is also one of those who had to slay his dragon and test his strength.

"Whenever I'm back in L.A., in order to hang out with my old friends I go where they go, and they go to parties. But at least in L.A. some of my regular friends are supportive of my sobriety. They even tell me, 'If you drink, we'll break your godddamned legs.' "

But Mark knows that parties are slippery places.

I probably shouldn't put myself in that position, because when I go to parties I usually end up getting stressed out. My problem is that I don't know where to draw the line. I don't know when to leave. As soon as my friends see me they say to me, "We feel guilty drinking around you," and I jump to reassure them. I tell them, "Look, if I'm here at this party it's because I *want* to be here. It's my choice to be in this situation. If I want to leave, I'll leave. So don't feel guilty. Go ahead and drink. It doesn't affect me." And then I sit there and repeat that to myself. "It doesn't affect me. It doesn't affect me. It doesn't affect me." I guess if it *really* didn't affect me, I wouldn't have to sit there telling myself it doesn't would I?

Mark burst out laughing here as he caught himself in the act of self-deception. Then he quickly moved on to discuss a possible solution to his partying problem.

Lately I've been trying to avoid at least some of the situations I know I'll have trouble getting out of. I just don't go. Back at the base when some of the guys asked me to drive them to a club so *they* could drink, I refused. I was really angry that they even asked me to do such a thing. I should have told them, "Look, I don't want you coming to me drunk, and expecting me to drive you to some damn club!" But I didn't say anything. At least I realized I was angry. That's progress. And at least I was able to refuse to go instead of giving in. That's a *lot* of progress.

The biggest danger for Mark at this point, of course, is cutting down on his own AA meetings, and that's exactly what he's been doing.

Sylvia: I'm sure you're aware of how risky that is?

Mark: I know in my *head* the things I have to do to stay sober, like going to meetings, but it's so easy to get sidetracked. When I was in the hospital, I went to an AA meeting every day for thirty days. The first week after my discharge, I went to three. The next week, only one or two, then none. But you know what? The next week that I didn't go to any meetings, I didn't feel guilty at all. It's easy to get rid of that guilt by making up excuses, like I don't have a ride, I'm too tired, there's nobody there my age, or I don't need it because I feel so much better about myself. I keep forgetting that what makes me feel really good about myself is *not drinking*, and going to meetings of Alcoholics Anonymous! Whenever I waltz out of an AA meeting, I feel great, a lot better than when I walked in. If every night, just by going someplace for an hour and a half, you can walk out feeling great instead of lousy, it's worth it. AA definitely works, no doubt about that. [Mark takes a long pause here.] So this business of not going to meetings is really stupid of me, isn't it?

Mark has recently begun to feel his feelings.

Mark: The first six weeks I resisted feelings. I pushed them away. The feelings I was most scared of was depression because I'd tried suicide three times in my teens. The only thing that had ever helped me with depression was booze, and since that was no longer an option, I kept waiting for this huge depression to come and smack me in the face. I'd wake up and say, "Is today the day?" It finally hit a week or so after I got out of the hospital. I just said to myself, "Face the feeling, don't run away from it." I let myself *feel* the depression instead of fighting it. And you know what? It wasn't as bad as I thought it would be. I felt it, and it was over with, and that was that. I survived it. It felt good.

Sylvia: That's a pretty advanced technique for handling painful emotions for somebody so new in AA. How did you learn to do that?

Mark: I don't know how I came to that conclusion. I think I just got tired of trying to deny or ignore my feelings. It takes more work to do that than it does to accept them, feel them, and then just let them go.

Another frightening first for Mark in sobriety has been dating women:

Mark: I've already been burned a few times! As soon as I tell a girl I'm a recovering alcoholic, she avoids me. I think it turns young girls off, at least high school-age girls. They think the only way to have fun is with alcohol. About three weeks ago I met this seventeen-year-old girl who really seemed to like me, but when I told her, "I'm an alcoholic. I go to AA and I don't drink," you know what she said? She said, "How boring. How can you have fun if you don't drink?" And I said, "Hey, I'm having fun." I tried to tell her what the meetings were like, but she blew me off. She said, "I don't want to hear it." And she was guzzling a beer when she said it! I was pissed! If she'd been a guy, I'd have hit her in the face.

But I can't let that get to me, because my main job right now is to be totally honest with people. That's what felt so good when I was in the hospital. I've begun to realize that in order for me to stay sober, I may have to upset some people along the way.

Sylvia: Then how are you going to handle this dating situation?

Mark: In the last couple of weeks I've met some older women, twenty-one or twenty-two, who are more understanding. They respect a guy for doing something to help himself. I'll keep looking for women like that and steer clear of the others.

Sylvia: How do you see yourself in the *next* thirty days?

Mark: I see myself going to more AA meetings and getting more honest with myself. Like it's not honest for me to say it's hard to find people my age who don't drink. I just haven't looked for them. I see myself spending some time looking for friends my own age who don't drink and hanging out with them.

Mark, of course, like most newly sober alcoholics and addicts, wants it all *now.*

Mark: I get confused sometimes between getting better and reaching goals—like getting a girlfriend, going to school, making money—but the real goal is sobriety. I'm lucky, though. I have good support at home. My mom is especially helpful because of her experience in AA, so I feel confident that I'll be able to stay sober, stop procrastinating, and go to meetings.

What I like most about AA is they don't pass judgment on you. They don't worry about what you're wearing or how fat or thin you are. In high school, if I had to talk in front of a class of only thirty people, my knees would be shaking because I knew they were judging me, but when I was in the treatment center, I actually got up in front of about two hundred people at an AA meeting and talked about myself, and I was fine. They don't judge you there. They want to hear what you have to say. They realize you're there to save your life.

4

THE ARMPIT OF SOBRIETY:
Norman, Sober 120 Days

I'm going through a major crisis. It's hitting me from ten different directions. After being asleep for thirty-six years, like Rip Van Winkle, I'm waking up to find that I'm not in love with my wife, I'm burned out as an engineer, and I have no idea who I am or what I want. Before, I could medicate myself with alcohol and sometimes speed to make pain go away, but I can't do that anymore. So I'm stuck. Paralyzed. In fact, the thought of suicide is on my mind daily.

Renewed craving, anxiety, depression, insomnia, clouded thinking, lousy concentration, irritability, tremulousness. Sound like the symptoms of an awful illness? Well, not exactly. They are symptoms of healing, the phase of the recovery process that Dr. Paul Grossman, in his colorful way, calls "the armpit of sobriety."

Dr. Grossman: When I talk about the "armpit of sobriety," I'm referring to what's been called "the post acute withdrawal syndrome," or the "post drug impairment syndrome." It can hit at about three or four months and in some cases can last for most of the first year.

In the beginning, the recovering person feels optimistic. He's dedicated to sobriety. He remembers his drinking episodes, how horrible he felt, how demeaning it was. It's all very fresh in his mind. He thinks he's been through the worst of it and that from here on sobriety is going to be wonderful. Then he gets hit with these symptoms, and it knocks him for a loop. The honeymoon is over. A lot of people don't make it through.

Sylvia: What approach do you use when you suspect that one of your recovering alcoholic patients is in the armpit phase?

Dr. Grossman: I casually say to him, "Oh, yes, you've entered the armpit of sobriety," and usually when the patient realizes this phase is something that's been codefied and described and documented, he feels tremendously relieved. Until then he thinks he's been doing something wrong. It's comforting to know this is only temporary.

Here's what our friend, Jack, has to say about the armpit phase from a sponsor's point of view:

> It's in these months of sobriety that the newcomer is asked to handle his worst problems when he has the least ability or experience to do so. Almost always, everything in his life is in a shambles. He's getting a divorce; he's sleeping on somebody's couch in their garage; he's lost (or is losing, or can't even get) his job; he's filing for bankruptcy; he's been accused of abusing his wife or kid; he's been unfaithful; he may have injured or even killed somebody with his car. At AA meetings they tell him to be patient and "work the program," and he says, "But you don't understand, I have *problems*!" Then they just smile and say, "Keep coming back." It's disconcerting to say the least.

Depression

The emotion most common to the recovering man in the armpit stage of sobriety is depression. Most people who have alcoholism also suffer from depression, because alcohol is a depressive drug. Drinking may start out as a feel-good activity, but it can end up getting a man down. However, the majority of recovering alcoholics who have stopped drinking report that their depression lifts and within weeks they feel better. Even during the armpit stage, bad as it is, life is still better than it was. As AAs are fond of saying, "My worst day sober is still better than my best day drinking." According to Dr. Paul L. Rosenberg, another Los Angeles-based psychiatrist who treats alcoholics, these are the people who are called "primary alcoholics." Alcoholism is their main problem. AA says, "If you just come to AA and stop drinking, get a sponsor, and work the steps, your life will get better." While this is true for about 90 percent of the newly sober, it's a different story for the other 10 percent. After *they* quit drinking, their depression gets worse. "They are called secondary alcoholics," says Dr. Rosenberg.

> Their primary problem is depression, possibly biochemical, which they've been self-treating with alcohol, and their secondary problem is alcoholism. When AA tells them to "stop drinking and your life will look rosy," they feel lied to because that isn't what happens. Instead, their lives look drearier than ever. Unfortunately, AA doesn't seem to distinguish between these two groups, so the secondary alcoholic in AA who isn't getting cheerier feels like a failure. Sometimes a *non*-mind-altering medication, such as an antidepressant—something the recovering alcoholic can take without blowing his sobriety—is helpful here.

Knowledge of the existence of these two distinct groups of people who recover from alcoholism is helpful—both for the recovering man himself as well as his helpers and his family. Dr. Rosenberg advises:

> If you yourself are feeling worse after a few months of sobriety, or if you are working with someone who feels worse, then the diagnosis of secondary alcoholism should be considered. At the same time, it's very important to remember that most alcoholics are depressed when they first come into treatment, so don't jump the gun and assume that they are secondary alcoholics. Let time

go by. Only if their depression remains after weeks or months of sobriety should a diagnosis of secondary alcoholism be assumed.

Depression surfaces in the recovery process from other drugs as well, such as cocaine. New evidence suggests that long-term cocaine use can reduce—perhaps even destroy—the brain's natural ability to manufacture pleasure-producing chemicals. For these addicts, sobriety brings no joy at all, which may be why so many decide to return to the only thing that *does* bring them pleasure—cocaine. They, too, can be helped by antidepressants, along with vitamins, exercise, participation in self-help groups—and *time*.

Anxiety

The other emotion that plagues newcomers, especially in the armpit phase, is anxiety. One AA sponsor follows this rule of thumb: "Once detox is over with, having anxiety means you're either doing something you *shouldn't* be doing, or you're *not* doing something you *should* be doing. Period!" Mother Nature gives us anxiety for a reason, to warn us that something is wrong, that maybe we're up to no good. But, of course, most newcomers don't pay any attention to their body's warning system. They plow right on ahead and then express amazement when they don't feel well emotionally! A newly recovered alcoholic can write bad checks, sleep with his wife's best friend, and break promises to his children, and then say, looking innocent and wide-eyed, "Yesterday I had the biggest anxiety attack of my life, and I have no idea what caused it."

Rarely does the newcomer make a connection between how he feels emotionally and his daily behavior. That's too simple. He figures anxiety must stem from something more complicated than that. He's like someone who hits himself on the head with a hammer and then wonders why he has a headache. That's why newcomers' lives are so full of drama, like soap operas. They keep misbehaving. Old-timers, in contrast, have very little daily drama going on. They've finally figured out that when they behave well, with integrity, life goes smoothly. Integrity "works!"

Emotional Involvements

The worrisome thing about the recovering alcoholic man who's depressed is, What is he going to do about it? Commit suicide? (Some do.) Relapse? (Many do that.) Or find some kind of quick-fix distraction? (Many do that, too.) One of the most common distractions from the pain of the armpit phase is getting romantically involved, something AA warns against. As we've already noted, it doesn't matter how many times the newcomer is told that sex and early sobriety don't mix; few listen. As one cynical old-timer put it: "Usually the only newcomers who don't manage to get emotionally involved in their first year weren't asked!" Some grasp for romantic liaisons even before they've been discharged from the treatment center. Occasionally, when boy meets girl in the CD unit or on the AA campus, one of them is married to somebody else, but that doesn't stop them, even though AA quietly attempts to discourage infidelity. Infidelity simply doesn't jibe with the principles of AA's twelve-step program.

Sponsor Jack relates his own personal experience with the fidelity issue.

> When I first got sober eighteen years ago, my own sponsor had to bring to my attention a few things I hadn't noticed, like the fact that I was married. He told me, and I now tell other newcomers, that if you want to stay sober you've got to be honest, and honest means keeping your promises, including the promise of fidelity. You're not being faithful to the woman, you're being faithful to

71

the promise you made. So it doesn't matter if the woman isn't as pretty or as young as somebody else. It has nothing to do with the woman but everything to do with the promise.

Of course, when I first heard this I lamented, "Let me outta here! I'm not going to be able to do this." But my sponsor warned, "If you don't stay faithful, you're going to drink." When I replied by threatening to leave my marriage, he said, "You can't do that because you can't make any major decisions in your first year of sobriety." So I was in a Catch-22 situation. Finally I said, "Okay, okay, I'll try." And that's what I did.

After three-and-a-half years I called him up to complain that even though his advice was working and I was staying sober, my wife *still* didn't trust me. "How long did it take you to teach her *not* to trust you?" my sponsor asked me. "Seventeen years," I said. "When you get to be seventeen years sober and *faithful*," my sponsor concluded, "then the score will be even." And I said, "Thanks a lot!" Well, on the very day that I was seventeen years sober and faithful, my wife gave me this gold charm I'm wearing around my neck. It says "17-Even."

What I discovered is that for the first seventeen years of my marriage I had essentially the same experience with a variety of women, and in the last eighteen years since I've been sober I've had a variety of experiences with the same woman, which is a much better deal.

Living in West Hollywood, I sponsor a lot of gay guys, and I've insisted on their fidelity too. Years ago I used to get arguments saying, "You don't understand. We're a different culture, and that's not our lifestyle," and I'd counter with "No, you don't understand, that's the *principle.*"

I'm not advocating that people stay in a relationship that isn't working, but what I *am* saying is that in any committed, loving relationship you have to be faithful and hang in there in order to earn the gifts of sobriety. I think we can give each other a great deal by walking through those dark moments together. That's when you become willing to confront issues and look for ways to make things *work*, instead of searching for ways to skip and run.

Our armpit man, Norman, has much to learn on this score.

NORMAN

*I've spent my whole life in places I didn't want to be in, with peo-
ple I didn't want to be with, doing things I didn't want to do. I've
been unhappy as long as I can remember, and I'm tired of it.
Now I'm going to do something about it.*

Norman is a big, blue-eyed, first-generation Estonian, with a
long, curly blond beard that makes him look more like a
Tennessee mountain man than the engineer he is. He appears
older than his thirty-six years. English is his second language.

Norman's parents were both born in Estonia. They met and
married in Los Angeles. When the Germans marched through
Estonia in World War II, Norman's father was drafted into the
German army. After he defected to the NATO forces, he became a
prison guard in Nuremberg during the trials. He came to America
after the war, initially settling in Kansas. Norman's mother and
grandmother spent five years in a German camp for displaced persons before coming to the States. At age fifteen she married
Norman's father and had just turned sixteen when Norman was
born. The birth of Norman's sister followed only two years later.

Like many alcoholics, Norman states that from an early age he
felt a tremendous pressure to please others, what AA refers to as
"people-pleasing."

I was always trying to achieve things to please my parents. I
thought being elected class president in the sixth grade, in a
school of about 600 kids, would please them, but I don't think
they even understood what that meant. All they cared about as
foreigners was that we did things the "right" way, the "American
way." It was especially important to them at the time because it
was during the Cold War. Being Estonians meant we were
regarded as Russians, which meant *Communists*. I was even
shunned at school. Later on, my mother was upset with me for
being the first divorce in the family, not to mention the first alcoholic. She took my "failures" personally.

Now 120 days into his second serious attempt at sobriety, Norman is having a hard time of it. Such a hard time, in fact, that at first glance he looks as though he might fall into the category of a secondary alcoholic whose primary problem is depression and whose secondary problem is alcoholism. Norman looks, talks, and even walks depressed. He's slowed down. And even though nearly all newcomers are hard on themselves, he is mercilessly so. During various times within the course of the interview, he referred to himself as worthless, a wreck, a mess, an emotional robot, and an asshole. He states that he has been depressed since childhood and has attempted suicide twice.

> In seventh grade I tried to poison myself by drinking iodine. In the hospital the doctor told my parents, "It's just a childhood thing," and not much more was said about it. Then years later I tried to kill myself after my first marriage broke up by driving my car into a tree.

Adding to his depression is the fact that Norman appears to be a chronic "stuffer," swallowing his feelings, wants, needs, and opinions instead of expressing them and acting on them.

> I've always been so worried about trying to fulfill the expectations of others that I never asked myself, "Yes, but what do I want?" I stuffed all that. I married my first wife to save her from a bad home situation. I was being Mr. Nice Guy. I moved her out of her house and set her up in an apartment. I supported her so she could finish high school. I let her use my car. And then, all of a sudden, she was my girlfriend. So to do the right thing, the expected thing, I married her.
> I married my second wife because she listened to me talk about my problems, probably my problems with my first wife! I met her in a bar, and when I talked she actually listened. Then I moved in with her because I didn't have anyplace else to go, and after three years we got married. She's a nice person. She's supportive. She's good with my kids. But until I got sober, I didn't realize I didn't love her. Now I don't think I want to be there.

Clearly, once feelings start getting *un*stuffed in sobriety, they can raise havoc.

Norman is equally ambivalent about work, but rather than deal with it directly, he's handling it in a passive-aggressive way, which he appears to have mastered to an art. He handles situations by *not* handling them, by sidestepping to avoid confrontation, by not taking a stand, none of which is very heroic. But if he stays sober, this will change.

Norman as yet doesn't seem to have much insight into what's behind his problems at work.

Sylvia: You said that you're burned out on your job, that you've slowed down and are functioning at about one-tenth of your capacity. Do you think you're *on strike*?

Norman: No, I don't think I'm on strike. I think I *should* be able to do what they want me to do. I'm beating myself up over the fact that I just can't seem to make myself do my job, even though I know how to do it. I just don't know *why* I can't.

Sylvia: Maybe because you're on strike! Instead of saying directly, "I don't want to!" you're doing it indirectly by saying, "I can't."

Norman: I've never let myself say I don't want to do something.

Sylvia: Well, it looks like you're saying it now.

Norman plans to resolve his work situation by getting his psychiatrist to put him on disability for "stress." Norman seems convinced that he's emotionally disabled to the point of being suicidal, and he may be right. With his history, his psychiatrist no doubt is concerned about this possibility.

Norman: I'm at the point where I can't be there at work one more minute. I'm not functioning. It's all I can do to keep myself from running. I keep hoping somebody will make an illegal left turn in front of me so I'll have an accident and won't have to go to work.

With any suicidal newcomer alcoholic, a balance has to be achieved between the principles of the AA program, which encourage being self-supporting and *dis*courage accepting outside financial help (which is what disability is) unless it's absolutely necessary, and raw survival. Obviously, life comes first. Norman's primary concern must be to stay alive, and then later he can worry about his character.

Whatever decision Norman makes, he should do so with the help of a sponsor since his own judgment, at present, is flawed. This is true for all newcomers. Unfortunately, Norman doesn't yet have a sponsor, so he's really skating on thin ice.

To "treat" the searing pain of his depression and anxiety, Norman has been self-medicating with an extramarital affair. He met the woman, *A.*, when he was in the treatment center for the second time. Since *A.* has about the same amount of sobriety, give or take a week, that means she's also been going through the armpit stage. Like two drowning people, Norman and *A.* are clinging to each other, and the scenario has two possible outcomes: either they will save each other (sometimes these relationships do wonders, risky as they are) or they will pull each other under. Only time will tell. If Norman had a sponsor, he'd probably be praying by now and holding his breath!

Norman: *A.* and I first became close friends and then we got sexually involved, which was very confusing to me since I was in the middle of trying to evaluate my marriage.

Sylvia: Does your wife know about *A.*?

Norman: Yes, she saw it coming and even cautioned me, "Don't get yourself in trouble. A. is freshly out of a marriage and vulnerable, too," but it was too late. I'd already fallen in love with A. I feel like I've found my best friend for the first time. It's my first glimmer of happiness. We just click. We're good for each other. Talking to her is the only thing I look forward to. And now my wife doesn't want the name of A. mentioned in the house.

Sylvia: Where will it go from here?

Norman: I don't know. I'm going to counseling with my wife. I haven't written my marriage off. I'm giving it as much of a chance as I can. I know my wife is feeling very threatened right now, and she's working hard to be there for me, to be intimate, to do all the things she thinks A. is doing for me, but my heart just isn't in it. I'm not happy. I think I'm just there out of guilt. And I'm so afraid of losing A., even though she understands what I'm doing. A. knows me better than anybody in the world, including my psychiatrist.

Newcomers have a strong need to be "understood," even though they have no understanding of themselves. Most of them are also oblivious to the impact that their actions have on other people. In Norman's case, imagine how the following series of events must have been experienced from A.'s point of view:

> I was so confused after A. and I got involved sexually that for a while I called a stop to the sexual part. Then I moved out of my house and into A.'s. A few days later, I left A.'s house and moved back in with my wife. A. said that when I moved in, it was the happiest day of her life. Then all of a sudden I packed my bags and left. It destroyed her. She felt so bad that she ran away to Oakland. But we've been talking it through on the phone, and at this very moment she's driving back down the coast to L.A. She'll be here on Friday.

It's not hard to see why old-timers also warn other AA members, even those with some sobriety, not to get involved with newcomers. They're lethal! Their emotions will change so rapidly that what they want today will probably change 180 degrees six months from now. Fortunately, they grow up. For example, if *A.* stays sober, chances are good that one day she'll wake up and wonder why she keeps putting up with a man whose shoes are usually under somebody else's bed. At that time she'll be able to make whatever decision she needs to save herself. Or Norman himself may decide to fish or cut bait. Again, time will tell.

At present, Norman remains one of those typical newcomers, mystified by his own emotions. Here he is, cheating on his wife, boomeranging back and forth with *A.*, giving of himself only half-heartedly (if that) on the job, plotting to quit, stuffing his feelings, and financially burying himself. Yet he wonders why he has anxiety attacks and feels depressed.

More will be revealed.

At least Norman has had enough psychotherapy and exposure to AA so that he should begin to catch on fairly soon, and begin to see that his behavior *is* affecting him and that changing his behavior will bring relief.

> I've been going through a great internal struggle. I believe in God and consider myself a Christian, but I've been going against all the teachings I had about divorce, commitments, and fidelity. To go out and cheat on my wife—I've never done that before. And I've been feeling guilty. But it just happened.

Recently, Norman has been looking to the future.

"My biggest problem right now isn't alcohol, it's adjusting to life. I don't see myself as being a recovered, productive person for at least three or four years."

He's probably right. A woman involved with a "Norman" should listen well and be prepared, because you can't hot-house a recovering alcoholic. Time is of the essence here.

On the more positive side, Norman is continuing to hang in there and stay clean and sober—despite all the stress and pain and the fact that some of his peers have already relapsed. Each day he does this, he gets stronger.

"I feel like maybe I'm finally beginning to crawl out of the armpit and up onto the shoulder of sobriety. There's a much better view from there."

5

ON BEING A RAVING LUNATIC ABOUT SOBRIETY:
"Charlie Brown," Sober One Year

Basically, I was a wanna-be tough guy who kept starting fights and ended up losing. But now I'm experiencing life for the first time. It's the best life I've ever had, and it's all because of this program. So nobody's going to endanger this program for me or take any piece of it away. This is real serious for me, this is number one. I don't care who you are, nobody's getting in my way. In fact, just like I used to mess around with people when I was drinking. Now I feel I would kill for this program.

Overdoing a Good Thing

Most nonalcoholics don't fully appreciate that it takes more than courage for a man to get sober and stay sober; it takes fanaticism, especially in the first year. If the recovering alcoholic *doesn't* overdo it, chances are he'll fail.

Dr. Paul Grossman is acutely aware of this in his treatment of recovering addicts and alcoholics.

The new man can't be nonchalant about sobriety. He can't say, "Well, AA is okay, but I'm not a joiner. I'm just a kick-back kind of a guy." That won't work. Alcohol is such a powerful medicine that he has to fight it with something equally powerful and strong. He has to become a zealot with a religious fervor. When he can become a raving lunatic about sobriety, then *maybe* he has a chance.

Stated in a less picturesque way, this is what the AA old-timers mean when they say that a newcomer won't make it unless he is willing to "go to any lengths."

Being a fanatic in AA terms means taking actions. It means reciting those AA clichés until their messages have become internalized: *One day at a time. First things first. Don't drink or use—no matter what. Easy does it. Don't take that first drink. Use the phone,* and so on and so on. It means going to meetings—every day, even two or three times a day. This isn't as nuts as it sounds. If people can't afford treatment centers and if local clinics are booked, a few meetings a day (they're free) may do the trick. Many have gone this route. If that's what it takes for a man to stay clean and sober, then that's what he's got to do. If he has to change jobs in order to do it, then *that's* what he's got to do. If he refuses, then maybe he's not enough of a fanatic to get sober. Doing whatever is necessary to ensure sobriety—even if it's uncomfortable, inconvenient, or difficult—is the number one priority.

By his first AA birthday or anniversary, the recovering alcoholic man who has been a fanatic about his sobriety has probably lost his sense of humor. Most fanatics do. He's been too busy guarding his sobriety to be jovial. But that won't last. He'll get back in balance eventually. Family and friends tell him to "lighten up," but that's as useless as trying to make those guards outside Buckingham Palace smile.

The first-year man is in a life-and-death drama. For him, just as for the early adolescent, everything is *A Big Deal.* At times he's even paranoid. A neighbor's friendly invitation to a cocktail party is interpreted as a calculated threat to his sobriety: "Why would they invite me to a cocktail party when they *know* I can't drink?" He feels safer inside AA's walls, trusting his new AA "family" more than his own. AA "understands" him. He is openly and unashamedly dependent on AA, often to the point where he's accused of using AA "as a crutch," a criticism that usually hits him right in the gut. While part of him still thinks it's bad to rely on anything or anyone, if he's a true lunatic about his sobriety he won't let that deter him.

First Go-Round With the Twelve Steps

By his first AA birthday or anniversary, the recovering alcoholic man has usually made a stab at "working" all twelve of the AA steps, even if it's only in a perfunctory manner. There is no official "right" way to work these steps, and no set time to begin. That's up to the individual. Some think they should be done in order; others say the steps should be used as needed, as tools to help a man deal with problems as they come up. While one sponsor may want the newcomer to write his "fearless and searching moral inventory" (fourth step) and then read it to somebody (fifth step) by the end of his first year, another won't push this. Yet most will agree that if the alcoholic procrastinates about this for too long, he runs the risk of drinking again.

The so-called "amends steps," steps eight and nine, read as follows:

Step 8: Made a list of all persons we had harmed and became willing to make amends to them all.

Step 9: Made direct amends, wherever possible, except when to do so would injure them, or others.

For many people, the amends steps are scary, especially if the men have hurt people along the way (and that's usually the case). But AA says that until these amends are made, the alcoholic won't feel free.

Some AAs impulsively tackle their amends before they're ready, which isn't advised. Others put them off for years, which isn't advised either. In most cases, the careful guidance of a sponsor is necessary to help the newcomer avoid doing more harm than good. People running amok through the amends without guidance can be deadly. One example is the man who decided he was going to be "open and honest" with his wife about all the affairs he'd had while he was drinking, so he went home and told her all about it, naming names. He thought he was "making amends," but what he was really doing was dumping. And because the wife had been blissfully unaware of his infidelities, she was devastated. It was a cruel and unnecessary confession on his part, and one his wife probably would have done better without. Had he worked on this step with his sponsor, this damage might have been avoided.

It is also during this first year that the alcoholic begins to discover that he has "character defects." This is usually a huge surprise to him. And, what's more, once he finds them he's supposed to do something about them (steps six and seven). Anger, resentment, dishonesty, and judgmentalness are often at the top of this list. He also has to learn to stay put. Most men come into sobriety with only two ways of handling problems: fight or flight. AA teaches him that there's a middle ground, which involves communicating feelings and listening without getting defensive.

The recovering alcoholic never finishes "working the steps." They are coping tools, not chores to be crossed off a "to do" list. Probably the most important step to do over and over is step twelve, "working with others." AAs are fond of saying, "You don't get to keep it [meaning sobriety] unless you're willing to give it away [meaning helping others]." That's the formula discovered by Bill W. and Dr. Bob, the magic of "one drunk talking to another."

ON BEING A RAVING LUNATIC ABOUT SOBRIETY

Breaking the "Don't-Get-Involved" Rule

Even though "everybody knows" that the recovering alcoholic man is probably incapable of having a mature, healthy relationship with a woman before he's two years sober, if then, so by the time his second "birthday" arrives he may have already broken the unwritten "Don't-get-emotionally-involved-in-your-first-year" rule. (Even if he's married, as we saw in the last chapter, he may have broken it.) While emotional involvements are certainly educational, they're risky. Most end in breakups. So if you're a woman, unless you're married to the recovering alcoholic, try *not* to be his first or second relationship in his new sobriety. All he's doing is going to school on *you*. Nice for him—after all, he's got to start somewhere—but maybe not so nice for you. Hopefully the recovering man in lust has a good working relationship with his sponsor, because he's going to need it. Left to his own devices, he'll wreck his love life for sure. With a sponsor's help, however, he might at least be able to work through it with a bit of class.

Utilizing the Sponsor

Picking a sponsor is nerve-racking enough. *Utilizing* that sponsor can be even harder. It means "sharing feelings," which is *not* something that most men are accustomed to doing. (Women usually find this aspect of sponsorship much easier.) If asked how they feel, most first-year men will fall back on, "I'm just fine." A man will say this even if he's dying inside. He holds his mud. And he does the same with women, like the man who, when asked by his lady to share how he was feeling about the relationship, immediately gripped onto the arms of his chair, looked panic-stricken, and wailed, "Oh, God!"

The first-year man is a secret-keeper. What secrets? Everything. About how he feels. About how his obsession for his drug of choice is still plaguing him. About how he's suddenly afraid of things. About how he's impotent. About how he's got a sudden sweet tooth and he's getting fat. When he's finally able to "share" (not a real macho word!), he discovers that everybody goes through this stuff, that it passes. He's relieved. Even though the successful utilization of a sponsor is dependent on truthful sharing, it usually takes a man awhile before he's willing to establish this kind of relationship with somebody.

The changes that occur in the life of the recovering alcoholic man in his first year are dramatic. This is where that greenhouse effect really becomes apparent. He looks forward to his one-year birthday/anniversary with great anticipation. It's by far the biggest milestone in the recovering person's life. No other year—not five, ten, or even twenty-five years on the program—has the impact of that first one. He may be feeling for the very first time that he's finally getting the knack of this "sobriety thing." He's got a little confidence now. Occasionally, he lets himself risk some fun. And from time to time he becomes aware of the presence of a brand new and quite unfamiliar feeling—happiness.

"CHARLIE BROWN"

I loved to cut people up. I got a lot of pleasure out of it. If they said stop, I kept beating them. Then I'd push them over a cliff. Sometimes I'd see my father's face on theirs, and it was too late for mercy.

If any of the interviewees for this book began his sobriety as an antihero it was "Charlie Brown." A member of a motorcycle gang for twenty-two years, Charlie Brown is the only interviewee who was nervous about being identified. He felt it might endanger

86

him. "If I should suddenly get diarrhea of the mouth, I could send a whole lot of people to prison for a long time."

In order to stay clean and sober, he felt he had to resign from the gang.

It's a gang you don't resign from. Club membership is supposed to be until death. They don't just let you go with a pat on the back. I've been called all kinds of names—wussy, wimp, snitch, disloyal. I've taken quite a risk getting sober. There are very few club members who make it. They still check up on me. In fact, when I took my nine-month chip at an AA meeting, I noticed a couple of the motorcycle club guys standing in the back of the room. They were just there to see what I was saying from the podium. They talked to me after the meeting, and that was it.

Charlie Brown, who just turned forty, is a stocky, cuddly-looking (believe it or not!) man with a Fu Manchu mustache, and graying dark hair, which had been long until the day before, but he'd just had it cut short for an upcoming job interview with a corporation. He wore the railroad cap he'd recently bought on a visit to Traveltown.

Born in Quebec, Charlie Brown is still a Canadian citizen. While he was growing up, his sister was "the good one" in the family and he was the bad one. At fifteen, he started drinking and smoking pot. His father, the man who is the focus of so much of the anger that has overwhelmed Charlie Brown's life, was a self-made millionaire by the age of twenty-five and an advocate of the "boys don't cry" school of child rearing.

He was a real tough cookie. He beat up on me and my mother constantly. He's only 5 foot 6 and suffered from the Little Big Man syndrome. He flaunted his money by driving around in a limousine and wearing full-length fur coats. But he never gave me a personal gift, not even a card with his name on it. Only checks. When I was a kid I'd say things like, "I'd like a sweater, you know, something you *buy* me," and he'd throw a fit. Money was all he knew.

The one thing dad did buy for Charlie Brown was a motorcycle, which was probably a mistake. "I immediately started to hang out with tough guys and outcasts. I developed a fascination for knives. At seventeen, I rode off to see the world and never returned."

He proved himself to be enough of a tough guy to be invited to join a motorcycle club and became deeply involved in their life-style, even taking a job in a club-owned restaurant. That's where he earned the money to buy his first Harley Davidson. "And that's when I became an associate of the organization."

Charlie Brown describes the motorcycle club as a tightly knit society.

> *They* became my family. They were my identity. Sometimes there would be a thousand of us, coming from all parts of the country, and that was always a lot of fun. In a way, I miss the camaraderie of that lifestyle, even today. The closest thing I've found to it is AA. There was also a definite daily routine. We'd hang out at the clubhouses, drink, throw knives, and work on our motorcycles.

However, it wasn't long before Charlie Brown, even in a club where violence was a way of life, began to stand out as trouble. Club members viewed his undisciplined anger as excessive, and his knife fascination particularly worried them. They were also concerned about his drinking.

> I was full of denial about the drinking. In order to drink on motorcycle runs, I'd pretend I was having trouble with my bike so I could pull off to the side of the road, and then I'd take a swig from the flask inside my vest while I made like I was looking at my motorcycle.

Since he was so busy with his motorcycle and his boozing, the last thing on his mind was marriage, but he nevertheless got entangled.

I really wasn't into women. I could go without sex for a year. In fact, I'd never even had a real relationship. In the club, the most important thing is your motorcycle, then your brothers, then your dog, and *then* your girlfriend or wife. Mostly women were just for sex, and if we couldn't get it we'd rape. That was just the mode of operation. We figured it was *her* fault, you know, for getting too close. I myself did a whole lot of raping. But one night I saw this dark-eyed cutie pie sitting at the bar. I thought she was the most beautiful woman I'd ever seen. Before I could go up and talk to her, I saw a guy in the parking lot, looking at my motorcycle. I took offense and went out and stuck him with my knife. When I turned around, the cutie pie was smiling at me through the window.

A short time later, they were married.

Today, Charlie Brown has a bit more insight into their mutual attraction.

Women who are attracted to motorcycle gang members are sick in their own way. My wife certainly was. She came from a violent alcoholic family, and she kept seeking that out. The guy she was seeing before me went into a bar one night and didn't come out alive. I thought she really loved me, but basically she hated men. What she loved was my lifestyle, my friends. The more violent they were, the more she liked them. And I had so little self-esteem that I used to love it when people told me I had a gorgeous wife, even though she'd chew me up emotionally and spit me out. I got so I'd rather have a man beat me up than be subjected to her lip.

His wife came into the marriage with two children. "Her daughter was less than a year old, and her son was barely three. I raised them. Now they're fourteen and sixteen, and when we got divorced it ripped them apart. I'm the only dad they've ever known."

Drinking was the one thing his wife *didn't* like about his lifestyle, and she pushed him to go to AA. "In one five-year period I was in and out of AA seven times. I bought the AA 'Big Book,' and each time I'd get sober I'd write my new sobriety date in the front of it. Then each time I'd slip, I'd cross it out."

Sylvia: What kept making you slip?

Charlie Brown: I'd come home from an AA meeting and my wife would say, "You're okay. You can smoke a joint now." So even though I wasn't drinking, I was doing every other drug in town. I even took an AA birthday cake with cocaine running out of my nose. She thought that was wonderful. Sooner or later I'd start sneaking booze again, and I'd drop out of AA altogether.

What triggered the moment of clarity that finally got him sober for good was the time he was so drunk that he left his motorcycle right out on the street in front of the house, unlocked, all night long. "I'd never done that. That's when I got scared and I said to myself, 'I think there's a problem here.' "

Charlie Brown eventually returned to AA, befriended another sober biker—"bikers can smell one another"—and in the next ninety days he attended 150 AA meetings. He's been sober ever since.

Charlie Brown: Those first days were the hardest of my life. I don't know how people make it through. I wanted to sneak a drink so bad, but I knew it would kill me. I was at meetings day and night. I'd get there early and help set up the chairs. Sometimes I'd be there so early I'd be the only one sitting in the room. People would ask, "How are you doing?" and I'd just say, "Fine. Glad to be here!"

Sylvia: Did you have a sponsor?

Charlie Brown: I finally got one. One night a guy at a meeting asked me, "How are you doing?" I gave him that "Fine. Glad to be here" routine. And he said, "Let's sit down and talk about it." That's the guy I asked to be my sponsor.

Sylvia: How did he start helping you?

Charlie Brown: He told me to divorce my wife. He felt she was a serious threat to my sobriety. Not only was she drinking herself but she kept on telling me it was okay to smoke pot. At first I fought my sponsor because I was still so attracted to my wife's physical beauty. But I knew he was right. In the end I filed for divorce.

With his sponsor's guidance, he tackled his amends (steps eight and nine).

> For the longest time my sponsor told me to hold off on my amends, especially the one to my dad. So I started out writing letters to other relatives, and making financial amends and amends for the stabbings and rapings. When he finally gave me the go-ahead to approach my dad, I called him—he's eighty now—and I told him I was in AA. His response was "Well, it's good for you. A lot of famous people go there." I went on to tell him that the reason I was calling was because I wanted to make amends to him for my behavior. I said, "I did this, and I did that," and of course my dad, being my dad, took it from there. He said, "Yeah, not only that, but you did this and you did that." That was the extent of our conversation. But my sponsor had prepared me for this, so I knew the only thing I was supposed to worry about was cleaning up my side of the street, not his. When I told my sponsor about my dad's response, he asked me, "Wasn't that what you expected?" and I said, "Yes, but it's not what I wanted." But the funny thing is, a couple of weeks later I called my dad again, and this time he started asking me questions about AA and then more questions.

A short time later, Charlie Brown's father flew to California and father and son met face-to-face for the first time in twenty-two years. "It went fine," Charlie says. "He found out that I like chili and soft drinks. I was able to be *me* in front of him. It went just fine."

A few months ago, Charlie Brown broke the unwritten rule. He fell in love.

Charlie Brown: I know AA says no relationships under a year, but she's the most wonderful thing that ever happened to me. I was always attracted to dark-haired, dark-eyed beauties, but this lady is a blue-eyed blond. She has five years sobriety. I didn't think I ever wanted a woman again, but we've become girlfriend and boyfriend, and everything's fine.

These days I use the word *share*. That never used to be a part of my vocabulary! And a while back I even caught myself using the word *love*. I was writing in my journal, "Dear God, thanks for a good day. Love, Charlie Brown." Then I wrote, "God, do you believe I just wrote the word *love*! I think maybe I believe in you now." I told my sponsor all about it, and he was so happy. He's a big 260-pound man, and he gave me a hug, belly against belly.

His sponsor has been working closely with him on his new relationship so he doesn't destroy it.

Charlie Brown: Once I was supposed to call my lady and I forgot. She was upset. Then *I* got upset because *she* was upset. I said, "Well, if you're going to get upset, then maybe we shouldn't be together. I can't afford to have scenes because they screw around with my sobriety." Then I stormed off. Fortunately, I called my sponsor and ran it by him. He says, "Oh, don't worry about having a fight. That's normal. Not everybody gets along fine all the time." I never knew that before. It made me feel better. It taught me that I could actually learn how to talk through a problem.

Sylvia: What did you use to do when you had a fight?

Charlie Brown: I'd get on my motorcycle and leave. I was great at that. I'd ride for a few hours and then I'd go get shitfaced somewhere. By the time I got home everybody would be asleep, and I wouldn't have to deal with it. That's how I handled it!

Because of his new relationship, Charlie Brown is beginning to let himself have fun.

Charlie Brown: We do things together. We ride our bikes. We go to the beach. We walk our dogs. We garden. If you saw her house now you'd think a kid walked all around it with a paintbrush, there are so many flowers, in so many different colors. I go up there every night just to water. I get serenity by watering the flowers and looking at the stars.

I'm having fun being a normal person. I like driving around. I like the zoo. I like movies. I hadn't seen a movie since I was a kid. I even like waiting in movie lines. Once when I took my lady friend to San Francisco, the steward on the plane said, "You two have to be the happiest people I've ever seen." I just like life.

A few months ago, Charlie Brown took what was for him a big chance: he got his motorcycle out of mothballs.

Charlie Brown: My first six months I was too afraid to ride my motorcycle because I thought the minute I got on it, I'd revert to my old way of life and start drinking again. But so far it hasn't taken me back. And I realized it's okay to ride it dressed like a citizen. I don't have to have long hair and wear chains.

To make sure that he hangs onto his sobriety, Charlie Brown does "service."

I go to five AA meetings a week, I'm secretary of one of the meetings, and I work with newcomers. But what I really want to do someday is take my message of sobriety right into the prisons. Because of my criminal record, I know I'm going to have trouble doing that, but I'm filling out all the forms anyway. I never thought I'd be begging to get *into* a prison! Anyway, I want to go in there and talk to the scooter tramps and the bikers, because they're too tough and too mean to listen to anybody else. They'd rather do time for the rest of their lives than admit they need AA.

So I'd like to go in there and say, hey, look at me! This is where I came from and this is where I am today, and they can say, "If *he* can make it, then *I* can make it."

At the time of the interview, Charlie Brown was just a week or two away from that all-important first AA birthday/anniversary. He sums it up:

Looking back on this year, it hasn't all been good. I've had a lot of shit happen in sobriety. I got a divorce. I lost my job. I had court hearings. I was robbed. I have liver trouble. And I still have a lot of anger. But at least I don't have to stab people anymore just because I don't like them. I consider that growth.

What I used to be was an insane, violent guy, like a turned-loose pitbull. I related to movies like *In Cold Blood*. I could stroll by somebody in a public place, stab them, and then calmly, get on my bike, and ride away. I was nuts. I just loved to get on that motorcycle and ride right into trouble.

I don't *need* to be angry anymore. Today I have peace of mind and a direction to my life, a purpose. Today people seem to like me. Today I not only stop and smell the roses, I *plant* them.

I don't want to go back where I used to be, or do what I used to do, ever again. And I have the power to keep all this, so long as I don't drink or use today.

Perhaps the most graphic example of how Charlie Brown has changed in his brief year of sobriety is what he's done with his fish tank.

"I used to have an aquarium with piranhas and other carnivorous fish in it. Just recently I set up the aquarium again, only now I raise guppies and goldfish. And there's sand at the bottom of the tank where I've stuck some lavender plastic flowers."

6

MATCHING THE WALK TO THE TALK:
Lenny, Sober Two Years

The Second Burrito
It was the day before payday, and I was down to $1.79. I was hungry, but I was trying to learn to live on my salary, so I wasn't going to borrow. I went to a take-out place. What I wanted was two burritos and a Coke, but I only had enough money for one burrito and a Coke, so that's what I ordered. I paid for it up front. When my order came, there were two burritos in the bag, so I had a little debate with myself: Should I tell him he'd given me two burritos? I even prayed to God: "Do you want me to have two burritos, or not?" Then I decided that since I'm trying to work an honest AA program, I'd have to tell him—even though I didn't want to. "Hey, you gave me two burritos and I ordered only one," I said. "It's my mistake," the cook said, "so you can keep it."
—Ramon, sober 18 months

While the first year is about getting sober and staying sober, the second year is about living sober. The recovering alcoholic is now expected to go forth into the world and put what he's learned to good use. "Apply the principles of this program to your everyday affairs," AA says. "This is an action program. Go out there and walk like you talk." As Ramon's burrito story illustrates, it's not enough for a man to talk about honesty and integrity; he has to live it.

The new expectation to get off one's duff and into action usually comes as a shock. The minute the recovering alcoholic has his one-year AA birthday or anniversary, he loses his "newcomer" status and privileges. No longer is it enough for him just to "suit up and show up." No longer is he applauded for simply getting up in the morning without using a chemical, which is something most people in the world do as a matter of course. No longer is he His Majesty, the Baby. He's been dethroned and six other new-comers have rushed in to take his place. Ah, how fleeting was his fame! Now *they* are getting all the attention, the pats on the head for merely breathing in and out. He's on his own now, and if he wants to survive he has to learn more about how to "work the program" fast—that is, he has to begin doing some of the dirty work like facing himself, working on his character defects, writing out his moral inventory (if he hasn't done so already), and mak-ing his amends. All those character issues that were put on hold his first year so he could focus on staying alive and staying sober now have to be dealt with. Work problems, money problems, family problems, legal problems, all need to be worked on—and with integrity. That's a tall order!

The two-year recovering man has probably been to several AA funerals, which may have shocked him out of taking the AA pro-gram and his sobriety so casually. "My God!" he says as he sees one after another of his comrades fall. "They're using real bullets here!" If a study were conducted, it would probably reveal that AA members attend more funerals in a five-year span than the average man. *People die of alcoholism.* For example, of the three funerals attended by one recovering alcoholic in his first year, one was for a man in his twenties who owned his own plane, drank again, flew it, and crashed into Santa Monica Bay; the second was for a man in his forties who drank again, smoked in bed, and burned to death when he set his house on fire; and the third was for an AA old-timer in his seventies who died sober. Sometimes it's a shocking revelation to the newcomer that sobriety doesn't make a man immortal. Even AAs don't live forever. Such a reality jars the newcomer's nerves.

"I was a nervous wreck wondering if I was going to be next to slip," said one man in the beginning of his second year, "until I realized that slipping isn't done by *lottery*. There's nobody out there picking numbers out of a hat to determine who'll slip next. *I'm* the one who's in control of that! If I don't drink or use, I won't slip. It's that simple."

That's called "taking responsibility" for one's sobriety.

The second year is a risky time for heroes-in-the-making because it's easy to get distracted from the goal. Once the recovering person puts his energies into something other than raw sobriety, like work or a relationship, the risk is that he'll forget his number one problem—his addiction—and he'll drink or use again. According to Barry, a Beverly Hills psychotherapist and recovering alcoholic (he's also our interviewee in Chapter 10), "The battle for sobriety is still there in the second year, but it doesn't maintain that *hotness* that it did the first year."

During the second year, the principles of the program become internalized. "What's to prevent an AA member from sneaking a drink now and then? And who would know?" are questions often contemplated by a newcomer in his first year but rarely asked by a second-year man. By now he knows that the reason he can't sneak a drink isn't because he'd get caught but rather because it would hurt *his* life. And that makes all the difference.

Out of the Mothballs

Finally, the two-year man begins to move out into the world. He's less self-centered, more aware of what's going on around him. He may even subscribe to the morning paper and watch the news on television. He has less need to "be strong" and "tough it out" and more willingness to ask for—and accept—direction from others, such as a sponsor. (Hopefully, he has one by now.) In the work area, he has settled down a bit. His work ethic has improved. He shows up, for one thing. That alone is an improvement. He may even be on time.

If he has a relationship with a wife or girlfriend, this is the year he starts to come out of his fog of self-obsession long enough to notice her. He begins to pay her little attentions. He may even pencil her in for a night out together instead of going to another AA meeting. (Although he should never neglect those meetings!) He also starts to realize that *she* has a life, too, and problems of her own—that she exists independent of him, that she is not his satellite. None of this has ever occurred to him before.

Sponsor Jack tells how this blazing insight—that his own wife had a life apart from him—was revealed in his second year.

> I was unemployed, but my wife was working. She'd come home at 5:30, make dinner for the kids and me, vacuum the house, and then go to an Al-Anon [self-help group for family and friends of alcoholics] meeting. When she'd finally get home after 10:00, I'd meet her at the door with my awful battle cry, "What's the matter? Why aren't you paying more attention to me? What have *I* done now?" One night she said, "Jack, did it ever occur to you that I could be tired or upset, and it would have nothing to do with you?" I said, "No! Of course not! How could that be?" But from then on I decided to make an effort to at least consider the possibility that her mood has nothing to do with me. Now, that's not my *first* thought, but I try hard to at least make it be my second thought. "Maybe it has nothing to do with me."

Anyone who lives with a recovering alcoholic quickly learns how thin-skinned they are. Get used to it! It can go on for years.

Psychiatrist Paul Grossman runs into this in his practice with alcoholics all the time. I asked him how he deals with the supersensitive ones.

I end up having to soothe and reassure them. I say things to them like, "No, you don't understand, when your wife says you don't listen to her enough, she's not attacking you for being a bad husband. She thinks you're a *good* husband. She just wants you to listen to her and understand how *she* feels about things once in awhile. So don't get defensive. It's not an attack on your value as a man. All you need to do is sit in your chair, keep your mouth shut, and listen. It couldn't be any simpler."

According to Sponsor Jack, there's a positive "flip side" that a woman can come to appreciate in her thin-skinned man. "Hard as it is to live with us sensitive alcoholics, the plus side is that as we become more sensitive to other people's moods, especially those we care about, we develop antennae. As a result, we can end up more nurturing, and in more imaginative and creative ways, than the average fellow. And God knows we're not dull."

It's not just *her* feelings that scare the recovering alcoholic man to death; it's his own. Feelings—from *whatever* source—are seen as a real threat, and because he has thawed out enough by now to have a whole myriad of feelings, the two-year man is very uncomfortable. Says Dr. Grossman, "He has a persecutory attitude about feelings. He thinks feelings are after him, and he wishes they would go away." Again, reassurance that feelings are normal—and that *he's* normal for having them—helps.

The joke about a man in his first few years of sobriety is "He's not free, he's loose." In other words, watch out! All dressed up in a clean shirt, self-assured from the experience of having spoken to audiences from an AA podium, he looks good and sounds good, but dating him can mean heartbreak. This man may have been sober long enough to notice a woman, to pay attention to her, even to listen to her, but he's usually not ready for commitment. The rule of thumb here is that it takes five years for a man to be a good catch. The woman should realize he's "in process," improving every day. The best advice for her, then, is to be patient and work on her *own* issues.

The "God Bit"

Though many manage to avoid it, most alcoholics, by the time they're two years sober, have to deal with the fact that AA is billed as a "spiritual program." At one time or another, they're going to want to ask themselves what that means. Some refer to this subject as the "God bit" in AA. Sooner or later most AA members begin to ask themselves some philosophical questions: "What is God? What do I believe in? What is spirituality to me?" For some, spirituality means the God of their childhood. For others, it means, simply, behaving well. "To me," says the psychotherapist Barry (from Chapter 10), "spirituality means ethical behavior. I have to walk the way I talk; I have to be faithful to my woman, and honest in all my daily activities. When I do that, I feel better. That's why I do it. Virtue *is* its own reward."

These are all issues our two-year man, Lenny, currently faces.

LENNY

I have a lady in my life, and for me the biggest change in sobriety has been learning not to act on my continuing lustful feelings for other women, even though these feelings are still lurking. I can admit I have these feelings, but I don't have to act on them, just like I can admit I have urges for alcohol from time to time, but I don't have to act on them. For me, continuing my promiscuity and giving in to my lustful feelings would be like taking a drink. In fact, it would probably lead to my taking a drink. So I can't do it.

Lenny, forty-four, was born in Huntington Beach, California, the oldest of four children and the only boy. He wears his hair long and dresses biker-style.

He seems to have come by his alcoholism genetically, although not from his parents. His great grandmother was a bootlegger in Oklahoma. His maternal grandfather was an alcoholic, as was his paternal grandmother, who sobered up as the result of what she called a "spiritual experience" and went on to become a minister of a mission to help other alcoholics.

When Lenny was twenty-two, one of his sisters was killed by a drunk driver. The night of her death, Lenny got drunk and drove around in his car.

A sometime actor/singer, during the late sixties he got one of the two leads in a road company of *Hair*. While on the road, he and his then "old lady" became parents of a daughter who is now eighteen years old. Even though the couple separated, Lenny has remained close to his daughter. Currently he's living with a woman he met in AA.

Lenny's background belies the "unhappy childhood" myth about alcoholism.

"I came from a real loving, warm family. I had the kind of family that led other kids to say, 'I wish I had parents like yours.' My dad was a cub master and built soapbox racers, and my mom was a den mother."

In spite of this boy-next-door upbringing, Lenny veered off in another direction.

I started drinking and being promiscuous at an early age. Of course, it was the sixties, when drugs and sex were free-flowing, but I kept right on doing it all through the seventies and the eighties. Even when I was with my daughter's mother I was promiscuous. She was my "old lady" and I was her "old man," but we didn't promise to be sexually faithful. That was our arrangement which I took advantage of a lot more than she did. As a hippie, I felt I had a certain image to keep up. The truth was, it was a fun image to maintain. When I started cocaine, it got worse. The cocaine world has so much sexual fantasy in it. There

101

were so many times I said to somebody, blatantly, "Okay, since you want a half-gram of coke and you don't have any money, then let's have sex." There were a bunch of women who knew if they came over and had sex with me, I'd keep them in cocaine all night. Group sex was common. It was all part of the deal. It comes with the dinner.

Lenny went from actor to prop man at the movie studios. His addictions caught up with him.

For years, I had a reputation in the movie studios as a good worker. They'd see me and say, "Oh, good, Lenny's here." But that changed as my addiction got worse, and it got to the point where they'd see me and say, "Oh, great, this is all I need! Lenny's here." I was the prop man on a TV show for years—as well as the head coke dealer. I knew which stars were coked out because they were getting it from me. (I was drinking Bushmill's Irish whiskey and doing two grams of coke a day myself.) I met this actress once, and I called her up and said, "I think I have what you want." When she found out that what I had was 1,000 Quaaludes, she not only came right over to my house, she moved in.

As Lenny's drinking and drugging progressed, he started missing work, sometimes disappearing for days at a time. Eventually fired from the TV show, he ended up parking cars at the Aquarius Theatre where he'd once starred in *Hair*.

"I'd tell people, 'I used to be in *Hair*. I was the star.' And they'd say, 'That's nice,' but probably thought, 'That parking attendant really has quite an imagination.'"

It was Lenny's addiction to sex—as much as his addiction to booze—that nearly killed him.

My girlfriend *T*. [not his daughter's mother] and I had been partying all night with a married couple, and at dawn I decided to go out to the store to get breakfast and bring it back. The other guy's wife went with me. On the way to the store we decided it would be nice to have sex in the great outdoors, only it was downtown L.A. at six in the morning. It wasn't like we could go off into the forest. Instead, we found this four-story parking structure at County Hospital. We parked on the highest level. Our plan was to go up the fire escape to the roof that had a wall around it and make love in the great outdoors there, but the door was locked. So I said, okay, no problem, it's got to open up from the other side. So I got up on the wall and then jumped up to grab hold of the wall on the roof level. [An alcoholic's judgment leaves something to be desired!] I was going to hoist myself up. But the wall was thicker than I expected it to be, and I couldn't get a grip on it. I ended up falling four stories and landing on my feet, barefoot. I broke my pelvis in two places, and my heel broke completely off my foot. The woman with me turned out to be awful in a crisis. First, she started to run away. Then she changed her mind and called her husband and my girlfriend from a phone booth in the hospital emergency room. It never occurred to her to tell anybody in the emergency room that a man had just fallen four stories and was still lying there! So her husband and *T.* came over and *they* carried me into the hospital. I had an alcohol level of 4.0 when I was admitted, but I didn't think I was drunk. I was there for three weeks. And I'd only recently recovered from a broken shoulder that I'd gotten skiing, off a cliff, drunk. I thought it would be a fun jump!

The last straw happened one night after Lenny had opened a bottle of Bushmill's, his favorite brew. He tripped and spilled some of the whiskey on his bedspread.

I caught it right away, so I had plenty left in the bottle. But nonetheless, I threw myself down on my knees by the side of the bed and started sucking the whiskey out of the bedspread. Then, suddenly, I had this moment of clarity, like I stood back from myself and I could see myself, holding this bottle in my hands with plenty of booze in it, sucking the whiskey out of the bedspread. I wasn't who I wanted to be! I had other plans! And so I said, not believing there was a God, "God, if you're there, help me now," and then I felt that feeling I'd read about—a warmth, a cloud, a comfort, and a *dis*comfort. And just like that, I knew that there's a God. I absolutely *knew* it. Until then, the closest thing I had ever had to a spiritual awakening was when I took acid and PCP. I thought, "You're really there, aren't you? And you're hearing me say all this bullshit, aren't you?"

Lenny likened his spiritual experience to the one his grandmother had described so many times that had sobered her up. Almost to test it, he drank one more time thirteen days later, but his heart wasn't in it. He knew his days of drinking and using were over. He's been sober ever since.

Lenny describes his first year in AA as a "honeymoon," although, like childbirth, once the experience is over, some of the pain of it may be forgotten.

In his second year, Lenny began to work on his "character defects," one of his biggest, of course, being his lust.

Knowing what a womanizer I'd always been, God turned the tables on me when I got to the program. It's as if he said, "Look, Lenny, you can't stay sober if you're going to be chasing skirts all over the place, so I'll give you the *best* woman in AA right off the bat, but you've got to be faithful." And that's what He did. She was two-and-a-half years sober at the time, and because my sexual needs were taken care of, I could concentrate on staying sober and on making a living without having to worry about who I was going to coerce into bed with me.

In his second year, Lenny's internal struggle has been to *keep* the pledge of fidelity he made in his first year. AA, after all, is a candy store, especially in Southern California. It was while writing his fourth step (the "fearless and searching moral inventory") that Lenny discovered how, for him, compulsive, sexual acting-out was just like booze: it had enabled him to avoid unpleasant thoughts and feelings.

While I was writing my inventory and dredging up all kinds of memories from the past that were stressful, things I didn't want to remember, I'd escape the stress by masturbating. As soon as I'd have a memory or a feeling I didn't like, I'd stick in a porno tape in the VCR, masturbate, relieve the stress, and then go back to writing my inventory. At first I thought there was something strange about that, but since then whenever I talk about it at men's AA stag meetings, usually three or four guys will come up and tell me they did the same thing!

In the job area, Lenny has had to "work the program," too. While some men—the ones AA calls "high-bottom drunks"— come into sobriety with their careers relatively intact, a far greater number have turned their work life into a shambles. Lenny's work record in sobriety has been eclectic, to say the least: he's been a musician, an actor, singer, songwriter, sculptor, ambulance driver, welder, stagehand, and an artist.

Part of getting one's work life back on track is dealing with the wreckage of the past. Sometimes this means making amends. These can be planned out in advance—letters written or appointments made with the specific purpose of making amends. Or they can happen spontaneously.

I got a welding call to a studio where I hadn't worked since I'd gotten sober. I went in with my helmet and gloves, and the minute the guy saw me he got "that look" on his face and said, "Oh, did you get a welding call?" I said yes. And he said, "Well, the thing is, our welder was out sick but he's back now, so what you can do instead is just sweep up, and we'll pay you the welding rate because we *did* make the call." So I said, "Look, last time I was here I was a hopeless drunk and I know I cost you a lot of money, but I'm not drunk now. I'm sober in AA." The guy smiled and said, "I knew you had a problem, and I'm glad you're doing something about it. We're really behind here, so just grab that welding machine over there and go to work!" The change was like that. And he had been willing to pay eight hours at the welding rate for me to sweep the floor, just to avoid having me touch anything.

That's "making amends." And because the situation presented itself spontaneously, it wasn't something Lenny was able to prepare for. But when the opportunity arose, our hero met it admirably. He might easily have tried to squirm out of it.

During his second year of sobriety, Lenny has been leaning toward work that's closer to his heart: his art, especially his wood carving. It's amazing how many talents spring up once sobriety enters the picture.

> Mostly I carve guitars for musicians. I carved a set of plaques for the AA meeting hall where I'm secretary, once for each of the Twelve Steps. And I'm doing leather work. I just got a call from an actor who wants some chairs leathertooled for his house in Malibu. So who knows.

AA promises the alcoholic that if he stays clean and sober, he can eventually end up getting paid to do what he loves to do. It looks as though Lenny is on his way.

Throughout his second year, Lenny has worked hard on his relationships with both his live-in girlfriend and his daughter.

"I see my relationship with my girlfriend as a gift from God. She has her life and her AA program, and I have mine. She never says to me, 'Don't you think you should go to more AA meetings?'"

When it comes to feelings, Lenny is perhaps atypical of the men we talked about earlier who "stuff" emotions that make them feel weak and vulnerable.

> I was never crazy about guilt, but when it came to tender feelings, I didn't stuff those. Nor did I ever have a problem crying. I'd cry in front of my parents, or any ladies I was with. Today at AA meetings I can be talking, with no intention of crying, and suddenly it will well up inside of me. It's just not a big deal to me to do that.

Recently, to celebrate the wedding of friends, Lenny wrote a song about finally finding love after traveling a long, rough road. He calls it "Journey":

Every bridge I've crossed over,
Every tunnel I've passed through,
Every highway brought me closer,
Closer to you.
I might have found some consolation
On the long and rocky ride,
Had I known my destination
Would be here by your side.

When the subject of his daughter comes up, Lenny melts.

She goes to a private rich kid's high school with a lot of celebrities' kids and she just graduated valedictorian of her class. She got every honor—for drama, even for French. To hear my daughter singled out and introduced by the dean in glowing terms was incredible. And her speech was brilliant and witty, the kind I would have written if I could have. I was sitting there with tears rolling down my face, thinking of all the times I wasn't there for her and feeling so incredibly lucky to have her. She loved me through all my drinking and never said a thing about it, but at the same time she refused to enable me. Once when I was making some half-assed attempt to get sober in a treatment center, I asked her to come for Family Day. She said, "No, Daddy, I've seen you in hospitals." But when I finally got serious, she was at my side.

When the graduation ceremony was over, I told her how proud I was of her, and she told me, "Dad, I'm real proud of you, too." And then I said, "Oh, no, you're not as proud of me as I'm proud of you." We actually had a *proud* contest! It was a wonderful thing. This coming Sunday, which also happens to be Father's Day, she's going to my AA meeting with me to give me my two-year AA birthday cake.

107

As Lenny gets up to take that two-year cake, he'll no doubt be thinking of two other alcoholics in his life who didn't make it. During this second year, Lenny attended two funerals. The first was for an AA friend who died of a drug overdose in a motel room. "He'd just sold his car and remaining possessions for cocaine. When they found him, there was a sheet of paper on the desk with the phone numbers of some AA guys on it. I don't know if he actually tried to call them." The second funeral was for his grandmother, who died of cancer—*sober*.

To maintain his own sobriety, Lenny does "twelve-step" work or "service."

"I took a guy to an AA meeting who drank again after twenty-six years of sobriety. At the meeting, he passed out on a table and people laughed. I got mad. 'This drunk that you're all laughing at just went out after twenty-six years, so you'd better pay attention. If it can happen to him, then none of us here is home free!' "

AA has an expression to cover painful situations like the one above: "Some must die so that others may live." To that, the recovering alcoholic who is truly honest will add: "Better him than me." He knows that the name of the game is survival.

7

IS THAT ALL THERE IS?:
Gil, Sober Three Years

Until a couple of months ago I thought I had everything I ever wanted—a job, a car, a girlfriend, money. I was working out in the gym four days a week and going to lots of AA meetings. I was getting along great with my mom. My self-esteem was high. I was feeling good. But a couple of months ago I began getting lazy about the program. I'd better do something about it, too, because I don't want to drink or use again.

A Path Through a Mine Field

By the time the recovering alcoholic man has reached three years of sobriety, he's experienced a lot. Sometimes his journey resembles a walk through a mine field: so many potential perils surround him that survival itself is an accomplishment. He's survived a multitude of temptations, the main one, of course, being the urge to drink or use; he's survived the discovery (or rediscovery) of his feelings; he's survived a relationship or two; and he's survived "doing" his inventory, "taking it" (reading it aloud to somebody else), and making his major amends. By now, there may even be a couple of newcomers running around calling *him* "sponsor."

By three, our hero usually feels confident that he's learned how to avoid the mines, that he's gotten the hang of this sobriety business. He's comfortable in the program. Abstinence is practically automatic, and to his amazement, some of those so-called "coping skills" he was taught really do work. In addition, some of the "promises" from page 86 of the AA "Big Book" have come true. For example, as is stated in Chapter 1, the book promises him that if he stays sober he will "intuitively know how to handle situations" that used to baffle him. Well, it's true. The three-year man notices that sometimes he can be in a tense situation where he needs his wits and the right words seem to flow forth. Who's in there? he wonders. Who said that?

He has "bonded" with friends, many of whom (if they manage to stay sober) he will have for life. No matter what their age is, they are his peers, his classmates, "the 'class of '87 or '97." What this means is they got sober at approximately the same time, within a few weeks or months of one another. Unlike college, AAs never graduate, so the focus is on when they entered sobriety, not when they left. Those who have the same sponsor ("parent") see one another as brothers and sisters who "grew up together." And their sponsor's sponsor is their "grandsponsor." The "baby," or "sponsee," may even be older than his sponsor. Again, when it comes to wisdom, no matter if he's twenty or forty, it's years of sobriety rather than chronological years that count the most.

On the whole, the three-year man starts out his fourth year feeling pretty wonderful and pretty proud of himself. He's actually happy. And he may even think he's got this program licked. There's a tendency to justify slacking off on the basics: "I feel so good, I don't need to go to meetings."

One Day at a Time—Forever

The trouble is, it's still a mine field out there, and he can't afford to run out of steam or get bored or disillusioned. Still, he does. At some point during the past year it has dawned on him that on the sobriety journey, there's no "arriving." There's no time when he's finally at his destination, at which point life goes smoothly and the rewards pour in. Instead, he discovers that sobriety is one day at a time—for life. There are ups and downs for recovering alcoholics just as there are ups and downs for other people. Sobriety gives no special immunity to pain. The man begins to wonder, "Is that all there is?"

Sponsor Jack, who has not only been through this phase himself but has walked dozens of his "babies" through it, has some thoughts on the subject.

> The guy suddenly realizes, "My God, this is going to go on forever." And just because he's sober now doesn't mean he can control the universe. It's as unmanageable as ever. He still can't control other people, their emotions, his own emotions, the business world, the traffic, the terrorists, air pollution. And it all just goes on and on. It can be unnerving.

Says psychotherapist Barry:

> The reality sinks in that this is what life is all about. This is it. There are going to be good days and bad days, and all the coping mechanisms in the world aren't going to keep problems from happening. What a shock! The recovering man is suddenly faced with accepting life on life's terms. Just because he's sober doesn't mean he's going to get everything he wants. The idea that if he just stays clean and sober and "turns it over" and prays, everything will go his way turns out to be a myth.

Sponsor Jack states this concept very succinctly:

> What the recovering alcoholic learns is that you can take a courageous risk in life—and *lose*. What happens is that some people drink around this time of sobriety, not because they're depressed—that's an earlier-phase reason for drinking—but because they feel an overwhelming loss of control over life's happenings.

This reality hits some people hard.

Because he's not perfect yet, the three-year man is likely to be overly self-critical, which adds to his discouragement and waning enthusiasm. But AA is not an unreasonable taskmaster. It stresses "progress, not perfection," and now is a good time for the three-year man to remember that. He's not finished yet.

With this in mind, let's meet our three-year man, Gil, who appears to be entering this uncertain phase after really flying high for a while.

GIL

Lately I just haven't been feeling comfortable. But since all the outside stuff in my life is fine, I have a feeling the problem is within.

At seventeen, Gil, who is tall, tanned, and handsome and loves wearing tank tops to show off his gym-made muscles, is our youngest hero-in-training, having gotten sober at the tender age of fourteen. His family is rife with alcoholism. Among those he mentioned in the interview as being alcoholic were his mother, father, maternal grandmother, and all three of his brothers (he's the third of four boys). Since he dropped out of high school, Gil has been working in the roofing business. He currently lives with his mother and youngest brother in San Diego and attends acting classes at night as well as classes to get his high school diploma.

Gil isn't the only member of his family to get sober. His father, whom he rarely sees, now has fourteen years of sobriety and recently showed up at one of Gil's regular AA meetings. His mother has been sober six years. One of his brothers did have two years of sobriety but went back "out there" again. Within AA there are many such examples of family members who are now in recovery as the result of one member's having gotten sober and then influencing the others to follow suit.

The first time Gil drank beer and smoked pot he was only six years old. He began drinking and using in earnest by age nine, even in front of his mother (who was by then divorced) and his older brothers, who "thought it was funny seeing this little kid running around stoned."

> I just wanted to get high and have people leave me alone. And by now I was even getting my little brother loaded, just like my brothers had gotten me loaded. He was really hitting it. [Today the brother is still using and drinking and has even joined a gang.] He had that ego and that attitude where he blamed everybody else for all his problems—just like me. But at the time I didn't even care what was happening to him. I was irresponsible, without morals. After my mom joined AA, she'd come home and say, "You're drunk," and I'd deny it. Then she'd say, "You're an alcoholic. You have the disease," and I'd say, "No, *you* have the disease. *You're* the one who goes to those stupid meetings." I remember deeply resenting her.

Unable to make it financially in San Diego, Gil's mother decided to move to Utah. She issued Gil an ultimatum: "We're moving. If you're sober, you can come. If you're not sober, you can't."

He wasn't sober, so his mother left him behind. Gil then went to live with his grandmother.

"My grandmother was a practicing alcoholic, so we got along just fine! I lived in a shed in the backyard. My buddies would come over and we'd be drinking and smoking pot in the shed while my grandmother was getting drunk in the house." Eventually, Gil's mother gave in to her enabling tendencies and sent Gil a plane ticket to come to Utah. "But all I did was continue my drinking there."

When the family moved back to California, Gil agreed to try AA, hoping it would get his mother off his back. He stayed "dry" but not "sober," which in AA terms means you're sober but miserable, a bite-the-bullet kind of sobriety. "Plus I still had a rotten attitude."

Not surprisingly, after thirty days, Gil had a slip. "I decided to go to this party and told my friends, 'If I go, make sure I don't drink.' "

Gil was doing what a lot of people do. He was trying to make others responsible for his sobriety.

My mom said, "You shouldn't go to that party," and I said, "Oh, it's okay," but she insisted, "No, you shouldn't go. It's a slippery place." And then she said, "If you do go, take all your stuff with you because you're not coming back." "Fine," I replied. And I went. I ended up using and partying out for four days. At one point I found myself in Hollywood with people I didn't know, doing things I shouldn't have been doing. I lost all my self-respect. When I compared the creeps I was hanging around with to the people I'd met in AA, there was no comparison. I guess that was my moment of clarity. I slunk home.

I was in the process of gathering up my gear to move out when my mother came home. She could see that something was different about me. She ended up giving me a hug and telling me to stay, and I remember feeling numb and lost, hugging her and telling her I wanted to get sober. I knew that I wanted to change something. I knew in my gut that it was going to be all right.

I called AA and they arranged to have a man pick me up and take me to a meeting. Looking back, it was a pretty funny sight. He was dressed in a business suit and had this nice car, and I was all rock-and-rolled out. I had on steel-toed boots, torn Levi's, a "party animal" shirt, long earrings, dog chains around my wrist and neck, and bandanas tied all over. I was a real costume party.

At the AA meeting I sat way down front because I wanted to pretend I had time on the program, that I wasn't a newcomer. I thought I was conning them pretty well, but about ten people came up to me and said, "Hi, you new?" so I guess I wasn't doing that great a job!

Getting sober and staying sober at age fourteen is no easy task, especially in the face of peer pressure to drink. Gil got sober before he was legally even old enough to drink! And because his friends drank and used, it meant he had to stay away from them, a price most young alcoholics are not willing to pay.

"I still can't believe that I drank, hit bottom, and got sober that young. And the older I get, and the more I look back on it, the more amazed I am."

In his first years, Gil was a classic example of what Dr. Paul Grossman talked about in an earlier chapter. He became "a raving maniac about sobriety."

> I was totally amped out and excited about AA. I loved being sober. I really wanted to change, so I went all out for the program. I was going to meetings every night and I was willing to do anything. I really listened, and I parroted all the clichés of the program. I had a lot of hope. I was obsessed with it. I started changing my appearance on the outside. I cut my hair and toned down how I dressed, and that began to have an effect on who I was inside. It was incredible. I felt as though I actually *created* who I am now.

But in spite of his enthusiasm, deep down Gil had a "secret"— a very common one among recovering alcoholics—namely, "I really didn't think that I was an alcoholic." Although this secret clearly jeopardized Gil's sobriety, he was fortunate to have experienced a second moment of clarity without having to go out and "experiment."

Gil: One night I was lying in my bed and I asked myself some questions: "Is this what I want to do with my life? Am I ready to make a commitment to live this life of sobriety and never drink again?" I knew I was going to have to make the decision. And then, deep from inside, the answer came back, "Yes." Without realizing it at the time, I was actually taking the first of the AA twelve steps, which is admitting at *depth* that I was an alcoholic, not just saying it with my mouth. That was my surrender. I suddenly felt as though I had a purpose in life. That's when I really started to change.

Sylvia: What kind of changes?

Gil: Feelings. All through my first year or two of sobriety, I didn't show anything but my tough-guy attitude. I just went around saying, "I'm fine, I'm fine," even though I wasn't fine at all.

Sylvia: Then what went wrong? Why do you think you're in a rut now? What's that all about?

Gil: Lately I've stopped opening my ears and taking advice. I just say, "Yeah, yeah," but I'm not listening. That's dangerous. And what's bizarre is that I know other guys who have about the same time as I do who are doing the same thing. We've hit a danger zone. In the beginning we went to lots of meetings and totally went full force, but now after three years we're saying things like "Gosh, I've been doing my time; now I want to do a little relaxing, you know, I want to be with my girlfriend at night." That's the justification for missing meetings and for not working with more newcomers. I'm resisting.

Resisting psychological growth is common to alcoholic and nonalcoholic alike. If change were comfortable, everybody would be changing all the time. Change hurts, though, so people fight it. But in AA there is pressure *not* to resist growth. The theory is, if you don't grow spiritually and psychologically, old thinking will lure you back to drinking, and if you drink again you'll probably die. So change is necessary for survival. It's very practical.

Gil, who is pretty sophisticated for his age, is onto himself here:

I've really been resisting growing. Whenever it's time to move on to another level, I try all kinds of things to make it work where I am, rather than press on. Until the last few months, I was grateful for everything I had. I'd look out my window and see my new van and be totally grateful for that. That's how I like to be, grateful for things. But lately I've been self-centered, and when that happens I stop being grateful.

One of the things that may be adding to Gil's wavering commitment to AA is the fact that he's distracted by a new relationship that's probably over his head. Not only is she an "older woman" of twenty-two, but she's also the mother of two small children, which puts her into a whole new category. Gil admits to being both excited and overwhelmed.

She's been sober ten months, and she's exactly what I prayed for in a relationship. I'm trying very hard not to get obsessed with her so that I don't end up burning the relationship out. I love her kids, but when they start crying it sort of changes my outlook on getting married. I don't think I'll be ready for that for at least ten years. Not until after I've got my house and all my toys.

A few weeks after this interview, Gil's girlfriend broke up with him.

One of the feelings that has given Gil the most trouble this past year has been *anger,* much of it stemming from having grown up in an alcoholic home. He's been getting in touch with anger at his mother for the fact that she drank until he was eleven, at his older brother for slipping, and at his father for abandoning him. He admits to being less in touch with his feelings about his father. "I hardly ever see my father" is all he had to say about him. Where his mother is concerned, he's more verbal.

I used to have all this hatred for her. I'd swear at her and call her names. But this past year I've been working hard on learning

117

how to bite my tongue and be civil. I started being nicer to her and discovered that when I sit down and talk to her, it really makes a difference in how I feel. I've finally started being able to love her.

Still, it's not all roses. Gil is obviously feeling pressured by his mother's apparent neediness and dependence on him, plus he finds himself worrying about *her* sobriety as well as his own. This is an additional burden.

Gil: My mom isn't going to many meetings. I don't know why. She says "Well, I'm close to God" or "I'm too tired." Excuses! And because she doesn't go to meetings, she doesn't have many friends. It's like right now I'm her *only* friend.

Sylvia: Does it put pressure on you?

Gil: It does, to tell you the truth, but I don't tell her that. We used to spend more time together, but now that I'm in a relationship I'm not home a lot. If I phone her from my girlfriend's house, she'll say things like "I miss you" and stuff. It seems like my mother is jealous.

Responsible as Gil has become in some areas of his life, he's dragging his feet in others, particularly in his acting. He *says* he "badly wants" to become an actor, yet he's doing things to sabotage it. I experienced his self-sabotage firsthand.

I'd written an educational film about "Working the [AA] Program" with four scenes in it, each of which called for two or three actors. One of the scenes was about a teenager who gets sober, and I thought Gil would cast well in this role. In addition to paying $200.00, it would have been his first professional "credit," and he'd also have a piece of film of his acting, which could potentially help him obtain future jobs. I told him to send me a photo of himself as soon as possible so I could submit it.

Well, Gil kept "forgetting" to send me his picture. When he finally did it was only a photocopy of a picture, and it certainly didn't do him justice. I submitted it anyway, plus I gave him all the information about where he could get good photos taken inexpensively. Despite the photocopy, the filmmaker liked Gil's looks and tried to reach him but none of his messages were returned. The filmmaker then called me, and getting into a little enabling myself, I tracked down Gil and told him to contact the filmmaker, whose office, coincidentally, was right across the street from Gil's acting school. I wrote down all the technical information on a piece of paper and gave it to him. A week later Gil called me to say he'd lost the piece of paper. I gave it to him again. Gil *did* call this time, and an audition was set up. He never made it. Weeks later I ran into Gil and asked him, "Did you get the part?" He looked sheepish and answered, "No, I lost the guy's phone number and address again." It hadn't occurred to him, he said, either to call me or to walk across the street and into the building where he knew the filmmaker's office was located and look at the board in the lobby to see if one of the names rang a bell. Instead, he had let the whole opportunity fizzle.

I gave him a scolding, right in front of his girlfriend (this was before she'd left him), and then rewrote all the information so he could call the filmmaker and make amends for standing him up and maybe try to get a shot at another acting job down the line.

"Put the information in your wallet for safekeeping," I told Gil. "I don't have a wallet" was his answer. At this point, Gil's girlfriend, who seemed a tad exasperated with him, grabbed the piece of paper and said, "Here, *I'll* keep it for you!"

Sylvia: Gil, you know a little psychology. Why do you think you messed up this movie opportunity?

Gil (grins): Fear of success?

"Fear of success" is a term that covers a lot of territory, but I'm sure there's truth in it for Gil. Self-sabotage at this stage of sobriety isn't at all unusual. Perhaps it stems from leftover guilt about being an alcoholic or addict. Perhaps Gil doesn't *fear* success so much as he doesn't think he *deserves* it, the rationale being that because he's "bad," he needs to undermine success by being a flake.

Gil obviously has some of his work for the coming year cut out for him. He seems to be trying to pull himself out of his current "Is this it?" mood and regain some of his former passion for his sobriety.

> Talking with you about what I've been going through lately has helped me to see it more clearly. I realize I'd better do something fast. I think what I should do is work with others more. I'll probably do a panel [when a couple of sober AAs take a traveling AA meeting into a prison, treatment center, or hospital]. I know if I work with others and keep my ears open I'm going to benefit from what I hear.

Gil has always been one of those people who learns from observing others, including his brothers.

> One of my brothers moved to London and got in with a crowd who drank and used. He called home and was real convincing about how he wanted to come home and get sober, so I enabled him. I sent him the money for the plane ticket. My mom had refused this time. And, of course, two days after he got here he was out drinking and using again. However, in a way it's good for me to see him, because right in front of me, in black and white, I can see how he's going backward in life and I'm going forward. I can look at him and say to myself, "Here's using, and here's sobriety—which do you want?" And there's no question in my mind that I want to go forward. My brother kept saying things like "The program isn't working for me anymore." But of course I know the problem is that he's not doing the things you have to

do to *make* it work. So I tell him, "Fine, do it your way and see how far you go."

From my own experience I think when a person wants to stay sober, he's willing to listen. He's like a sponge, ready to absorb any information that might make things better. But my brother's not doing that. And now *I'm* starting to do the same and tune out. I need to open up my ears and listen again.

Gil's immediate task is to find a way to get through his burnout without relapsing. "It's progress and not perfection," Gil reminds himself.

For the most part, I *am* pretty responsible today, and I know that my whole attitude about life is totally different. Today I *am* what I used to see in other guys—and put down, probably because I was envious. Now I'm there, too. And I know one thing for sure: If I don't drink or use, eventually I'll be successful. Mostly I think I have a good program, although I realize now that I need to get out there and give back some of what I've gotten. I really feel I've come a long way. I've got responsibilities. I've got bills. And when I'm eighteen, my mother says I have to pay half of my obligations at home: rent, food, everything. But I'm actually looking forward to it. I'm becoming a man.

8

SOPHOMORITIS:
Rusty, Sober Four Years

Sophomoric (definition): From the Greek sophos, *wise, plus* moros, *foolish. Self-assured, opinionated, though immature.*
—Webster's New World Dictionary

Siren's Song

As Ulysses' ship approached the Siren's island, the sea was calm, and over the waters came the notes of music so ravishing and attractive that Ulysses struggled to get loose, and by cries and signs to his people begged to be released; but they, obedient to his previous orders, sprang forward and bound him still faster. They held on their course, and the music grew fainter till it ceased to be heard, when with joy Ulysses gave his companions the signal to unseal their ears, and they relieved him from his bonds.

—*Bulfinch's Mythology*

The Greek hero Ulysses was certainly brave. During his long odyssey he faced—and survived—many dangers. He was also wise, wise enough to know that as a mere mortal he had human weaknesses. One was his susceptibility to the seductive song of the sirens, sea nymphs who lived on the Siren's island. In order to make it safely past the island, Ulysses needed the help of his loyal crew. He had them tie him to the mast of his ship to prevent him from jumping overboard to his destruction in response to the sirens' song. And Ulysses, in turn, helped his crew avoid the same fate by insisting that they put wax in their ears so *they* wouldn't succumb to the charm of the sirens' seductive strain. As a result, both Ulysses *and* his crew survived.

The recovering alcoholic hero is in a similar position. To bypass the various dangers and temptations facing him on his own long journey, he needs two things: first, the wisdom to understand that, like Ulysses, he still has human weaknesses, and, second, the realization that he needs the help of other people. No matter how smart he is, no matter how long he's been sober, he simply cannot make a successful journey through life alone. And, as Ulysses knew so well, he can't let down his guard simply because he survives one danger. There's always another threat lurking around the next bend.

The stage during which the recovering alcoholic man is gaining this knowledge is the awkward period of sobriety before the five-year milestone, usually around year four, when the man suffers from what some AAs call "sophomoritis," or "wise foolishness." Like an adolescent, he is neither fish nor fowl, neither wise nor totally foolish, but a little of each. One minute he's an adult, the next a child. One minute he's up, the next down. One minute he's arrogant, the next he's humble.

Beyond Wise Foolishness

The cure for sophomoritis or wise foolishness is for each man to recognize, as Ulysses did, that he is human and therefore vulnerable, and to find ways of working with these inherent qualities so that his flaws don't kill him. The truly wise man knows that he is foolish. The true fool thinks himself to be wise and denies his foolishness. As Socrates said, "The wise man knows that he knows nothing." AA asks each man to make friends with his own foolishness instead of denying it. Those who fail to find Ulysses' solution are doomed.

A man in the "moros" (foolish) phase of sophomoritis may have the illusion, for example, that he is cut out for something special in life, that he has unique talents; but as we saw with Gil in the last chapter, he's often not willing to put these talents to the test. He may hide behind a respectable-sounding excuse like "fear of success," but it's probably closer to the truth to say that he has a fear of finding out that he has no talent after all. It takes a lot of courage for the recovering alcoholic to risk the discovery that he's average. Even nonalcoholics have to face this dragon.

Also in the last chapter, we saw the beginnings of sophomoritis in Gil, who was questioning "Is that all there is?" Any recovering man who begins to run out of steam in his third, fourth, or fifth year, who is no longer gung ho, may attribute this to an assumption that he's learned everything there is to know about AA and about sobriety—a very dangerous assumption indeed. Once he starts thinking, "If I survived my first few years, I can survive anything," sophomoritis has set in. He becomes complacent, thinking *he* could never slip; he stops calling his sponsor because he doesn't think the sponsor has anything else to teach him; he begins to think of himself as someone who has "graduated," so he no longer sees himself as a student with work to do; and he forgets his weaknesses and behaves as if he's immortal. He thinks, for example, that because he's sober, he can drive 85 mph and not have an accident, and even if he does, that he's impervious to injury or death. Nothing bad can happen to *him*—he's in AA now. "Wise foolishness," of course, is *very* foolish.

125

We saw Gil flirting with this conclusion. Fortunately, Gil seemed to recognize—at least intellectually—the danger of this thinking, the foolhardiness of believing he could skip meetings, stop working with newcomers, sabotage himself in his career, and obsess over a woman who's inappropriate for him without eventually drinking again. The theme of the struggle each man has with his own wise foolishness continues in this chapter when we meet our four-year man, Rusty.

The Right Stuff

Sponsor Jack has nursed many a recovering alcoholic man through sophomoritis. "Some of them think they know everything there is to know about the program. You can't tell them anything. They think they've been through their tests, and because they survived four years they're impervious now. Invulnerable. Invincible. They are damned near perfect. You can see it. It shows all over. They become, in a word, insufferable."

When a man in the "moros" (foolish) part of his sophomoritis calls his sponsor, it isn't so much to ask for help as it is to *announce* some decision. After all, if you think you're John Wayne, you don't need to ask for help.

> Sponsor Jack: I had one of these guys call me after two months of silence, just to inform me that he'd been offered a job for a certain amount of money. He said, "What do you think?" I said, "I think you're going to drink," and he said, "What?" I repeated, "I think you're going to drink. For two months I've been waiting for you to ask me a question, any question. I think you're being totally arrogant and off-base. You're pretending to yourself to be spiritual, when in fact you think you're God. You really better be careful." I scared him enough to get his attention, and he started calling me again. Eventually he got through it.

126

The tremendous drop-off in AA membership shortly before the five-year milestone clearly attests to the dangers of the sophomoritis phase. These men were able to survive the hurdles of the first few years but just didn't have the "right stuff" to survive sophomoritis. They couldn't make the transition from foolish to wise. Fortunately Rusty, though he's sometimes uncomfortable in his skin, seems to be making the transition pretty well.

RUSTY

Last night I was feeling victimized on my job, so my dueling head started up: "I'm going to march right in there to my boss, and I'm going to do this, and I'm going to say that, and then I'm going to smack him one!" But, of course, when reality finally came through to me, I knew I wasn't going to do any of those things.

Rusty, thirty, is good-looking, 6 foot 4, and loves motorcycles. In some ways, Rusty seems to take up where Gil leaves off in the last chapter; in fact, he could easily be Gil's big brother. Where Gil was just entering into the sophomoritis stage, Rusty seems to be pulling out of it. His sense of humor—though self-deprecating—has undoubtedly helped to save him from disaster. He is wise enough to have some perspective about himself, even about those things that may seem foolish. For example, when I commented that because he'd started drinking so young (age eleven) he'd missed his adolescence, Rusty shot back, "I'm having it now."

Rusty was born in Pennsylvania, the youngest of three children. His father was in middle management and the family moved from place to place when Rusty was growing up. Though neither of his parents was an alcoholic, Rusty points out that the extended families on both sides are "laced with alcoholism." In fact, he adds, "I was named after an uncle who died of alcoholism." Like Gil, Rusty drank young, grew up fast, and preferred the company of older people. "I don't mix with peers," he says with a little twinkle in his eye. "They don't give me the respect I deserve."

For nearly half his life, since age sixteen, Rusty has held the same job (for an alcoholic to stay put in one job is unusual) as a night stock clerk in a supermarket. He sees his job consistency as a flaw. "My problem is that I dig myself into a rut, and then I furnish it until it's so comfortable I don't want to move on."

Like so many alcoholics, Rusty remembers feeling "different"as a kid. "I always knew there was something *wrong* with me, only I didn't know what it was, so I used to tell people I had diabetes. I *didn't* have diabetes, but I figured that would do until I discovered what *was* wrong. Of course, it never once occurred to me that what was 'different' about me was that I drank a case of beer every day and did drugs. My friends would say, 'Jeeze, Rusty you drink a lot of beer. Maybe you should try something else' And I'd say, 'No, I think if I tried anything else I might get a drinking problem.' "

Rusty feels he's always had a fatal attraction for alcoholics and addicts.

"There was a married couple in our building when I was a kid and they were always coming home drunk. The guy would stagger in and his wife would pass out in the car. I thought they were great. I remember thinking, 'Boy, they really know how to do it.' "

This couple inspired Rusty's first big drunk at age eleven, a two-day affair during which he had to fight to keep the alcohol down. "Each time I threw up, I'd say to myself, 'If *they* can do it right, then *I* can do it right.' "

Finally, he did it right.

Although alcohol was Rusty's drug of choice ("I used to crack open a can of beer in the morning with my cornflakes") he was not a "pure" alcoholic. As a kid he experimented with "pot",

Pertussin, and Nyquil. He even sniffed Bactine spray and airplane glue. At the same time, Rusty played Little League and was a cub scout.

"I was convinced that I must be demonically possessed. It was the only thing I could think of that could explain how a kid like me, who helped old ladies across the street and was named Paperboy of the Year, could turn around and steal anything that wasn't bolted down to buy drugs."

In his twenties, when he started using cocaine, things got worse, especially when he found himself involved with the notorious Colombian Mafia.

> I met the Colombians through my friend, R., who was one of their top salesmen, and soon after, I became a dealer. The Colombians would give me an ounce of blow [cocaine] one week, I'd sell it, and I'd pay them $2,000 the following week. Then they'd give me another ounce. I had visions of making $10,000 a week. All I could think of was how many motorcycles I could buy selling drugs. I became a ruthless character. Amazing the backstabbing I did. I just leap-frogged my way right up to the head of this particular organization, right over the back of my friend, R. I became a total dictator. If you owed me $90, I'd take the wheels off your car or I'd kick your door in and take your stereo or threaten your wife. I'd say, "I'm sorry. It's not personal. It's just business." But later on, when the tables turned and people started doing this to me, I'd say, "Well, it goes to show you the only person you can rely on is yourself." The truth was, I couldn't even do that. I couldn't even trust *myself*.

By now Rusty was in trouble with the Colombians.

> I had a $300 to $400-a-day cocaine maintenance habit. I had become my own best customer. To cover myself, I had this rotation of Colombian connections, and I'd take one guy's stuff to pay another guy off. One year I made $30,000 legitimately from my job, on top of whatever I made dealing, and it *all* went for cocaine. Here I was, thousands of dollars in debt to people who had stated

very clearly that they'd break my legs or kill me, and I *still* couldn't stop. I'd use. Then I'd try to fall asleep, but I couldn't because the bag of coke was talking to me, so I'd do another gram, pace around cursing myself, and use again. Finally I had a brilliant thought: "There's something wrong here."

What Rusty did next was rather unique. "I went to the Colombians and I told them, 'Look, I messed up. I got myself into this, and I'm going to get myself out of it. I owe you X amount of money and I'm going to pay you back.' "

And that's exactly what he did. He paid back every cent, in installments, for over two years—just as he might have paid off a refrigerator at Sears. Even more remarkable is the fact that the Colombians consented to this arrangement. "They kept threatening to break my bones in between payments, but they didn't do it."

Paying back the Colombians stopped Rusty from dealing cocaine, but not from using it.

I spent my salary on cocaine. My living conditions stank. I lost my girlfriend, even my car. Every day on the way to work I smoked pot. My employer was watching me and I was paranoid as hell. On New Year's Eve I found myself alone with a beer, a little cocaine, and a pack of cigarettes, watching MTV's "Million Dollar Cash Giveaway," saying "Tomorrow will be different." I had this feeling that "Something was in the works," only I didn't know what it was. I thought it had to do with winning a lot of money, so I kept dialing MTV like crazy.

Then I walked into the bathroom and looked in the mirror, and I saw, as though for the first time, who was really there—not what I wanted to see, not the man I should have been, but who was *really* there. I weighed only 155 pounds and looked deathly white. My eyes were sunken and dilated, and in them I could see the reflection of the reflection of the reflection . . .

Suddenly I knew that *I* was the problem. It wasn't the law, or the Colombians, or my ex-girlfriend. My parents hadn't done this to me. All the misunderstandings I'd had with people couldn't be blamed on them. I couldn't blame them for why I was alone on

New Year's Eve, where the high point of the evening was dialing MTV. I found myself praying to God, "Look at the life you gave me, and I've messed it up; so if you think there's anything here that's salvageable, could you please come do something about it? I can't go on like this any longer."

A week later Rusty was arrested for drunk driving in a parking lot. He was sentenced to a yearlong driving program at the National Council on Alcoholism (NCA) and told to go to AA. Rusty balked. "I told them, 'AA's just a cult, man, it's not going anywhere,' but they insisted. When I walked into an AA club-house and saw the bumper stickers and the pictures of Bill W. and Dr. Bob on the wall, I thought, 'Oh, God, Jonestown here we come!'"

Nonetheless, Rusty stuck it out, even though his first few weeks were physically miserable since he didn't go through a treatment center and had to detox himself.

I broke down with the DTs [delirium tremens] after forty-eight hours. I couldn't talk or stop shaking or take enough showers. I was convinced I was going insane. I'd seen those winos on the street, and I couldn't believe this was happening to a young guy like me. But I was still so much into "looking good" that I would-n't tell anybody what I was going through. I just stuffed it. I went into work hallucinating!

When Rusty started to feel a little better, he made a remark-able discovery: "There are gorgeous girls in AA!" That kept him going back to meetings. But, as AA says, "whatever it takes!"

He managed to survive his first year under difficult circum-stances. His friend and roommate R., was still drinking and deal-ing cocaine out of the house. And Rusty's buddies were continually trying to sabotage his sobriety by offering him free lines of cocaine. "It seemed like people started coming out of the woodwork, just to get me high. I was sure it was the devil coming to claim me. So I just kept saying, 'I don't do that anymore,' and I kept going to meetings."

Once Rusty came within a hair of giving in to a "freebie," but R. saved him.

> R. was with me and I was just about to say yes to this guy when suddenly R. said, "Leave Rusty alone! He's got seven days in AA!" And I could tell by the look in R.'s eyes that he was proud, *really* proud of me. And I said to myself, "Hey, he's right. I've got seven days. Tomorrow I'll have eight days, then I'll have nine days, then I'll have a thirty-day chip!" *That's* when I finally got the concept of one day at a time.

Soon afterward, R. got sober too. "Sobriety spreads like wild-fire," Rusty says.

> But I was still uncomfortable at AA meetings. I stood up at the back of the room and wouldn't talk to anybody, until one night this girl walked up to me and said, "What are you, the bathroom monitor?" After that I started opening my mouth.
>
> "I became a meeting junkie. I bought the AA "Big Book" for all my friends as Christmas presents—and lost a lot of friends. Then I started working the Twelve Steps."

In his second year, Rusty worked on some of his *trickier* amends, the ones that had to do with his cocaine dealing. "I had a lot of guilt over the fact that I sold drugs to people who were hurt by them."

Sylvia: How did you make amends to those people?

Rusty: Many of them were coming into AA themselves, so when they arrived, I was at the door to greet them. I'd offer them assistance in any way I could, like I'd drive them to meetings. It made me feel good.

During the past year or two, Rusty admits he's been fighting sophomoritis but feels the worst of it is over, that he's "wising" up and coming out the other side. For a while there, he was beginning to think that he had it all together.

> I was full of it. For example, when the supermarket chain I work for decided to stay open twenty-four hours a day and I was switched from the night to the all-night shift, I was sure it was because I was so together and was such a good AA member that God wanted me to work the all-night shift so I'd be there to save all the drug addicts and alcoholics who frequent supermarkets at those hours. Instead, what's happened is that all this year I've had a front-row seat to the all-night Misery Parade. Our store is in a very nice neighborhood that just happens to be in the grips of the whole crack scene. So I get to see it, and I get to realize that that could have been *me*! It's humbling. Every day when I see those guys, I want to get down on my knees and thank God for my sobriety. I'm so grateful that I don't have to live like that anymore.
>
> So it turns out that it's not me saving the alcoholics and addicts by getting *them* sober; it's the alcoholics and addicts saving me by keeping *me* sober!

A very wise conclusion. This sophomore has obviously gained some critical wisdom.

Sylvia: What else was "sophomoric" about you?

Rusty: I guess it was arrogant of me to get so complacent about the program. I was starting to take AA and sobriety for granted.

Sylvia: What changed your mind?

Rusty: A number of my close friends, guys I hung out with who got sober with me, went back out there [relapsed] this year. That has made me more appreciative of just how lucky I am to still be here. It's made me realize that staying sober may just be a little harder than I'd thought.

What Rusty has done consistently (and this, like his sense of humor, may be another factor that has saved him) is to rely, like Ulysses, on the help and support of others. Despite an admitted "problem with authority," he's overcome it enough to allow himself to call his sponsor and he's continued to "do service" by helping others, again as Ulysses the hero did. Working with others, taking them to meetings and going on panels into hospitals and prisons all serve to remind him of where he came from not too long ago.

Rusty still displays some foolishness in the areas of love and work, but he's working hard on wising up. He admits to getting obsessed with women, which only distracts him from his program. And at work, there's some self-sabotaging going on, just as there was with Gil.

> When I stopped being the bathroom monitor at AA meetings, I started chasing women. And once I caught a few, I realized I was afraid of them. I don't think I'd ever made love to a woman without being high. So I had to learn how to be with a woman from scratch. Of course, once I started doing it, I got addicted. Women have become my new drug of choice, and for me it's a destructive one, because the women I choose to become obsessed with are unavailable types. The more unavailable they are, the harder I try.

Again, while Rusty may be foolish enough to get obsessed with unavailable women, he's "wise" enough not to try to handle the problem alone. He keeps his sponsor and friends appraised of what he's up to. Sometimes he even lets them "tie him to the deck" so he doesn't destroy himself.

> My sponsor and other AA guys are teaching me that, since I have an obsessive personality and probably always will, I should learn to *transfer* my obsessiveness over to positive things that can benefit my life instead of hurt me. For example, it's safer for me to be addicted to exercise than it is for me to be addicted to an unavailable woman!

Sophomoritis also surfaces in Rusty's struggle to get along at work.

> I'm basically antisocial and rebellious, so I don't deal well with authority and supervision. When somebody puts their foot in my behind, I just react. On the other hand, when *I'm* in charge, it's even worse. I turn into a control freak. So it's best if I keep myself out of both of these extremes by working the graveyard shift and steering clear of people. They leave me alone, and I leave them alone.

Here again, the "wise" part of Rusty is that he knows he has limitations in the work area and he makes allowances for them to minimize the risk both to himself and to others. The all-night shift, like being tied to the deck, keeps him out of trouble.

Self-restraint is also wisdom for someone who's been impulsive all his life. The tendencies are still there, as seen in the quote at the beginning of this section where he wanted to confront his boss and "smack him one," but he didn't do it. He recognized that if you smack the boss, you get fired! Today, he can admit the impulse without following it through.

Rusty, like Gil, complains of a "fear of success," but more likely it's a fear that he'll turn out not to be special after all. Even though he says he wants a career beyond being a stock clerk at the supermarket, for now he's still wary about committing himself to picking a goal and doing something about it.

> I *still* don't know what I want to be when I grow up! I have all kinds of dreams. I always wanted to race motorcycles, or become an actor or an athlete or a rock star. I'd like that on-stage kind of life. And the law has always interested me—I was in trouble with it so much! Maybe I should become a lawyer. I took some communications courses, and now I want to take broadcasting, guitar, and writing—although maybe writing is a gift you shouldn't pollute by studying it. I used to write a lot of poetry; now I'd like to try writing songs. I think someday I'd like to move to Santa Barbara.

To say that Rusty is unfocused is an understatement. It looks as though he has next year's AA work cut out for him.

Sylvia: What's holding you up from pursuing one of these goals?

Rusty: Fear. Fear of success. Fear of failure. Fear of looking bad. Fear of not getting what I want. Fear of losing what I have. Fear that I don't deserve success. Last week I won a motorcycle race, and immediately I thought to myself, "They must have made a mistake. They must have scored that wrong! Should I tell them?" It's all just fear. [He laughs.] *Just!* And because of fear, I keep denying myself my dreams. I sabotage myself so there's no way they can come true. For example, this guy I know gave me an application card to join a club that could potentially be beneficial to me with my song writing. He told me to call the president of the club. He said, "Tell him I told you to call." Well, I still haven't called. I'm too worried the guy will think I'm some kind of gate-crasher. I'm too worried about what other people think!

On the other hand, maybe it's just sloth. Maybe I just want it all dumped in my lap. Maybe I'm disappointed to find out that things take work.

Sylvia: What has your own bout with sophomoritis taught you?

Rusty: Not to think that I have it all together. I *don't* have it all together. My life is equally, if not *more*, unmanageable today than it was the day I walked into Alcoholics Anonymous. Or maybe its just that today the fact that my life is unmanageable is more *apparent* to me!

Also, I think I've learned not to take myself so seriously. I'm even starting to let people joke with me about myself, which is a huge change. In the past, I wouldn't allow anybody to make me the butt of a joke, but today I can take it. I say things like "You must have me confused with someone who can take a joke," and I can laugh it off.

Today I realize that sobriety is a gift that I had absolutely nothing to do with. That's certainly taken me down a few pegs. I'm not God's gift to AA. I'm just here by accident.

Sylvia: What else can help people through this wise-foolish phase?

Rusty: A few good kicks in the teeth.

9

SECOND SURRENDER:
John, Sober Seven Years

I'd been trying to walk on water, and I almost drowned. It all came to a head one day when I stormed into my office and started bawling someone out for a mistake anybody could have made. Suddenly, I caught a glimpse of my reflection in the window and I said, "Oh-oh, Dr. Jekyll had faded away, and now Mr. Hyde is back out of the cupboard." That's when I saw how far off course I'd gone.

Second Milestone

Getting past the five-year AA birthday or anniversary may not be quite as magical as getting past the first one, but it's an important milestone nonetheless. Life on the other side of five is a lot better. It's also a lot lonelier. Most of the troops our hero has been fighting alongside during his early years have fallen, gone back "out there" somewhere. They've become the AA equivalents of the *desaparecidos*, the "disappeared ones," and the majority are never heard from again. When the still-sober man attends an AA meeting, 90 percent of the faces in the room are newer than he is. Here he is feeling as though he's barely learned to tie his shoes in sobriety, and now these newcomers are looking at *him* as an old-timer.

No matter how long an alcoholic has been clean and sober, he still plays a little game in his head. He likes to ask himself, "What's still out there that could make me drink or use? If X happened, would I drink or use over it?" He imagines all the horrendous things that "X" could be—the death of a child, a terminal illness, financial ruin, even war. He likes to believe he'd be strong, but now that he'd passed through the cocky, sophomoritis stage, he won't swear to it. He knows it's always possible that something could come along that could shake him off his ledge. God knows, he's certainly seen it happen to others countless times. It's newcomers who say things like, "Oh, if X happened to *me*, I'd never drink over it!"

During this time, some recovering alcoholics experience the "second surrender." Having first surrendered by making the initial commitment to the program, the recovering alcoholic now *recommits* to the sobriety journey after having perhaps wavered a bit during his year or two of sophomoritis. The second surrender often goes hand in hand with the recovering alcoholic's increasing interest in his spiritual and philosophical life. In many cases, the second surrender is triggered by a shock, an upset, or a crisis, which snaps him out of his complacency.

The crisis for one man who has been sober six years was when his sponsor drank again: "If there was anyone I thought would never slip, it was him. I'd have bet anything on his sobriety. I realized that if *he* could drink again, anybody could drink again. *I* could drink again. It scared the hell out of me. It made me realize that there's no safety, no guarantee. I don't like knowing that."

"As If" Courage

God, grant me the serenity to accept the things I cannot change,
the courage to changes the things I can,
and the wisdom to know the difference.
—Serenity Prayer, author unknown

Once the man has recommitted to his sobriety, changes begin to happen fast and happen big. One of the most remarkable changes is in his vastly improved ability to take action *in spite of* his fear. Unlike the men in the previous two chapters, the five-year-plus man doesn't let "fear of success" or "fear of failure" (depending on the nature of his focus) hold him back. He's learned that in order to "change the things you can," as the Serenity Prayer says, he has to act "as if," meaning he acts as if he had no fear when, of course, he still does. *That* takes courage! (His journey is becoming more and more heroic all the time.)

Roughly, *before* five is paying dues; *after* five is getting on with the business of living. The issues he put on hold while he got his sobriety act together can now be addressed. Maybe he's been hanging onto an unhappy marriage to see if sobriety improves it—if it does, great; if it doesn't, then perhaps this is the time he gets divorced. Or if he's been avoiding a love commitment, this may be the time he makes it. The five-year-plus man is probably on the verge of being able to have a real relationship. In the work area, this may be the time the man finally quits show business to go to dental school or quits dental school to become an actor. In sobriety, all things are possible.

Some see the second surrender stage as basically a spiritual crisis. There's less emphasis on material things, and more emphasis on the good old-fashioned virtues of integrity, rigorous honesty, and responsibility. There's also the attendant irony—as the man soon discovers—that these virtues are what really bring success, *including* material success.

For many recovering alcoholics, spirituality is defined as good reality testing and good behavior, pure and simple. As one man puts it, "Spirituality is doing the right thing."

141

Letting Go of the Branch

A man is hanging out over a cliff with only a tiny branch to cling onto. Down below is certain death. So he looks up to the heavens and shouts, "If there is a God, help me now!" A voice answers, "Let go of the branch!" And the man says, "Let go? Are you kidding? Only a fool would let go at a time like this!"

Recovering alcoholics hearing this story are likely to smile. They know that being on the healing path eventually means that they'll have to "let go" of trying to control people and events and of trying to predict the outcome of their actions. They have to learn to trust the process, to have faith that if they take the right actions the right result will follow—MAYBE. But if they *don't* take a chance, if they don't risk trying something new—even if there is no guarantee of success—they'll never know what might have been.

Such an approach isn't easy for the man who has spent his whole life avoiding things because he has been afraid. To get to the point where he's willing to act "as if" and take an action when his fear is still pounding at him takes tremendous faith, let alone courage. It's letting go of the branch at the very moment when letting go looks as though it will lead to sure disaster. Our seven-year man, John, is finally attempting this challenge.

JOHN

Whenever some new challenge comes up and I'm scared to let go and trust, what keeps me going is reminding myself of how good it felt to walk through the fear the last time, how nice it was to get to the other side, and I'm greedy enough to want that feeling again.

John, a small, wiry, high-energy man of forty-three, was born in Greenock, Scotland, a town on the west coast about 25 miles from Glasgow. It was there that he found Alcoholics Anonymous. Of all the interviewees in this book, John was possibly the sickest physically, having come close to death a number of times because of a torn esophagus. John is currently working in a chemical dependency treatment center as an aide and is also in school, studying to become an alcoholism counselor. He has retained his thick Scottish accent.

John was named for his grandfather, a 1920s IRA hero who, to this day, is still considered a saint in the town of Greenock. The oldest of eight children, John felt pressure from his relatives, his town, and his church (which he calls "Our Lady of Guilt"), to do something saintly himself, or at least something respectable.

> My family was shooting for me to become the first Scottish Pope. At Halloween, they dressed me up as a little priest. And when all my friends had pictures of girls on their bedroom walls, I had 10 by 8s of Spencer Tracy as Father Flannigan in the movie *Boy's Town*. As it turned out, I was incapable of bringing them the respectability they wanted. I guess I let them down badly.

John got off on the wrong foot when he failed the examination that all Scottish students had to take at age twelve.

> Your whole life depended on that exam. It determined whether you went to professional school or trade school, whether you were going to spend your life in a white shirt or in coveralls. As a result of it, I was sent to trade school when my whole personality cried out for communication—the theater, the movies—not holding a wrench.

What made it worse was the fact that John's friends passed the examination and were sent to professional school.

> I'd meet them in the pub after school, but I felt isolated from them. They never actually did anything to make me feel that way, I just felt that way—until I discovered alcohol. One scotch would fix me immediately, like Popeye with his spinach. One scotch made me bulletproof, muscular, and handsome. One scotch, and I could now expound on any subject—even subjects

like sports which I knew nothing about. And then, of course, it was two scotches. Then three."

Ironically, while alcohol initially helped John feel closer to his friends, it ultimately isolated him from them. "I began to want to drink more than I wanted to be with my friends, so I'd go off to low-class bars where they couldn't find me." The other irony was the fact that it was alcohol, not trade school, that finally put John in those dreaded coveralls.

After I graduated from trade school, I managed to get a job in a department store, which meant that I at least got to wear a suit and a tie instead of coveralls. But I regularly began to drink at lunchtime, which of course wasn't allowed. We had very high-class customers, a lot of blue-rinse-tone ladies, and I knew that eventually one of them would report me.

Then one day a crew of painters came to paint the store.

I noticed that at lunchtime the painters went out to the pub. They drank openly and nobody gave a hang. I remember thinking to myself, "You know, Johnny, you never liked those blue-rinse-tone ladies anyway." So one day when the painters made their daily jaunt to the pub, I left with them and never went back to work.

Instead, he put on coveralls and became a painter. "Now I had no interest in painting, especially since it dirtied my hands and made me lower class, but I wanted to drink the way painters drank."

At twenty-eight, John the Painter fell in love, a romance doomed from the start by alcohol.

She wasn't like my usual bubbleheaded dollybirds. She wore glasses and looked like a secretary, and the first time I saw her I saw the whole relationship—including the end of it. Because of my drinking, she gave up on me, as I knew she would. "If this is what you're like before we get married, what are you going to be like afterward?" she said to me. And then, after a long sigh, she'd use a line I think she stole from a movie: "I can't marry you, John, because you're already married to—the bottle!" So that was it.

I ran away to London to live with my sister. She was a stewardess and frequently out of town, so I had the run of her beautiful apartment that was stocked with bottles of scotch and TV dinners. And it was upstairs from a fancy bar. For awhile I thought I'd found heaven, but in the end the life brought me to my knees. I went back to Scotland, took a job, and made a pledge to myself that if I ever got fired, *then* I'd stop drinking.

Well, it happened. John got fired. He also kept his promise to himself. After going to a bar and downing six double scotches, he turned himself in to a treatment center for alcoholism.

Our town had an asylum up on the hill. When we were kids, our mothers would say, "You be good or we're sending you to the loony bin." This asylum had a little annex next to it, and those of us who'd seen the movie *Psycho* called it the Bates Motel. It was really a detox center. And that's where I went. I was only twenty-nine. In Scotland, it was unheard of for an alcoholic to hang up his guns at such a young age. Alcoholism has been in Scotland as long as there's been a Scottish nation, and everybody *knows* there's no cure. When an alcoholic with liver failure gets rushed down the corridor of a hospital, he has his bottle on the gurney with him. So the detox nurses were fascinated with me. They gave me the star treatment, which included tranquilizers. I'd never taken them in my whole life, and I thought they were wonderful. So for six weeks the first thing I'd do in the morning was go get my tranquilizer, and then I'd sit down in the dayroom and conduct the Scottish symphony. When it was time to be discharged, I didn't want to leave. At least I managed to bamboozle an extra day's supply of tranquilizers out of them by faking an anxiety attack at the front door.

John stayed sober for nine months. "It never occurred to me that I was supposed to give up booze *forever*. Are you kidding?"

On the first day of the tenth month, he drank. "And then one wet and windy day, I was back at the Bates Motel."

It was during his second detoxification that John was introduced to Alcoholics Anonymous.

> They told me to go down to Room 207 and when I opened the door, there were two gentlemen waiting to see me, smoking pipes, looking like head principals. "John, come on in, my boy," they said. And I thought, "Oh-oh, what's this?" I even checked behind the door. "Sit down," they said. "We hear you have a problem with the old booze." And then they went on to tell me their own personal stories.
>
> There in Scotland, we're raised to be independent, self-sufficient, and never, never to rely on anybody. We're raised to build a farm in a blizzard. That's why we make such good soldiers. There were Scotsmen at the Alamo. So when these two AA guys started talking to me about their feelings, I was shocked. "Hey, easy guys, lower your voices?" I said. "I don't even tell that kind of stuff in confession." But it was like they were reading my mail. They knew the secrets in my heart, and they won me over. Every Wednesday they came up to see me at the detox center and later I got a pass to go to their AA meeting in town. I had the address on a piece of paper, and when it turned out to be a nice-looking office building I thought, "This can't be it. What I'm looking for is a hobo campfire." Then I opened a door and saw a classic AA scene—a room with fifteen or twenty people and cigarette smoke as thick as a London fog.

This time John stayed sober six months, but he relapsed again. One major obstacle was his youth. Everyone else in the Greenock AA group was much older, so he had no AA social life. The social part of recovery is important for everyone, especially for an outgoing person like John. His spiritual void was also a major problem: "I never replaced the booze with anything else, outside *or* inside, and as a result the obsession for booze never left me. I was dry but not sober."

Each time John relapsed, he got worse. He already had liver damage, and this time he tore a hole in his esophagus and nearly died.

> I remember drinking a cup of coffee and it went down through the hole in my innards. I screamed out like a Scottish banshee.
>
> My family had decided to make arrangements for my tombstone. "It's not that we hate you, John. It's just that we hate what you've become," my aunt said, stealing a line from a movie herself. And I, of course, responded, "Not half as much as I do." Later I thought, "You know, John, they're right. It's getting near the end. You don't have a lot of time left. You're going to die, and when you do it's going to kill your mother, so you'd better get out of town so you won't be here underfoot when it happens." I decided to go to America, see the Alamo, and then lie down and die.

Instead of the Alamo, John ended up on skid row in Los Angeles. When he realized after a few weeks that he was still alive, he decided he'd try *"one* more AA meeting." He's been sober ever since.

Considering his stoic, "farm-in-a-blizzard" kind of upbringing, one of the hardest aspects of the program for John has been admitting, talking about, and then confronting his feelings. His heroic grandfather's ghost still hovers overhead. "I drank to stop feelings," he says. "I drank to be John Wayne."

It was while writing his fourth-step inventory that John began to see how some of his family's expectations of him were excessive. "All my life I've felt guilty for not becoming a Pope, and now I realize I only have to be myself. What freedom!" he says.

In sobriety, John has gone back to school where he's studying to become an addiction counselor. "I even learned to drive a car on this program. I'd never driven on a freeway before, and my first time I was sure I was going to die. But then I said to myself, 'Just think, John, if you die you'll be a martyr, and AA will talk about you for years.' Suddenly, I couldn't wait to get on that freeway."

147

John's second surrender, when he was about six years sober, came on the heels of his own bout with sophomoritis, an episode he now believes almost did him in.

> I got hung up on money, property, and prestige, and I forgot the program. Somebody had said to me, "If you're going to be in the addiction recovery field for the rest of your life, before you settle down in it why don't you do something else first, something you've always wanted to do?" So I took a job driving a limo, and I loved it. In fact, I loved it *too* much. I learned every nook and cranny of Los Angeles and I was going to all kinds of interesting places—nightclubs, parties, big hotels, and the airport, where I met lots of celebrities. But it turned out to be a serious crisis for me. I dropped all my AA meetings. I'd drive around town, right by some of my old meetings as they were in progress, playing country and western music as loud as I could, and I'd think, "I really should get to a meeting." But then the old thinking would come back in: "I'm coming up in the world. I've got money now." I was making about $100 a night and had started to get a bad case of big-shot-ism. I became aggressive and quick with people. I'd lose control of my shark-infested mouth and hurt people. Once somebody even asked me if I had a license for my sharp tongue because I was using it as a dangerous weapon. I remember one run-in I had with a couple of drunks, and I was incredibly judgmental and impatient with them—like I'd never been a drunk myself! It was as if I'd forgotten where I came from.

Shortly after his confrontation with the drunks, John blew up at somebody in the office of the limo company, caught that glimpse of his reflection in the window, and saw what a monster he'd become. The shock of it triggered his second surrender. He quit his limo job and scurried back to AA. Had he not done so, chances are he'd have relapsed, and given his physical condition, he'd probably have been dead by now. It was a close call, one that certainly humbled him.

From this point on, John began to focus more on his *own* limitations and less on the limitations of others.

> Initially, I wanted to interview everybody new who walked into Alcoholics Anonymous to see if they were fit to be members of this select clan of chosen people who had stopped killing themselves. Later, I realized that my AA "contract" only requires that I stay sober, go to meetings, and *help*—*not* judge—those who are coming behind me. At any given moment in this country there are millions of people out there slowly but surely making their way to AA's doors. When they arrive, we in AA may be their last hope, because *we* are the only ones who really understand what they've been going through. We are the sentinels at the gate. That's our job. Today I consider myself a walking copy of the AA "Big Book," and I treat people accordingly. Before, if I didn't think somebody was worthy of AA, my attitude was "Get out of here, you bum!" Today I realize that "there but for the grace of God go I." It's as if God said to me, "John, you're going to work with these alcoholic people and what you think of them personally is of no consequence." Now my ego is always a problem here, especially if it gets trampled because people don't treat me as I think they should, if they don't appreciate *who* I am. But what I feel about it and what I *do* about it are two different things. Today I behave in an orderly fashion while all this is going on, a very hard task for me, but I do it. For me, spirituality is my behavior with these people.

In the relationship area, John has made huge leaps into accepting who he is and is beginning to recognize just what kind of woman he can and cannot handle. Recently he has been put to the test by a pretty AA blond (just the type he says he *can't* handle) who has been pursuing him. (Many AA women, especially the newcomers, are very aggressive in love!)

> I get hit on by women, I think especially because of my accent, but this girl alarms me. She'll call me up instead of waiting for me to call her, and she's so beautiful, she doesn't need to do that.

149

I admit to being kind of intrigued, but something tells me no. I found out that she dates a lot of high-flying guys with lots of money, and I know I can't compete with that. Once she called me and said, "Come on over to the Rodeo Drive meeting in Beverly Hills and I'll introduce you to some people." Well, her timing was poor: it was the Friday before payday and I had only fifteen bucks left in my pocket. So I told her no, and why, and she said, "That doesn't matter. We're just going for coffee." And I said, "Yes, but the *possibility* is there." We might have ended up in some restaurant after all, and there was no way I was going to put myself in the mouth of that crocodile!

The other thing I've realized is that where women are concerned, I'm old-fashioned. When I learned that this girl had been with men I know well on the program, I guess I took her off the list. I want to believe a woman hasn't done anything until she meets me. I know that's unrealistic and may be unfair, but it *is* how I feel and it's what I have to work with. I guess I'm looking for the girl next door.

John's statement here is an important one, because it's such a healthy example of a man making friends with who he really is, not who he thinks he *should* be. If this is how he feels about women deep down (and Lord knows it took him long enough to even acknowledge those feelings.), then he will only be happy in a relationship if he honors such sentiments. For him to pretend to be more sophisticated and open-minded than he really is would be courting disaster.

It's possible that John may have found himself a "girl next door," but the trouble is, she's a newcomer. AA not only tells newcomers not to get emotionally involved too early, but it also advises old-timers not to get emotionally involved with newcomers. As we witnessed with the newly sober interviewees at the beginning of this book, newcomers are fickle, and old-timers aren't immune to getting their hearts broken. John is aware of this (at least intellectually), and he's handling this budding new relationship in the best way he can by openly and regularly discussing it with his sponsor and peers.

> I have to handle this very carefully. First of all, I had to tell this girl that I can't even go out on another date with her until she gets a sponsor. I could be cutting my own throat here, because that sponsor might turn around and say, "Drop that guy like a hot potato." The way I cover myself from my end is by telling everybody I know what I'm up to and enlisting their guidance. No more isolating myself from AA because I'm too busy with something else. That limo-driving job was a good lesson for me.

As the result of his second surrender, John no longer routinely lets his fears hold him back. He has enough faith in the whole recovery process to be willing to face new challenges.

> Sobriety has stretched me. It's given me the courage to attempt things I wouldn't have thought of trying before. School, for example. I had so many painful associations with school that when I did decide to go back, I was terrified. I thought they would laugh at me. I thought they would *know* I belonged in coveralls, and not in class, so the first day I arrived I felt queasy. Then the teacher said something wonderful: "This class is not about passing or failing, it's about learning." Instantly I felt great relief. I didn't have to be the best here, just John. From then on it was okay.

John also began to view his own drinking story from a different—and much healthier—perspective.

> My second surrender made me more aware of what and who I am. Before, I felt I was nothing, so that all I was was my war story [drinking story]. People seemed impressed by it. They'd stop me and say, "You're a walking miracle, John. To still be alive after all that!" It got so I was *proud* of my war story. I used to love standing up at the AA podium and giving them the Sam Peckinpah version of it, complete with the blood gushing out through the hole in my esophagus! But today I understand that I have more to offer than that. Today, I talk about recovery, about how even though I'm not as fortunate as I'd like to be, I'm grateful for what I have and I'm happier than I've ever been.

151

There's a saying in AA that every recovering alcoholic will have to reexperience, in sobriety, some of the significant events that happened to him when he was still out there drinking and using, just to see how he handles them clean and sober.

One of the events John reexperienced only a few weeks before this interview was getting fired. In this case, a personality clash with his boss had cost him the counseling job he loved in a residential drug treatment program.

But seven years of sobriety clearly changed the way John responded to his firing. Recall John's story of the first time he got fired back in Scotland, when he went to a pub, ordered six double scotches, and then checked himself into the "Bates Motel." This time he picked himself up, dusted himself off, and went out job hunting. "My main concern this time," he says, "was getting through it with some grace." While the idea of drinking may have flitted through his head—after all, he *remains* a recovering alcoholic—not once was it a serious consideration. Within a week, he had a new—and better—job, as an aide in a hospital-based chemical dependency treatment center. And while he still has some of his old insecurities about work (that coverall image dies hard), they don't render him dysfunctional.

Sometimes when I look ahead and think about being a counselor, I get scared. But then I see signs that it's going to be okay. In this new job I sit in with the counselors and therapists at staff meetings and give feedback about my work with the patients, how they relate to one another, how they handled themselves on pass, and so on, and I love it. One of the staff members told me that I was "a valuable addition to the team." It gives me a buzz to know I'm accepted.

It's incredible that they're paying me to do what I love to do, what I'd do for free. Just the other day, we had this wimpy guy try suicide, and later I talked to him. "You were trying to jump out the window, but if you'd succeeded you'd have killed the wrong person. You were trying to kill Mr. Hyde, but you'd have been taking Dr. Jekyll with you. You were going to kill that person inside you who has never even had a chance!" It was like I was talking to myself seven years ago. Thanks to AA, I gave that other person inside me a chance to come out—and he has.

I've been given what I always wanted: a life with some adventure to it. I stay sober not because I'll die if I drink. That's not enough of a deterrent. I stay sober because this is the best I've ever had and I want to see what happens next.

10

HITTING STRIDE:
Barry, Sober Ten Years

I've had eighteen years of psychoanalysis and ten years of sobriety, plus I'm a psychotherapist and licensed clinical psychologist. But once in a while I still get depressed. Well, I no longer assume that because I'm feeling down there's some psychopathology going on, or that I'm deficient or wrong. I no longer jump on my own case about it. Life really does have its ups and downs, and maybe I'm just feeling down because I'm human.

Becoming His Own Man

Until now we've focused mostly on similarities, on how all recovering alcoholics look alike. But as time goes on and the men fan out into their continuing sobriety, major differences appear. They begin to look more and more like individuals—like *themselves*. They become, as I said in an earlier chapter, whoever it was they were on their way to becoming before alcoholism intervened. This is just as it should be. While sobriety is AA's main goal, its secondary purpose is to help each man learn how to live successfully in the real world, not hide out from it. According to our consulting sponsor, Jack, "Around ten years of sobriety there's a kind of developmental leap, much like the one between adolescence and early adulthood. The man becomes defined. He learned what his powers are and what he can contribute. He now has an identity

155

all his own." Jack explains that even sponsors develop their own unique styles. "Some become quietly supportive, while others become flashy, authoritative, finger-shakers."

Back when he hit the five-year milestone, like Superman, the recovering alcoholic stepped out of his phone booth with a new attitude. He was ready for risks and took them. Even though he was afraid, he did it anyway. He acted "as if." By his tenth year of sobriety, he may have lost the fear itself. It simply went away. He's comfortable now. In fact, he has pretty much hit his stride. Things are going well and most of the time he feels okay. More important, even when things *aren't* going well, he's *still* okay. He's learned that being okay isn't dependent on his circumstances but rather on his attitude, how he holds those circumstances. As one eleven-year man said, "Right now everything in my life is a shambles, but *I'm* fine."

The ten-year man no longer uses his recovery process as an explanation or excuse for anything. He accepts responsibility for the state his life is in, good *and* bad, and accepts that what's going on today is mostly the result of choices he made yesterday. Heredity, background, childhood, experiences, age, health, even his unconscious mind all play a part, but his own choices are critical.

In short, after ten years the recovering alcoholic man is no longer searching to find himself. He's *found* himself. Re-schooling, re-training, re-marrying, and re-locating are most likely all behind him. There's no illusion now that if he could just take singing lessons he could be an opera star. He knows what he's *not*. Now he's busy hunkering down and doing whatever it is he's decided to do in depth. Success may not quite be his yet—after all, he was off track a long time and may still have dues to pay—but he's close.

Of course, this is the stage when a man's chronological age begins to make a significant difference. Thirty days sober was thirty days sober, no matter if the man was eighteen, thirty-six, or seventy. But now such generalizations can't be made. A twenty-five-year-old man who's been sober for ten years is going to be in a different place than a man of sixty-five who's been sober ten years. Nonetheless, because of the greenhouse phenomenon in AA that speeds up growth, that twenty-five-year-old AA guy with ten years of sobriety will probably have raced way ahead of his peers. He'll look much more grown up.

A Touch of Heroism

The ten-year man is likely to have developed a number of those hero qualities we've been talking about all along. He's honest (or more honest), he's responsible, he plays fair, he keeps his word. If he says he'll be someplace, he'll be there. Chances are the ten-year man who's married doesn't just talk about fidelity, he's faithful. It's not that he's out after a gold star; it's just that somewhere along the line he's discovered that in order to have a quality relationship, fidelity *works*. Through trial and error he has learned that in all areas of life, things go better—and he feels better—if he walks like he talks.

BARRY

By the time you've been sober ten years, you come to see that the joy of life and the pain of life are both experiences that can be handled sober.

Our ten-year man, Barry, is a slim, high-energy, forty-seven-year-old drummer-turned-psychologist. He has a long face, long nose, and graying hair and a way of leaning forward, like a race-horse about to take off.

He was born in East Los Angeles of parents who were both the black sheep of their respective families. His mother liked to play

157

cards and was, in Barry's words, "undisciplined and outrageous." She and Barry's father fought constantly, often to the point of violence. Barry has a half brother nine years older by his mother's first husband, who died in an auto accident. The brother moved out of the house when Barry was still young because he couldn't stand the "craziness" going on there.

Barry's mother often stayed out all night at card games. She had so much trouble getting up in the morning in order to get Barry off to school that after awhile she stopped trying. Once Barry hit second grade, she took him out of school altogether. "Basically, she wanted me there to be her companion. She wouldn't even let me go out and play ball. She was jealous of anyone else in my life and she wanted me bound to her, body and soul. If I tried to bring home a friend, she'd carry on and do one of her crazy trips in front of him until he fled. Then she'd be happy."

Barry's mother managed to keep him out of school until fifth grade. At that time, when her own mother died and left the family some money, they moved to an upper-crust neighborhood in West Los Angeles. That's when the rest of the family stepped in and laid down the law: Barry would have to go back to school and Barry's mother would have to go to work. As a result, her card playing lessened, but her fights with Barry's father did not. Barry longed for an escape.

> One day as I was coming out of temple with my parents, I saw some kids playing drums in a drum corps. They were parading by on Wilshire Boulevard. I fell in love. I begged my parents to get me drums. Amazingly, they did. After that, whenever they'd fight I'd escape to my room and play the drums. It drowned out their noise and made life more tolerable. I became obsessed with the drums—especially since I knew I was never going to be able to play ball or have any friends or have any happiness. My only happiness sprung from this dream of someday becoming a great drummer.

At fourteen, Barry began to study with an internationally acclaimed drum teacher, who took him on as his youngest student. "I think my parents' fighting helped me in this respect, because just to get away from them I practiced six or seven hours a day and I got to be very good."

By the time Barry completed his drum course with this teacher, he was twenty-three. He'd been married and divorced, had a son, lost his father, was drinking booze and using heroin, and had begun a psychoanalysis that was to continue for eighteen years.

At one point, he went to New York with the intention of entering the music business, but he found himself unable to meet the challenge.

> By then I was a full-fledged heroin addict so I turned around and came back to California and went to Synanon [a now-defunct drug treatment facility based in Santa Monica]. I stayed there six months. I left when they told me I couldn't drink. I didn't want to hear that. I was willing to stop heroin, but I *wasn't* willing to stop drinking.

Though certainly not "clean and sober" by AA standards, Barry was at least better. Heroin-free, his health improved and he began to make it in the music business. He joined a few bands that became really big. "It was the sixties, so it was okay to smoke pot and drink. The cocaine came later. As long as I stayed off heroin, I never considered anything else a problem."

Life went on like this for many years until Barry hurt his knee in an accident. "As I lay in bed in the hospital, I realized I didn't want to depend on being a drummer the rest of my life. I was like an auto mechanic. Without my hands, I wouldn't be able to work. Nor did I want to end up a sixty-year-old drummer schlepping my drums to play weddings on weekends like a lot of great drummers do."

Barry then switched to record producing. He married again. And again, he divorced. By now his addiction to other mind-altering chemicals was out of control. Pills. Vodka. Pot. (He was growing his own.) All the while, Barry thought he was doing just fine. "But after I told the president of a major record company to f— off, I didn't work for three years! He blackballed me in the record industry. I couldn't put a single deal together and I ended up with a job moving instruments."

It never once occurred to Barry to stop drinking or using.

Eventually, he got back into the record business. He even became president of a record company, but he continued to drink. Plus he was now free-basing cocaine. "I had the job opportunity of my dreams, yet I wasn't even showing up for work. I was depressed. Once I woke up and discovered I'd fallen asleep with a shotgun in my mouth."

Then, for the first time since Synanon, he started fixing heroin again. I remembered thinking, "This is the end. I've reached the end of the trail."

Barry begged his now second ex-wife to put him in a mental institution.

> But the first night I was there I heard a guy say, "Oh, boy, there's the new kid!" and right then and there I had some kind of moment of clarity. "I'm not crazy. I'm just a *drunk*," I shouted at the guy, and hurled my shaving lotion at him. Then I demanded that they let me out, which they gladly did.

He ran back to his psychoanalyst. "I think I'm an alcoholic," Barry told him. "Don't be ridiculous," the analyst said, trying to reassure him. But Barry pressed on. "I don't think you know your ass from a hole in the ground," he told the analyst, to which the analyst replied, "I know more about this than you'll ever know, and I say you're *not* an alcoholic."

Barry stormed out of the doctor's office and a few days later walked into a meeting of Alcoholics Anonymous. He's been clean and sober ever since.

Barry took to sobriety like the proverbial duck to water. While most of the interviewees we've met so far in this book had at least one slip before committing to AA, Barry got the message immediately. "At my first AA meeting a woman told me 'You can stay sober even if you're also crazy,' and I was very relieved. 'Great, there's some hope for me!' I thought, and I stayed." Even Barry's analyst had to admit there was a positive change in him. "I'm getting the feeling that you don't need me anymore," the analyst told him.

"Hum," Barry answered. "Only eighteen years of psychoanalysis, and cured already?"

The analysis was terminated two weeks later.

Barry continued in the music business for the first few years of his sobriety, but eventually he began to have second thoughts about it. "It's such a crazy business, I didn't think I'd be able to do it and stay sober. I'd ceased to enjoy it. Also, I consider music a business for young men, like being a ball player." So after all those years of studying and playing and producing, he just quit. It was a move that took courage—the kind of courage a man acquires by staying sober in Alcoholics Anonymous.

Barry began scanning the horizon for something else to do. "When a friend said, 'Why don't you become a psychologist?' it was like lightning. I thought, 'That's it! That's God talking to me.' " He completed his college degree ("I'd dropped out for sex, drugs, and rock 'n roll") and went on to graduate school for his Ph.D. in psychology, which took five years. "But I did it the same way I do things in AA. I simply followed their program, *one day at a time*." And ultimately, he got his graduate degree, then his psychology license, and then a job in a hospital chemical dependency treatment program, which he quit several months ago to set up his own private practice in Beverly Hills. A long way from East Los Angeles for a "crazy" kid who almost didn't make it past the second grade.

Today Barry has many recovering alcoholics in his practice, and he also has some definite ideas about diagnosing and treating them. For example, he is vehement about not blaming the disease of alcoholism for every character defect and personality quirk of the recovering alcoholic.

> I definitely believe in "dual diagnosis." I believe you can be both alcoholic *and* crazy, alcoholic *and* neurotic, alcoholic *and* obsessive-compulsive, alcoholic *and* borderline, or alcoholic *and* schizophrenic. I know alcoholics who are nuts, and I also know alcoholics who have no psychopathology other than their alcoholism. If you sober up a normal person, he returns to whatever the premorbid condition was and carries on with his life with great success. If you sober up a schizophrenic, what you get is a sober schizophrenic. If you sober up an asshole, what you get is a sober asshole.

Even after ten years, staying sober seems to come easy for Barry. He loves meetings, attends them often, has lots of AA friends, and sponsors newcomers. He's also secretary of an AA meeting and chairman of the speaker committee for an upcoming Cocaine Anonymous Convention. He seems to have sailed through some of the awkward stages—like sophomoritis and the second surrender—with relative ease. His initial commitment to his sobriety and to AA really stuck.

The spiritual side of the program, however, hasn't been such smooth sailing for Barry.

> I come from a Jewish intellectual background where believing in God is tantamount to believing in Santa Claus. It's the opiate of the masses and it's just not acceptable for educated people to do that. I've had to struggle with what "spirituality" means to me, and what I've concluded is that spirituality is behavioral, not verbal. It's walking like you talk. Even though I don't *talk* about God, I still have to *walk* a certain way. I can't be unfaithful and

then say, "Well, that's okay, because I'm an alcoholic; or I have problems in the area of intimacy, so I had sex with a woman I met at AA because I'm working on my problem." That's bullshit! You can't use the label "alcoholic" or "recovering alcoholic" to avoid personal responsibility for actions. This behavior is bad enough when people are still drinking, but I find it intolerable in sobriety. The reason I accept personal responsibility is because I feel better about doing it that way. Virtue *is* its own reward. I never used to believe that. I thought I could be dishonest in this little area over here, or over there, and that was okay. But it's not. You end up not feeling good. So walking like you talk is God to me.

Even though Barry, for the most part, seems satisfied with his present life, it doesn't mean he's going to stop working on himself. Currently, in fact, he's begun to question his basic worldview. His conclusion is that all his life he's lived by what he now calls the "sour milk organizing principle."

I was raised to see life as tragic. Imminent tragedy was the byword. Don't go outside or you'll be captured by the gypsies. Don't wear good clothes, because someone might give you the bad eye and you'll get sick. Don't go to a party, because you'll have a lousy time; besides, if you stay home you won't get germs. Don't get married, because you'll only get divorced and broken-hearted. Whatever it is, there's something wrong with it. Life was organized by a principle that said not only *can* bad things happen, they *will* happen. You can count on it. And it's going to be terrible.

It took Barry a number of years to begin to catch on that this "sour milk" organizing principle was not only affecting him negatively but was actually running his life.

When I finally began to see its influence on me and the problems it created, I was astounded. I remembered that back when I was drinking and I had a hit record that was Number 3 on the charts, I kept saying, "Yeah, but it's going to drop off the charts like an anchor.

It's going to go down to Number 100 in a second. In fact, it's going to be the record-breaking drop of the year." And whenever I got applause for my drumming, I'd say, "It's only because of my showmanship. I'm really a fraud." That kind of thinking continued for years into my sobriety. For example, when I decided to go back to school to become a psychologist, I'd catch myself thinking, "Why bother to go back to school when you're just going to die of cancer anyway?" Or, "Why bother to go back to school when you'll end up failing because it's too hard? You're a weak person and you'll just get sick and have to drop out." Even now I can still manage to come up with the worst-case scenario for anything that's going on in my life.

Barry still has to consciously work at shifting over to a more positive organizing principle.

Today I'm trying to retrain myself to realize that while life is not all a bowl of cherries, it's not all a vale of tears either. My old worldview was so pervasive that I have to be on the lookout so it doesn't rear its ugly head and swallow me up, especially when there are bumps in the road, when it's tempting to throw my hands up and say, "Ah-hah! I was right. Life *is* a vale of tears."

But reality moves back and forth in between. And today one of my major jobs is sustaining my new organizing principle that says that life can be happy, that I can go to a party and have a good time, that I can get married again and not have heartache and grief.

The last part of Barry's new angle on life is particularly pertinent now, since he is soon to remarry a fourth time (to a redheaded writer who is also in AA). That Barry is willing to try marriage again suggests that his new, positive organizing principle is working for him, because he has reason to be skittish.

My third wife, who was also in AA, came home one day and said, "Are you happy?" and I said, "Last time I checked I was." Then she said, "Well, I'm not, and I'm leaving." To this I replied, "Do you want to talk about it?" and she said, "No, my therapist told me I got married too early in sobriety, and I'm leaving." Then she left. That was it and, of course, I was devastated. But life isn't fair. What's important is, I didn't drink and she didn't drink. A few months later when it looked like she wanted back in again, I said no. I told her, "I can't live this way. I'm not going to be fifty-five or sixty and have you decide that you don't love me and walk out. We've got to move on with our own lives."

That's a pretty healthy response. A man with less sobriety might have caved in—out of loneliness, out of nostalgia, or out of convenience.

One major area of unfinished business in Barry's life involves his strained relationship with his son, now twenty-four, the product of Barry's first marriage when he was eighteen.

My son was only a few weeks old when my wife left me, and even though I was always available for a relationship with him, I don't think he ever wanted one with me. He has no feelings for me, for whatever reasons. I've reached out to him many times, but my phone calls are never returned. Basically, what he's been telling me for years is to buzz off.

Drawing on his newfound organizing principle, Barry refuses to be tragic about this, or even to dwell on it. "I have to accept that there are a number of things in the world that I do not understand, that I cannot understand, that I cannot control. My son is one of them." He moves on. "I have found that my relationships in Alcoholics Anonymous are much more nurturing and supportive than any of my familial relationships. I'm civil with members of my family, but the people I'm *close* to are all in AA.

"When it comes to marriage, I could *never* be married to anyone who wasn't on the program. And I don't mean Al-Anon, either, I mean Alcoholics Anonymous. It's important to me that she has experienced what I've experienced."

Interestingly, there are probably plenty of other ten-year men in AA who would disagree with Barry about this, who would just as passionately insist that when it comes to marriage it's a far, far better package to marry a woman who's *not* in AA, a "civilian."

But, of course, that's the whole point: By the time the recovering alcoholic man has reached ten years of sobriety, he has a mind of his own and he not only speaks it, he acts on it.

11

PERSISTENCE:
Arthur, Sober Fifteen Years

When I look back on a situation, I can see that persistence was probably what got me through it. But when I'm in the middle of something, it doesn't feel like persistence. All it feels like is trying to avoid the pain of whatever the hell is going on. It's hard to see jumping out of a hot frying pan as persistence.

Don't Quit Five Minutes Before the Miracle

There's a poster that many recovering alcoholics can smilingly identify with. It shows a photograph of a kitten clinging precariously onto a rope, and it reads, "Hang in there, baby!" AAs know that the secret of success in sobriety is hanging in. Persistence.

Persistence, which is defined as the refusal to give up in the face of opposition, adversity, or even boredom, is hard. "Endurance is one of the most difficult disciplines," the Buddha said, "but it is to the one who endures that the final victory comes." Hasn't every student at one point or another been told that "slow and steady wins the race"; that success is "1 percent inspiration and 99 percent perspiration"; or simply that it comes from "applying the seat of the pants to the seat of the chair"? During a recent telecast of the Emmy Awards, a ceremony honoring the best television performances, one winning actress proudly held up the statuette that symbolized her success and stated, "This shows that fifteen years of persistence paid off."

The same can be said for fifteen (or twenty or thirty) years of sobriety. Persistence definitely pays off, the biggest payoff, of course, being sobriety itself. But there are additional rewards, and by "hanging in there," the recovering alcoholic man can begin to reap the benefits of his labors. In some cases, this means material and financial success or creative success or even other intangible kinds of success. The implications of *success* depend on each man's definition of the word: for the man who has tried a new venture in sobriety and failed, the "success" part may be that he tried at all, that he gave it his best shot; for the man who kept himself impoverished for whatever neurotic reasons, success may be learning to hang onto a dollar; for the man who made a false God out of money, success may be losing it; and for the man who has abused himself physically all his life, success may be stopping other addictions in addition to drugs and alcohol, such as overeating and smoking.

Making a Dent

The fifteen-year recovering alcoholic man is making a dent in life, contributing something of value to the world. He knows what he cares about, what he believes in, and he's most likely standing up for it somewhere, being counted. During any given evening, I can sit in front of my television set, flip channels, and on every station see men I know to be recovering alcoholics—an actor in his own series, an astronaut, a newscaster, a politician, a writer being interviewed, a baseball player, a journalist, a musician, a talk show guest. They are all out there contributing their skills and talents to the rest of us.

Whatever work the recovering alcoholic man is doing, chances are that by the fifteenth year he's doing it better than ever. Sponsor Jack comments:

> Over the years, there's a subtle change in the *quality* of his work. I sponsor actors who were actors before they got sober, and they've stayed actors. With each year, the depth of what they have to offer improves. Their acting gets deeper. It seems to reach a certain wellspring of spirituality and strength. This happens, no matter what the "work" is. If you're a carpenter and initially your values are just to "get by," as time goes on your values will begin to change. Pretty soon the bench you "threw together" you now build with a loving care that reaches a depth of beauty you were incapable of before.

Beyond Survival Issues

In the earlier years of sobriety, the recovering alcoholic man had to deal with so many basic survival issues that he didn't have the time or energy to attend to such high-level issues as talent and creativity. In fact, newcomers are often afraid that if they have any talent, getting sober will have a negative effect on it. As mentioned earlier, years ago artists had the same apprehensions about entering psychotherapy or psychoanalysis. They feared their talent would be "analyzed" out of them, that their creative muse would be killed off. But for the truly creative person, sobriety only makes things better. Often the man doesn't even discover his talent until *after* he gets sober, like the man who unearthed a dormant talent for painting, worked at it for years, and ended up with his own gallery art shows. Such discoveries are what AAs gratefully call "the gifts of the program."

Of course, not everybody has a painter lurking within. They may have thought so, but what sobriety does for them is make them more honest with themselves. Sponsor Jack elaborates:

169

In the beginning, a carrot is dangled in front of the newcomer: If you stay sober, *all* your dreams will be realized. So what's your dream? What do you *really* want to be when you grow up? The theory is that if you can discover your talent or dream and do something about it, it will help you stay sober. That may be true, but unfortunately not everybody is clear about what his dream is. In my own case, what I've wanted has changed over the years. Once I wanted to be a wildly successful actor, but when I started seeing the nature of "the business" more clearly, I stopped finding that so interesting. In other words, for some of us the dream changes with new information.

Those who really *do* have an inner mission will discover it eventually. It will push its way up like a weed through a cement driveway, until it's noticed. Time, and persistence, will out.

ARTHUR

At fifteen years of sobriety, there's a sense that it's all survivable. You can trust that no matter what happens, no matter what you do, even if you're a less-than-willing participant, recovery is still not only possible but probable. All you have to do is show up.

Our fifteen-year man is a balding, soft-spoken, fifty-two-year-old public-relations man. Despite his warm, affable, nice-guy style, Arthur has an aura of sadness about him—like the sadness one imagines concealed behind the happy-face clown. He is just emerging from what he describes as a "three-year bout with depression," which may explain his demeanor. At 6 foot 1 Arthur is, in his own words, "disgustingly over two hundred pounds." This is recent. He quit smoking six months ago and put on the weight.

Arthur was born in Los Angeles of an Irish-English background; his maternal grandparents were Irish immigrants. He attended Catholic schools and, like our Scottish seven-year man John, he refers to his church as "Our Lady of Perpetual Guilt."

PERSISTENCE

to be Easter Sunday. I went over to her house with my little Easter plant and splattered my sobriety all over her house. And she, with her typical withholder's response, raised an eyebrow and said, "Oh, that's nice," and went right on talking. It hurt.

He had better luck with his daughter.

To *show* my daughter, who was then twelve, rather than just *tell* her about AA, I took her to a meeting. Driving home, she said to me, "You know, Daddy, I really like you so much better now that you're not drinking." When I heard that, I was puddles. I almost lost it right there on the freeway—me, the guy who stuffed feelings. And what's even more important is the fact that since then she's been an enormous support to my sobriety, the most vocal of my three kids in supporting me.

Arthur seems to have reached his current fifteen years of sobriety by simple plodding and perseverance, by being one of those "quietly supportive" people in Alcoholics Anonymous mentioned by Sponsor Jack. He goes to lots of meetings, he sponsors lots of guys, he's a good friend to many, he works diligently, and he is also one of those who augments his AA program with outside tools—workshops, therapy, self-help books. As a result, Arthur has been able to plod his way through some real-life problems that have arisen in his sobriety, problems that might have driven others back to the bottle.

When my daughter got to high school, she started running with some pretty rough kids and was probably smoking some dope. As a result, she was constantly truant and failed school. One night she showed up on my doorstep. She wanted to live with me instead of with her mother. I agreed, but only on one condition— that she attend at least one Alateen [for children of alcoholics] meeting a week. She went and loved it, and the fellowship turned her life around. She dropped the friends and the pot, and went back and finished school just like a normal kid.

173

Arthur's older son had an even rougher time. He, too, moved in with Arthur, but his drug use continued. Eventually Arthur had to go the old "tough love" route and kicked him out—probably the hardest thing a parent can do, especially when they know what can happen to a kid out there on the street and how the odds weigh against getting sober. But again, Arthur was persistent. Painful as it was, he knew what had to be done and he did it. For the next few years, Arthur's son continued to drink and use. But Arthur held his ground, despite the temptation to cave in and let the boy return home. Finally, a year and a half ago, Arthur's son got sober.

Arthur's younger son, on the other hand, "is so disgustingly normal I hardly know how to communicate with him. Sometimes I can't believe he's related to me. It must be a recessive gene or something."

After a few years of sobriety, Arthur married again. And like our ten-year man Barry, he chose an AA fellow traveler, which presented some blessings *and* some complications. There are definite pros and cons to AA marriages. If both partners stay sober, the relationship can be wonderful; but if one partner relapses, the sobriety of the other is threatened. The home itself becomes the kind of "slippery place" an alcoholic is not supposed to be in. Some AA couples, in fact, make deals with each other. If one of them slips, he or she will move out of the house until sobriety is regained so as not to endanger the other. In the meantime, the sober partner is supposed to handle the stress and the upset in the relationship by stepping up his or her own program by going to more meetings, keeping in close communication with his or her sponsor, and working with others. It's preventive medicine.

As it happened, Arthur's new wife slipped frequently on pills. At first she took the pills secretly, and, because pills don't smell, for a while she got away with it. But soon her increasingly bizarre behavior and mood swings made her slip obvious. She went into treatment, but slipped again. Without her sobriety, the relationship fell apart. The pair separated, then divorced. Some time later, Arthur's wife went to a long-term recovery house for women and did get sober again, but by then the marriage was beyond repair.

It was a staggering blow to Arthur. But one more time, just as he'd done when his kids were in trouble, he didn't choose the easy way out of his pain—drinking. He stayed sober, and he hurt.

The trouble is, Arthur *did nothing* about his hurt. He reverted to his long-entrenched pattern of "stuffing" his feelings, of being a "real man" by keeping a stiff upper lip. As a result, he became increasingly depressed.

> During the last few years, I've been digging back into my childhood and uncovering how I actually *felt* about growing up in an alcoholic home, feelings that I never let myself experience at the time. And I've learned that just because you stuff a feeling, it doesn't mean it goes away. It's just hiding from you. What it did to me was it gave me depression, a depression that was the culmination of a whole lifetime of unfelt feelings about things I wasn't allowed to discuss or react to—from my infant brother's death to my father's drinking to my divorces to my parents' deaths to recent career and financial problems, and even to the fact that in the last year my apartment was broken into and robbed three times. *None* of these things did I ever really let myself react to. I just shrugged and stuffed, shrugged and stuffed. And it all added up to one big depression.

As a therapeutic exercise, Arthur wrote a letter to himself as a little boy named "Artie." "All kinds of stuff that I had pocketed away in the dark began to emerge. And the more I wrote down in my letter to Artie, the more my depression lifted. It was quite remarkable."

Arthur says that what he now has to do to prevent the depression from recurring is consciously remind himself to *feel* his feelings and *react* to things, instead of retreating behind his old affable shrug. This includes saying "Ouch" when he's hurt, and "No" when something doesn't sit right.

Sylvia: Do you think that everybody has to go through this kind of process in order to stay sober?

Arthur: I suspect that this healing process is inevitable, unpreventable, and unavoidable. Whether you want to or not, you have to go through it; otherwise, you'll drink or go insane. In most cases, it just happens automatically. That pain pushes up from within, and suddenly you feel you're on an icy road without chains. And when the front end goes, the back end goes, and you know you have no choice but to take some kind of action fast. I suspect that even if I hadn't gone into therapy, even if I hadn't intentionally worked on healing my depression, it still would have happened. My recovery might have taken longer, but it would have happened eventually. I just didn't want to wait.

Of course, the one thing that can always prevent this natural healing process from taking place is booze. And that's the route many men—even after fifteen years of sobriety—choose to take. Arthur did not.

Another important issue for Arthur is his creative talent as a writer. He sees creativity not only as his livelihood but also as his source of strength and aliveness. It's one of the things that makes life worthwhile.

Throughout his career and well into sobriety, Arthur felt at the mercy of what he calls his "temperamental" creative muse. He lived in dread of the "creative block." But as the result of an artistic deadlock in sobriety, Arthur finally was able to do something about it.

I'd been hired to do the PR on a movie being filmed in Mexico. I was there for three weeks, and it went beautifully. I got great stuff. I had funny and moving stuff. Everything a PR man could possibly want to put into a press kit. When I got back to L.A., I set up all my work on the dining room table. I had my telephone here, and my paper there. I had all my notes and taped interviews. I put paper in my typewriter—and nothing happened! I found myself looking at the damn phone, trying to will it to ring. Then I'd make nonsense chat'-em-up calls to people. I'd diddle around with some of the lesser writing, but I just couldn't get the important work rolling. Well, one day the phone rang and it was a friend offering me a job at Columbia Pictures on a pilot. He also told me that if they sold the pilot, they'd obviously need to increase their staff, so I'd be auditioning as well. Well, I couldn't finish the movie PR job fast enough! Zoooooom! Done! *That's* when my moment of clarity came, when I realized that my own creative block stems from a fear that at the end of the project *there will be nothing.* End of work, *out* of work! As soon as there was work at the other end, the block "disappeared."

For Arthur, there has been great comfort in learning that his creative muse is neither tyrannical nor fragile.

Ironically, I've discovered that the creative muse is present in me more today than ever before. She's more quick to kick in, and she stays with me a lot longer. And she's much tougher than I ever imagined. Even if I tried, I couldn't drive her out. That's nice to know. Today I'm not afraid of writing because I know I won't have any real trouble with creative blocks, as long as I just hang in there and don't give up. I've even learned a few little tricks if I'm stuck, like I'll start on the third paragraph or the second page, and get through that somehow rather than try to hit the introduction head-on. Eventually I know I'll get around to it. As a result, I haven't been rendered incapable of performing my work in a long, long time.

Our hero faced his dragon and slew him.

Since his second divorce, Arthur has been cautious to the point of avoidance in the relationship area. But that doesn't keep women from approaching him. Yet Arthur, like so many men who are preoccupied with work and other things, is oblivious. He doesn't know that for women in certain age groups, men are scarce, which means that Arthur–despite being a little overweight, balding, and fifty-two—is definitely a "catch."

Sylvia: Do you think you are hit on a lot by women in AA?

Arthur: Hit on? I don't think so. I just don't know what a *hit* is. Maybe it happens, but I don't recognize it as a hit.

How true! Maybe in Arthur's case part of his obliviousness is self-protective. He knows he needs to do more healing in this area first.

> Right now I'm afraid that if I got involved with a woman it wouldn't work out. I do have a fear of commitment, which sort of condemns a relationship before it begins. At least now that I've worked my way through my depression my attitude about women is better. I'm much better raw material for a woman today than I was a few years ago. But I'm still a work junkie. I'll go to any far-flung movie location—even join the circus if I have to—just to be able to track down a good story. That kind of precludes my having a relationship, doesn't it?

But Arthur obviously isn't satisfied to leave it at that, or "leave well enough alone," as some might say. Previously, he used therapy to uncover the cause of his depression. Now he's using therapy to get some enlightenment about his relationship attitudes, even though he finds the process uncomfortable.

Only time will tell the outcome. Will Arthur join the circus and stay a work junkie for life? What if some assertive AA cutie calls him up one night and says, "Why don't you come over." Will he go?

This chapter in Arthur's life obviously isn't finished yet. But as they say in AA, the more he persists, the more will be revealed.

12

BALANCING ACT:
Roger and Ken, Sober Twenty Years

I was sitting on a beach in San Blas, Mexico, when suddenly I was transported into an ecstatic state of consciousness, drenched with peace, love, and bliss. I felt as though I were in love, in love with God. It left me grinning, with tears of joy streaming down my face. I knew that I'd been profoundly changed and that for the rest of my life I was going to be on some kind of spiritual path.
—Roger

I just wasn't interested in programming computers anymore. All I was interested in was sex.
—Ken

Overshooting the Mark

As we've observed in the last few chapters, men may start out their sobriety journey looking alike, but they end up looking very different and taking their own unique paths. As a group, longtime sober men are an extraordinarily diverse bunch, probably even more individualized than a group of so-called "normal" men who have never been exposed to the AA greenhouse, who have never really been encouraged to "find their own voice."

But can this recovering alcoholic "free spirit" go too far? Can he overshoot the mark? The answer is yes. Once an addict, always an addict. It's as easy for him to get addicted to a way of life as it was for him to get addicted to alcohol and drugs. It's so common, AA members joke about it: "If it's worth doing, it's worth *over*doing."

That's why one of the tasks for those with ongoing sobriety is to find, and then maintain, a balance. One's AA life, family life, work life, and spiritual life *all* need time and attention. This goes for the "normies," too, not just for the recovering alcoholics. There are religions and philosophies that stress balance as a goal, and so does AA. AA knows that its members are likely to overdo even a good thing and cautions them against it.

Maintaining this balance in life is tricky. Recovering alcoholics seem to have a knack for leaping from one obsession to another—from obsessive chemical abuse to obsessive sex to obsessive work to obsessive spiritual practices, even to obsessive AA participation, which is fine in early sobriety but not later on. A man can become so intent on going to AA meetings and on participating in AA activities that he ends up shortchanging his family, his work, even his own nature.

Most men make their AA journey in a sailboat, not a steamer. They don't go forward in a straight line. Instead, they spend their lives tacking from starboard to port, port to starboard. Whenever they find themselves off course, which could lead to relapse, they tack again to correct it. Their destination, strange as it sounds, is to *die* sober.

The Spiritual Path Versus the "Householder" Path

In this chapter, we'll be meeting two twenty-year men instead of just one. There's a reason for this. By comparing the two of them, it will be easier to see just how different AA paths can be. The two men started out looking very similar—one an aerospace engineer, the other a computer programmer. Once they got sober, they branched out onto totally different paths. One took the high road, or spiritual path; the other took the low road, the one Eastern philosophies call the "householder" path. (I like to think of them as "the Buddhist and the Bartender.") Both overshot the mark and had to "tack" to get themselves back on course—back in balance.

The lives of these two men—and the process they've both been involved in for twenty years—clearly shows that AA is no cookie mold. AA doesn't invent the men; the men invent themselves.

Are the two paths mutually exclusive? They don't have to be. They only become mutually exclusive when a man becomes so obsessive with one path that he neglects the other. In most cases, the recovering alcoholic will take on the two paths sequentially rather than simultaneously. He'll start off his sobriety by focusing on the "householder" concerns of work, love, sex, and money, and then later on turn his attention toward spiritual matters. Occasionally (as we'll see in this chapter), a man will do it in the reverse order—that is, he'll head down the spiritual road first and leave the householder challenges until later. Some see this as eating dessert before dinner.

Now, let's meet Roger and Ken who were introduced to each other at an AA meeting in Los Angeles. Roger had been sober only a few months; Ken was new. They immediately hit it off, and Roger became Ken's sponsor as well as his friend. AA advises newcomers to pick sponsors with at least one or two years of sobriety, but in this case the match worked well. From that day to the present, Roger has remained Ken's sponsor and his friend. Their relationship has survived both differences and distances. Roger has spent long periods of time in India on his spiritual quest; Ken moved to Seattle to accept a job promotion.

ROGER

What I know is that a spiritual experience—no matter how dramatic, all-consuming, or profound—still doesn't mean you're home free.

Roger, fifty-three, was born in Denver, the only child of a forty-one-year-old mother ("I'm sure I was unintended") who was plagued with health problems and a father who constantly threatened—and eventually committed—suicide. Roger is tall, angular, and somewhat awkward in his movements. He has uneven features, a wispy beard, and a sweet smile that lights up his face. Like his mother, he has health problems, including asthma and congenital scoliosis, a severe curvature of the spine.

> My parents weren't alcoholics, but the family was certainly dysfunctional, and I have some of the same characteristics as ACAs (Adult Children of Alcholics), such as not knowing what normal is, not relating to people, and wanting to rescue them. My father's suicide threats were his way of throwing temper tantrums. He'd storm out the back door saying, "You'll be sorry when they find me floating in the lake tomorrow."

Roger, like many alcoholics, describes himself as a loner.

> I always felt as though I came from another planet. I still don't feel comfortable with Earth people. It's lucky that I was an only child. I don't think I'd have wanted another kid around. I had a passion for electronics and spent all my time in the basement making radios. I think I was *born* an alcoholic because I can't remember a time when I *didn't* have that alcoholic sense of alienation and anxiety. Every morning I'd wake up in a panic attack. I needed a drink by the time I was three!

The minute Roger discovered alcohol, he used it. "It was the magic elixir that fixed everything." It helped him socialize enough to find himself a wife. After college, he married and got a job in aerospace. "My drinking progressed from drinking every weekend to *drunk* every weekend. I became not only an alcoholic, but also a workaholic. I'd work compulsively all week, and I'd drink compulsively all weekend."

After three years in aerospace, Roger decided along with his wife to enroll in graduate school at Berkeley, California (he for his Ph.D., she for her master's degree). During this period, Roger's mother died. Two days later, his father finally made good on his promise to kill himself. "He had cried wolf so often that when he finally did it, I was astounded." On top of all this, Roger's marriage was falling apart. "I turned out to be infertile. A good lover, but infertile. As soon as I got that diagnosis, my wife, who had been determined *not* to get pregnant, suddenly became obsessed with having a baby. In part, that's what caused the end of the marriage." Another part, of course, was his drinking.

Once out of graduate school, Roger got a job as an assistant professor in the engineering department of a Los Angeles area university. He began drinking during the week as well as on weekends. "As soon as I started that, the downward spiral began. It culminated in my setting my apartment on fire when I was in a blackout." Fortunately, someone on the street spotted the smoke and Roger was rescued.

This incident scared him. He decided to try AA, and that's when the process of coming in and out of AA's revolving door began. He'd get sober, then blow it, then get sober again, then blow it again. "Once I had three whole months of sobriety, but then I went to Europe for a technical conference, and as soon as I was away from my meetings I drank."

One of Roger's problems staying sober seemed to be his powerful intellect. He was "too smart for his own good."

I was an uptight engineer. My rational, linear, right-brain mind nearly killed me. I figured if information couldn't be analyzed and disputed, then I didn't want to know anything about it. I was raised to believe that good management of one's thoughts was a virtue. The man who manages his mind best and thinks the most positive thoughts wins. Well, it's stressful to try to control your every thought. It gave me free-floating anxiety and panic attacks. I thought that if I let my mind roam free, I'd go crazy and have to be apprehended by the authorities.

Roger had an "aha! insight," a moment of clarity, while he was reading the AA "Big Book."

I came across a sentence that said, in effect, that good mind management will *not* bring happiness, and that the notion that it *will* is an old idea that we should let go of. I realized that the AA program was based on a radically different philosophy than I'd been living by, and that my formula was all wrong. Suddenly, in a flash, in a microsecond, I had a thought that astounded me: "It's safe to let go. You gain control by letting go." That was it. It wasn't like a thought that came from my own head, but a thought that was fed into my head from someplace else. It made me realize that the thing for me to do henceforth was to deliver my mind and my life to God, and let Him take over. I was to become his cosmic puppet.

That was the first experience that put Roger on the spiritual path. The second was his "San Blas" experience (quoted at the beginning of this chapter) while sitting on a beach in Mexico. When it happened, an AA friend, who was sitting on the beach with him, looked at him and froze in fear: "Oh, my God! Somebody's given you grass!" But it wasn't grass. Roger was feeling high on God. It was a turning point in his sobriety, *the* event that changed the direction of his life.

Having such a grand spiritual experience so early in sobriety, one that catapulted him on the spiritual path through no choice of his own, made Roger's life no easier. In fact, it gave him problems aplenty, especially in the area of work.

> After my San Blas experience, I had a difficult time working. I just wasn't interested in anything except my spiritual life. My relationship with God, not with people, was what was important to me, and I felt that it was mandatory for me to maintain my spiritual condition with yoga and meditation, as well as with AA. My job just took me away from that. I thought, "Well, if I lose my job, I lose my job. So what?"

Roger's job productivity screeched to a halt.

> Alcohol was always a stimulant for me, not a depressant. It helped me function intellectually and enabled me to be creative. During the three years I'd been drinking on the job, I'd had a meteoric rise, and I'd built up enough revenue in terms of publications to get tenure. What they failed to notice was the fact that in the last year, since I'd gotten sober, I hadn't written anything new, hadn't done any research, hadn't supervised any students. I'd just been coasting along on my previous workaholism. I was like those alcoholic writers who don't write worth a damn once they sobered up. I never did get promoted to a full professor because of it. I'm an associate professor to this day.

His intense focus on spiritual matters also interfered with Roger's love life. He hadn't learned how to communicate very well with women, or even how to judge who'd be a good mate. "I believed that if I was ever going to relate to a woman, she'd have to understand my San Blas experience. I was looking for a saint, and I was having trouble finding one."

Finally Roger met *V.* at an AA New Year's Eve party. And even though she might not have looked much like a saint to anybody else, to Roger she did:

> *V.* was from North Carolina where she'd been arrested for selling LSD and was then sent to Synanon in Santa Monica, California.

But she split and got a job working for a porno film outfit in West Hollywood—not as a participant, but as a secretary. She was brand new in AA. In fact, she was still detoxing from LSD the night I met her. She had enough left in her system to make her pretty trippy, which made it easy for her to relate to me spiritually. We were instantly attracted like magnets. I was going to be able to convince her to stay sober, and *she* was going to understand. And that's exactly what happened. I sat *V.* down and explained AA to her—from a *spiritual* perspective—and she said, "Wow, far out!" She actually *got* it! She never drank or used again. And then I thought, "Oh, boy, now I've got what I wanted, somebody sober who can relate to my San Blas experience." So we got married.

But after that, the relationship went downhill. "The original magic faded. To our dismay, we just lost it. There was no excitement in the relationship, no fire. We ended up living like brother and sister. Even our spiritual conversations fell apart. I guess it was the Tower of Babel phenomenon. The words meant different things to each of us." Although they tried all kinds of things to repair the marriage—getting deeper into spiritual practices, yoga, even open marriage—nothing worked.

The union ended in divorce. *V.*, who had gone to India, remained there. "She still shows up back here about once a year to get her visa reinstated, but there's still no sexual affinity. We still can't talk. It's over."

By putting the cart before the horse and focusing with such intensity on his spiritual life before he'd had a chance to work on his "householder" concerns, Roger threw himself off balance. He's aware of this. At the same time, he feels he had no choice. He believes that his San Blas experience is what saved his life, and he wouldn't have traded it for anything. "I think in my case, I was so crazy when I first got sober that if I hadn't had a whopping spiritual experience right off, I'd never have made it."

One of Roger's tasks in sobriety—especially since his failed marriage—has been to attempt a better balance in life by getting in touch with his own feelings, which had always been a mystery to him. (He too, like many of our other interviewee-alcoholics, was a master stuffer.)

Sylvia: Have you had trouble getting in touch with your feelings since you've gotten sober?

Roger: Absolutely! It's taken me a long time. For years and years I read books about being in touch with one's feelings, but the books were opaque to me. I'd say to myself, "I know this stuff is important, but what the hell are they talking about?" But after my San Blas experience, especially after all the yoga and Reichian bodywork, I started to come out of my shell a bit and get in touch with all kinds of feelings I'd previously denied myself. Those books that were once opaque to me were now becoming transparent. I'd say, "Of course! How come I didn't see that before?"

Today, even though Roger hasn't remarried ("In that area, at least, I'm still a loner"), he's become much more of a people person. He has friends like Ken (our other twenty-year man), with whom he's remained close. "One of the ways I calibrate how I've changed is by how others see me. These days people say things to me like, 'You're very open, Roger. There's a feeling of kindness and love coming from you.' Now that's not at all how they used to see me, so I know something's different!"

Although Roger may not have achieved an ideal state of balance, he has vastly improved, particularly in the work area, where outside circumstances practically forced him to take action.

What happened involved the merging of our little department into the larger electrical engineering department, and they decided it was their mission to become one of the outstanding departments in their field. They were on a real productivity kick. It became obvious to me that unless I got busy and produced, I was going to end up doing all the schlock jobs. They couldn't fire me, but they could make my life very unpleasant. So to avoid that fate, for self-protection, I got busy.

Though Roger remains clear that obtaining—and maintaining—a more balanced life is necessary, at times he wishes he could pursue the spiritual life full-time. He also wishes others would join him and admits to getting frustrated when they don't share his enthusiasm for the spiritual path.

> I feel that I've discovered the key to alcoholism recovery, which is the spiritual awakening and the spiritual path, but I can't seem to interest anybody else in it! I tell newcomers about my San Blas experience, and they say, "Oh, that's nice." They just don't relate to what I'm saying. I sponsor a physician who's so totally left-brain [the rational side] that he can't even have a conversation with his wife without rehearsing it. He's just like I was, and I wish I could re-create for him what I experienced myself, but I can't. I encouraged another man I sponsor, who was having trouble getting in touch with his feelings, to go into therapy. He did, but he got nowhere. After a year, he quit. I encouraged another guy to take yoga because I'd had such fantastic results with it. He went to a yoga class regularly for four months and then dropped out. I asked him why? He said, "Because it makes my knee hurt"! I just can't seem to make my methods catch fire for others.

What Roger has discovered—and this is something every recovering alcoholic discovers sometime during this "service" to others—is that what's good for the goose isn't always good for the gander. What "works" for one man won't work for another. There's an infinite variety of ways to get sober and many paths to take afterward. Fortunately, Roger now recognizes this, which means he's also become more "in balance" as a sponsor.

What I've learned is that when I sponsor newcomers who don't seem attracted to the spiritual path, I have to sponsor them in a traditional way. If I do that, they're happy. They end up having what I consider a "conventional" recovery, but if that's what they want then I guess that's what counts. Still, at times I find it frustrating. I mean, here I am, convinced that these newcomers *need* what I have to teach them, and they're not interested. I guess what's really important, though, is that I know *I'm* interested.

KEN

I believe that every AA has two tasks in front of him. One has to do with the opposite sex, and all its various manifestations, and the other has to do with work and all the things that go along with that, like creativity and self-expression. I also know that the ultimate solutions to problems in these two areas of love and work lie in the spiritual realm.

Ken, fifty-one, was born in Massachusetts, the son of two alcoholics. His father died in a skid row gutter (literally) at age thirty-six. His mother drank daily, "to the exclusion of everything else, including me." She died of cancer in her early fifties. "But to say her cause of death was cancer is like saying that the cause of a suicide is a pistol. My mother's cancer arose out of her lifestyle, which was misery and alcoholism." Ken has two brothers and a sister.

Ken is 6 feet tall, balding, with sharp features and a beard, which is mostly white. He has a fine speaking voice and is one of those well-built men who wears clothes exceptionally well. Twice-divorced, he has a daughter by each marriage: one is twenty-six, the other nine. When Ken was drinking, he worked as a computer programmer. When he got sober, he threw all that to the winds and became a bartender. A few years ago he moved to Seattle to become assistant manager of a country club.

Alcohol was always Ken's drug of choice, and he contends that he was probably a drunk by the age of fifteen. "I loved the

THE ALCOHOLIC MAN

'drama' of drinking alcohol—the crying jags, and the 'maudlins.' In alcohol I found freedom and omnipotence, so as the years went by, I invested less time in trying to cope with the world and more time in ingesting alcohol." Of course, this caused problems for him. "I made resolutions. Heartfelt resolutions. But since I suffered from high-voltage anxiety, sooner or later I'd get the conviction, like an irresistible psychic force, that I had to have a drink."

Ken got arrested a lot: Drunk driving. Drunk walking. Common drunk. Breaking and entering in the night. He spent many nights in jail. And many evenings in AA. Between the ages of twenty and thirty-one, Ken was in and out of AA a dozen times. He became known as a "hopeless case"; it was his claim to fame.

> I went to psychologists, psychiatrists, social workers, priests, and ministers up and down the Boston-New York-Washington corridor, and from each I got the same diagnosis: hopeless case. Each time, I'd react by going out for a drink. Why not? After all, I was a hopeless case, so what the hell.

Although Ken felt pretty crazy on the inside, he looked fairly well put together. He was able to get married, father a child, and function in his job as a senior systems representative for an information systems company. But on one of his business trips, his image cracked open. "My pain got so bad that it finally obliterated every other concern I had. I realized that even if I lost my job, my marriage, and my money, I still had to find a way to stop drinking and *stay* stopped. I had to seek sobriety for its own sake."

A week later, on another business trip, Ken experienced his turning-point moment.

> I was at an AA meeting, and this old-timer took me aside and talked to me. He said, "You have to stop coming in and out of AA's revolving door, because the day will come when you'll be

caught out there and you won't be able to get back in. Do you understand?" I nodded dumbly. He went on: "Then do exactly as you're told to do. Get a sponsor. Work the Twelve Steps. And don't worry about anything except sobriety for at least five years. You're so self-destructive that it'll probably going to take you that long before your head clears enough for you to start learning how to *work* for things in life like other human beings have to do."

Ken had no fight left in him. He took it all in. "The idée fixe that I got out of that conversation was that my sobriety had to be unconditional, that I had to be obsessed with sobriety, that I couldn't do it alone. I haven't had another drink since."

A few months later his company transferred Ken to Los Angeles. It was *not* a promotion. His job was in jeopardy and so was his marriage. "I had a job and a wife and a child, and I felt no more equipped to handle those things than the man in the moon." His mother's death a few months after his transfer compounded his stress. By the time Ken had been sober a year, his marriage ended. "My wife kept telling me, 'I hate your f— face!' so I finally took the hint and left."

Initially, he didn't cope very well.

I shut off my emotions. There I was, an articulate, guilt-ridden, broken little boy in a grown-up body. My sobriety now seemed to be tenuously held together like some kind of Rube Goldberg device. Without alcohol, I hadn't a clue about how to live, so I shut off my emotions. Eventually I just went snap.

The snap, which Ken describes as a "brief psychotic break," landed him in a psychiatric hospital. "What I learned as the result of that unpleasant experience was that I couldn't survive if I continued to bury my feelings.

"So as soon as I was patched up enough to leave, I dragged my ass to lots of AA meetings, and, simply, whenever I felt sad, I cried."

191

It was at one of these meetings that Ken was introduced to Roger.

This time, Ken took off in AA like a rocket. No more revolving door. And though he found a path for himself, it definitely wasn't the one his new sponsor, Roger, had selected. Ken's was the path of sex.

> In my marriage, there had been very little physical intimacy. I was as close to a thirty-two-year-old virgin as you could get. Ahead of me lay the whole world of women and physical love. So in the next six or seven years, I think I had at least twenty-five intense love affairs with AA women. It was the most wonderful, painful, fruitful, terrible, rewarding time of my life. These women were gentle and nurturing and understanding, and I'm grateful for these gifts. I really never had a bad experience with any of them, even though a couple of them broke my heart. I survived. All in all, it was incredible to experience myself as a man at last, to be given compliments, to be told that I had a good body, that I wore clothes well, that I had good taste, that I was articulate. It made me realize that I'd been living in a desert all my life and didn't even know it.

Ken, like Roger, went a bit overboard frolicking down his newfound path, and his work and other responsibilities began to be affected.

> I quit my job. All I wanted to do was go to AA meetings and play with girls! Clearly, I was going through some developmental stages more appropriate to a teenager. At one point, I met a woman named *B.*, and we decided to take off on a three-month cross-country camping trip together. We packed up her little trailer with a Coleman stove, camera equipment, and stacks of books and headed north to Vancouver, then east all across Canada, then back through the States. It was a wonderful experience.

But when Ken returned, there was music to be faced: He found himself in court for nonpayment of child support.

I'd been out of work all those months, I'd just gotten a minimum-wage job, and I'd declared bankruptcy. I was living in a $72-a-month furnished room in a building in Venice [California] that was painted black. I knew I'd been irresponsible, but I'll tell you, it was all worth it! The scales had fallen from my eyes. I was alive. I remember I'd get these leaps inside, these epiphanies that made me feel connected to other people and to the world around me.

Over the next few years, Ken began to toe the line and meet his obligations as a father, which ultimately included having his daughter, come and live with him.

Although his lusty adventures still continued to take up most of his spare time, a sad event finally forced him into a better balance: his ex-wife committed suicide with pills. The suicide forced him to settle down considerably and begin focusing on his responsibilities both to his daughter and to his work.

I began to increasingly analyze my relationships with men, not in the sense of homosexuality, but in terms of how I related to them, how they, and authority in general, intimidated me. This, of course, tied in directly to work. I'd been working as a bartender in a beach club all those years for a boss, the club manager, who didn't really think much of me. I had to look at what I was doing, or *not* doing, which had brought on all his animosity toward me. I discovered some of my character defects—my lack of punctuality, my childishness, my resistance to authority. As a result, in a three-year period I was able to turn things around to the point where my boss ended up asking me to go with him when he moved to Seattle to manage another club. I went.

This time it *was* a promotion. Ken was made assistant manager. "I know today that I do my job well, even though it has problems attached to it that sometimes frustrate the hell out of me. But I no longer walk around wondering, 'Am I up to this?' I just *do* it."

Soon after Ken moved to Seattle, he married again—this time to a woman in AA—and had another daughter. This marriage, too, ended in divorce. Ken shares custody of the child with his ex-wife.

Today I consider myself a good, responsible parent, and I think my girls reflect it. My twenty-six-year-old daughter isn't self-destructive the way her mother and I were at her age. And just this afternoon I took my nine-year-old out in a boat on Puget Sound. We sat there together in the drizzle, under a raincoat, reading *The Hobbit*, and it was wonderful. Once upon a time I could never have done that without a drink.

Ken has a new lady in his life.

I've been living with a woman for about two years, and we fight and play and travel together. We just got back from London. And even though I still have a wandering eye, I don't act on it. I've made a commitment to this woman.

Though Ken's primary concerns in sobriety have remained pretty earthbound, he has recognized the need to balance it all out.

I had to let go of the idea that success in the areas of love and work would automatically bring me happiness. So while the first phase of my sobriety had a tremendous emphasis on women and the second phase on work, my recent concerns have involved issues of spiritual growth. In looking around, I've had the realization that we human beings are using only a small fraction of our capabilities. We barely touch our spiritual natures. Here we are, all five billion of us living on this planet, and most of us are on about the same emotional level as I was back when I was drinking. Species-wise, we need the kind of miracle that took place with me personally in Alcoholics Anonymous.

I've had mighty adventures in sobriety. I can enjoy a lot of things in my life now—baseball, the company of other people, time with my children. And I know that the most important thing for me is the maintenance of my sobriety, one day at a time, by maintaining a spiritual connection to God as I understand him.

It's a delicate balance. But I always think of what a man I met in my newcomer days said to me—that being in AA is like having two guys in front of you, forever unrolling a red carpet. But he also warned that there are another two guys right behind you, rolling that same carpet up. So if you don't look sharp, maintain your balance, and keep on walking, you might get rolled right up with it!

13

OLD IDEAS:
Walter and Dean,
Sober Twenty-two Years

When they say in AA that you have to give up your old ideas or the results will be nil, it's true. I had to give up my old ideas about everything.

—Walter

With plenty of help, I've been able to let go of a lot of my old ideas, and along the way I've been able to be of service to other people in AA by helping them give up some of their old ideas. And so it goes, one drunk helping another, so that each is transformed.

—Dean

Bad Versus Good "Old Ideas"

In Alcoholics Anonymous, when members talk about the importance of getting rid of "old ideas," they are referring specifically to the "bad" ones—those negative notions, attitudes, opinions, assumptions, or beliefs—be they conscious or unconscious—that end up interfering with a man's progress, that have a destructive effect on his daily life. Ultimately, old ideas are a threat to sobriety, which is the main reason they need to be given up. Discovering just what these old ideas are, and working to get rid of them, takes time. Sometimes years. "Good" old ideas, such as an admirable work ethic, aren't likely to give a man much trouble.

Onion Peeling

In this chapter we'll be meeting two more men, Walter and Dean, both of whom are twenty-two years sober. Although it would have been tidier to skip from twenty to twenty-five years of sobriety, Walter's and Dean's stories are just too good to pass up, especially because of how they relate to the theme of old ideas. Their stories also illustrate the fact that the longer a man has been sober, the farther back into his childhood and the deeper into his psyche he's able to go in order to ferret out the sources of his old ideas.

It's onion peeling. And the changes that can be the result of this process are often profound, even though from the outside they may not look all that dramatic. For example, Walter found himself faced with rediscovering and then reevaluating his old ideas (which he hadn't even realized were there) about being black. And Dean had to rediscover and reevaluate his old ideas about being an identical twin. Furthermore, both men had to carefully look at their old ideas about work, women, and fidelity. In the process, they changed their lives.

From the beginning, AA stresses that the sobriety journey is a never-ending process where progress not perfection, is the goal. It is assumed that each man will handle whatever obstacles he needs to handle in his own good time, including the obstacle of his old ideas.

WALTER

What I've learned in AA is that we get what we need if we're just patient.

Walter, sixty-five, is a trim black man of medium height, with a moustache and rimless glasses. He was born in New Jersey, the younger of two brothers. "Our parents were devoted, church-going people. Can't blame my alcoholism on them. They were wonderful and doted all over me. I always had their attention and consent." He had his first drink when he was thirteen.

Walter was trained as a singer, and while he was out there drinking he spent seventeen years as a member of a well-known singing group. After sobriety, he put in a full career with the post office. Since his retirement three years ago at sixty-two, Walter has returned to singing and acting. He recently completed a full-length movie and has been doing TV commercials. In addition, he's started his own business, a janitorial service. Married twice, he has two children by each marriage. His second wife A., to whom he has been married for twenty-seven years, is Chinese. Their two daughters are eighteen and twenty-six.

Walter first saw California from the window of a troop train during World War II. "It was in the dead of winter, and when I saw oranges hanging from trees I said, 'This is the place for me!'" What made him return to California years later was show business. "I thought show business was going to give me love, peace, money, and happiness. I was wrong."

Throughout Walter's life, the issue of being black has been a big one, more so than he ever realized until he got into AA and began investigating his old ideas on the subject.

I had a horrible image of blacks. I fought hard not to be like other blacks. I worried about my diction. I avoided talking flat, and I wouldn't say words like *dis*, *dem*, and *doze* because that's how blacks are supposed to talk. God, I never wanted to be Little Black Sambo. And when it came to women, having married a black woman the first time, I knew I could never marry one again because I was certain I'd never live up to her standards of what a real man should be. In my heart I was afraid I *wasn't* one. On the other hand, I knew I could never marry a white woman. I'd been out with white women and I remember walking down Hollywood Boulevard with one of them and somebody called her a nigger-lover. I realized right then and there she wasn't worth dying over!

So the second time out, I married an Oriental woman. At least that made me different. *A.* was this young [nineteen years his junior], innocent, old-culture Chinese girl. She used to feed me dinner in bed and sit on the floor and watch while I ate. She gave me a bell and told me to ring it whenever I wanted her. When our daughter was born, *A.* got me a second little bell so I could ring for her, too. And I thought *I* was doing her a favor by marrying her!

Prior to marrying *A.*, Walter had decided to quit drinking on his own, without AA, which he'd tried but hadn't liked.

I knew if I continued the way I was going, my singing career would be over. After all, I'd already had twenty arrests, been in a couple of nuthouses, messed up lots of career opportunities, and ruined my first marriage. So for twelve miserable years, I didn't drink, I didn't smoke, I wasn't profane. I was just sickenly wonderful!

Walter, however, wasn't wonderful enough to be loyal to his wife. He'd tell *A.* he wanted to take her out on the road with him, but he knew he didn't mean it. "I *played* when I was out on the road. Taking *A.* with me would have been like taking a sandwich to a banquet!" Having their first daughter conveniently kept his wife at home.

At the end of those twelve years of bite-the-bullet sobriety, Walter started drinking again. Without the help of an ongoing support group like AA, relapse was almost inevitable. Within no time, Walter was up to a fifth-and-a-half of scotch a day and was adding "bennies" [stimulants] to perform on stage. "My wife had absolutely no understanding of alcoholism. She said to me, 'Why don't you just stay home and rest for a couple of weeks? You'll be all right.' Like it was the flu!" And the more Walter drank, the more he played around. "I'd let *A.* find the letters and the pictures from the girls on the road, just to divert her attention away from the drinking. That's how desperate I was to protect my right to drink!"

Like so many practicing alcoholics, Walter expended a great deal of energy trying to maintain the *image* of a man in complete control of his life. He had many old ideas about what a "real man" is.

> Then I'd get drunk and blow my image to bits. People started telling me, 'Man, you need to get your shit together.' They wouldn't know that's what I'd been trying to do, get it together. I'd get it together—and go to jail. I'd get it together—and go to the nut ward.
>
> My life was a mess—*that* was the reality. I owed $40,000 to the mob, and I was frightened and paranoid because they'd promised to bury me. [After he got sober, Walter paid all the money back.] On stage, I performed with a .25 in my shirt, and I had a .44 under the seat of my car. Once a guy I worked with who had a resentment against me came right up on the stage in the club where I was singing and stabbed me in the back. Nobody even noticed! And I had such a need to be a macho man that I just kept right on singing while the blood was running out of me. Then, nonchalantly, I walked off the stage and ordered a drink. Only after that did I go up to somebody and say, "I think we'd better get me to a hospital and check out the damages."
>
> Meanwhile, when it was time for the guy who'd stabbed me to go out on stage, he took the mike and started singing a blues song, using lyrics to confess the crime as he went along: "I just stabbed a man in the back, and he's got blood running down all over the place. . . ." Nobody knew what the hell he was talking about.

The old ideas about what it takes to be a real man lingered long into Walter's sobriety.

> I've had three heart attacks since I quit drinking. The last one happened in my doctor's office when I was about fourteen years sober. He said, "Walter, I'm calling an ambulance," and I said, "And leave my car in your parking lot where it'll cost me $20.00? No way!" So I drove home.

Sylvia: That's sort of like finishing the nightclub act with a knife sticking out of your back.

201

Walter: Same thing. Same old idea that says, "Be a man!" So I drove home, and my wife drove me to the hospital. I walked up to the desk and said to a nurse, "My doctor says I should report to ICU [Intensive Care Unit]." Well, she jumped up, grabbed a gurney, and flew me down to ICU. Only then did I concede to myself, "Walter, I think you may be sick. Even if *you* don't think you're sick, you'd better act like it so you can get out of here and go see *A.* again." So I "pretended" to be sick so they could take care of me. That was as much reality as I could let myself tolerate. I'm not real big on reality.

But in AA I've learned that I don't have to be a "real man," that it's not a requirement for sobriety. All I have to do is learn how to be who I am, Walter. I don't have to walk around with that macho image anymore, making all that mantalk, doing all that tough stuff. Popeye the Sailor said it succinctly: "I am what I am." There's some softness in me now, and little by little I'm letting it come out. My daughter looked so gorgeous on her eighteeth birthday that I just broke out in tears—but they were tears of joy. That's one of the soft things I never would have let anyone see before.

Walter had his moment of clarity about his alcoholism one night in a club in Portland, Oregon, where the owner said to him, "Walter, you're too drunk to get up on *my* stage."

"That's all he said, but that was the end. I suddenly realized that I must be a lot sicker than I ever imagined. That's the moment I decided to give AA another shot and do whatever was necessary to stay sober."

One of the things he felt he had to do was steer clear of show business for awhile. In order to make a living and get to his nightly AA meetings, he took on a day job that he considered beneath him.

It was moving furniture and sweeping out the office and the street in front of the office. It was handkerchief-head work, real "black" work, but I was willing to do it because sobriety had become paramount in my life. Nothing else mattered, not even my "image." To stay sober, I was willing to pay any price.

One of Walter's "good" old ideas was his work ethic, learned from his parents. That was something he didn't have to give up.

I've always been a person who loved to work. There's something nurturing about it. I really think people in sobriety *need* to work for what we get. As a kid, if I'd say, "Mom, can I have a penny?" she'd say, "Well, maybe if you go down to the store for somebody they'll give you a penny." Of course, I wanted her to *give* it to me, but before long the work ethic—no matter what the job—was in me and it's never left. If there's one thing I've learned, it's that I'm *not* what I do.

After a few years of sobriety, Walter was finally ready to tackle some of his old notions about being black.

The attitudes I had were buried so deep that it took me that long before I could even *begin* to look at any of it honestly. One of the things I dug up was the fact that I'd always refused to eat watermelon because it was such a symbol of being black. I didn't want anybody getting that picture of me sitting on a white fence eating red watermelon. I wouldn't even eat it after I got sober. Then on my fourth AA birthday, a friend of mine gave me a watermelon with four candles on it instead of a birthday cake. From then on, I started collecting little knickknacks that had to do with watermelons. They were like a barometer of where I was emotionally on the subject of being a black man, a gauge of how much it still bothered me. I had ceramic watermelons, china watermelons, glass watermelons, even pictures of watermelons! My collection grew over a number of years, until I went to Johannesburg [South Africa] a few years ago to make a movie. It was my first feature role in a full-length movie. I took one of the figures from my collection with me, a watermelon slice with a little black face on it. I had it sitting in my hotel room.

203

While I was there, I went to visit some people in that cesspool, Soweto. A group of us were sitting with a black writer who'd just written his autobiography. At one point during the conversation, this writer edged over to me and rubbed his arm against mine. Then he said, "All my life I've wanted to rub up against the arm of a black American." When I heard that, I cried like a baby, because he was saying, "You're black and you'd better be *proud* of it." At that moment, I knew that slice of watermelon no longer existed in my life. I came back to America with a feeling of dignity.

Walter's old-idea search spread out and uncovered some troublesome attitudes about women and marriage. Basically, like most other self-obsessed alcoholics, Walter believed that he was the center of the universe and thus it wasn't necessary for him to have to *give* anything in a relationship, that it should all fall in place without his having to do any work. And whenever he felt that too many demands were being made upon him, he split.

I had to start looking at how I'd abused my marriage commitment, and when I did, I felt I owed it to my wife to leave her. Plus now she was putting salt on the wound by not letting go of the past, by constantly harping on what I'd done to her, so I *wanted* to leave. When I went to my sponsor and told him my intentions, he said, "Aren't you tired of running?" And *that* I was. So he said, "Then go home and learn how to be a good husband. Practice loving your wife and doing nice things for her for fun and for free." He then explained what "for fun and for free" meant: that if I did something nice—like wash the dishes or make the bed—and she thanked me, then it wasn't for fun and for free anymore, so I'd have to do something else. That's how I started learning how to be loving. After awhile, my little daughter began pitching in and we'd clean house together and have a grand old time.

One day while my daughter and I were doing our housework together, it suddenly occurred to me that I didn't want to run away from home anymore. I was where I wanted to be. An hour later, my wife walked in and told me that she was pregnant again. That clinched it. The day our second daughter was born, I had seven AA friends there in the waiting room with me, giving me support. We had an AA meeting right there in the hospital.

I consider that child a real gift of Alcoholics Anonymous, as is the fact that my wife and I are still together.

Every recovering alcoholic man eventually has to deal with his old ideas about how to handle his feelings. Walter was no exception.

Walter: I was taught that if I got angry at somebody, I shouldn't show it. But I'd always end up walking around with that person in my gut all day, which gave *him* all the power. In AA I learned that the only way I can get my power back is to tell that person how I feel.

I started practicing on my wife. Many times when I was on my way to work, she'd make a put-down remark, and I'd say nothing and I'd go get in the car mumbling to myself. I'd start to drive off, and there she'd still be, sitting right there in my gut. I'd think to myself, "Walter, you know you can't just drive off like this. You have to go back into the house and tell her how you feel." So in I'd go and usually say, "Your comment a few minutes ago really hurt me." Then I could get back in the car and leave, and she— and those feelings—would no longer be eating away my insides. By learning how to do that, I've been able to walk around freer than I've ever been.

Sylvia: What about the spiritual part of the program? Did you have any trouble with the old ideas about God?

Walter: Yes. Coming from a Pentecostal background, I was heaped and steeped in religion. I'd been brought up to see God as a punishing power, someone to be deathly afraid of. He was watching all the time. I feared God so much that when I went into

205

my first bar and ordered my first drink, I felt He had the power to strike my arm off, suspended in mid-air with the glass in my hand. When I'd see people maimed or crippled, I was sure that's what had happened to them. As a child, I knew I'd been so bad that there would be no heaven for me, only hell.

But in AA I've learned that heaven is here on earth. In early sobriety, the first time the word *shit* flew out of my mouth at an AA meeting, no one sucked their teeth, no one! It was such a far cry from sitting in one of those Holy Ghost churches, hearing somebody say, "Boy, the Lord's going to get you for that!" And I said to myself, "Ah, here's a Higher Power that lets me say shit, that once let me run around, cheat, drink, lie, and yet, even after all that, still loved and accepted me enough to bring me to AA and change my life. Now that's a Higher Power I can understand!"

DEAN

I'm having more fun than anybody reasonably ought to expect to have.

Dean, fifty-two, was born in Denver. Since his father was in the service they moved frequently, and in his late teens Dean lived in North Africa. His father was an alcoholic who, like Walter's father, had a strong work ethic. "Even though he was often sick, he always showed up for work." Dean is an identical twin, younger than his brother by seven minutes. He also has a sister four years younger and a brother twelve years younger. Married four times (twice while drinking, twice in sobriety), he has three sons from his first two marriages who were brought up by their mothers and with whom he has good "but not terribly close" relationships.

Once Dean's drinking began, there was a steady decline.

After college, it was dental school and getting thrown out; then the Marine Corps and getting popped out of there, even though honorably; then it was a job selling encyclopedias and losing it; then it was living in a garage and finally landing in jail. In fact, the person who took me to my first AA meeting was a bail bondsman. That first experience showed me people who were staying sober, and since I'm a guy who thrives on example, it worked. If I can see somebody else doing it, I can do it.

Later on, Dean picked a sponsor in much the same way. "I knew I needed someone who'd be a good example, so I picked a real authority figure—someone I could salute, somebody I'd listen to." The relationship worked so well that it still exists today, twenty-two years later.

After Dean had been around AA for awhile, he began to discover that some of his most cherished beliefs were really old ideas that were interfering with his life, especially in the area of work.

My main "old idea" about work was a strong objection to working itself. I didn't think I should *have* to go to work, and it's difficult to get something done if you object to it. The difficulty, of course, always lies in the objection and not in the task. Remove the objection and the task is easy. I realized that in order to fight my objection, I'd have to firm-up my discipline, keep my agreements, and follow the rules—like in the Marines. Once you decide you're going to follow the rules, for whatever reasons, it's so much easier. Since I was in sales, I learned to set appointments early in the day so I'd be out there. And I didn't give myself meritorious days off just because I'd done a lot of business or sold something. I also addressed my old attitudes about employers. I learned to salute them, not simply tolerate them. I became a good employee and, understandably, they liked me. In my first couple of years of sobriety, I sold encyclopedias, then ballpoint pens, dictating equipment, little computers, and then carpets, and in the process I developed good discipline and made good money. I was even given an award for being one of the top ten salesmen in the country.

Once Dean had learned how to work, he was then able to turn his attention to the work itself.

My heart wasn't in selling any longer. Something was missing. Then I heard a guy in AA say from the podium that if you're working five days a week just to get to the two free ones at the end, something is wrong. I realized that was me. That's when I began to look for a game worth playing.

The search was on. Dean had no idea what game he was looking for, only that he wanted

something that had creativity and excitement to it; something that could make a contribution; and most of all, something with respectability. I'd hungered for respectability all my life. One night I was talking to an AA guy who's a lawyer. I was sniveling about how I couldn't find a game worth playing when he said to me, "How about law school?" Funny, even though my twin brother had become a lawyer, I'd never even thought of that. I'd always seen law school as a big risk, and that was another old idea I had: If you take a Big Risk you lose, and you get humiliated in the process. I wasn't anxious to embrace that kind of humiliation.

However, when Dean realized that this was, indeed, just another old idea, he became willing to give law school a try. He used AA's one-task-at-a-time, one-day-at-a-time approach.

My first step was to take the LSAT [Law School Admissions Test]. Law schools are very interested in that test because it seems to measure that little bubble on your brain that accounts for whether you think like a lawyer or not. It's correlated with mathematical ability, musical ability, language ability, and the ability to hold abstract ideas in your head. I seem to have that little bubble on my brain, so I did very well. That gave me heart. Next I decided not to project into the future about becoming a lawyer, or even about going through law school, but just to focus on getting through one semester at a time. So that's what I did. When I got through one semester, I decided to go on to the second. Somewhere in the second semester, I got hooked. I began to believe that this was going to be a fascinating challenge, that it was going to be a game worth playing.

Law school was also, Dean says, "humbling."

> In law school I discovered something rather startling: There are better minds than mine! On the flip side of my old idea that if I ever took a big risk I'd fail was another old idea—that if I ever really put my mind to anything, I'd be spectacular at it. And the only reason I'd never done anything spectacular was because I'd never really tried. Well, in law school I *did* try. I lengthened my stride and went all out, 100 percent, and I discovered that I have some limitations. But rather than be a horrible discovery, I found that becoming aware of your limitations is actually a relief, because then you can compensate for them and won't be taken by surprise.

Law school also showed Dean that he possessed many skills of which he was previously unaware. "I learned that I can absorb more information than I thought I could, that I can write and articulate, and that I can really slug it out with somebody in a courtroom and not die."

So one day at a time, one task at a time, Dean graduated from law school, became a law clerk, took (and passed on the first try) the bar exam, and became a lawyer, his current profession and one he still finds exciting.

Dean found that being an identical twin had a lot of old ideas attached to it.

> When you spend the first fourteen years of your life with somebody and you're virtually always together, some things emerge that are not a part of everybody else's experience. In a twin relationship, communication gets very subtle. You read the other person extremely well: you know what they're thinking, what they want, how they feel, and vice-versa, and you know it without having to ask a lot of questions, or explain.

There was even a "loss of boundary," where Dean wasn't sure where he left off and his brother began. Dean felt that whatever his brother did, he did too—that his brother represented *him*.

> I got the notion that he is me. If he acted stupid, that embarrassed me. If he got into trouble, I felt guilty, so I'd have to be on my best behavior for awhile to make up for it. On the other hand, if my twin was good, that gave me license to do what I wanted. After all, that was *me* out there being just fine.

This overidentification and "merging" of feelings with his brother tainted all his other relationships. Dean was walking around with the basic premise (the old idea) that "I shouldn't have to explain. If you care about me, you'll know."

"Since my twin and I didn't have to work at communicating— it just happened at a very subtle level—I assumed I should be able to communicate with everybody this way. I had no idea how to relate to somebody who wasn't exactly like me."

Later, Dean was even able to trace his chronic habit of tardiness to work and other appointments back to another old idea that came out of his being a twin. From the beginning, people used to ask his parents,

> "Which one is the oldest?" and they'd say, "*E.* was born first and then Dean came along about seven minutes later." Well, your brain picks up on that, and after I'd been sober quite awhile I got this insight that somehow this related to my habit of showing up late at places by seven minutes. In fact, in my life that seven minutes pops up all over the place. It's as if somewhere along the line I got the message that seven minutes later is what I'm supposed to do! It's amazing what weird notions we pick up as kids that create problems later.
>
> I sponsor a guy who was willing to be fired from his job because he refused to cut his long hair. I got curious about it because the hippie thing is passé, and I couldn't see any fashion statement to be made here. When I asked him about it, he told

210

me that the long hair was to cover his big ears. Well, when he finally let me see his ears, they were normal size. Together, we dug back into his childhood to see what old idea was behind this. It turned out that as a kid he'd been hovering around when his mother was gossiping with a neighbor lady, and when she saw him she said to the neighbor, "Shh! Little pitchers have big ears." And he took her literally! This guy was ready to lose his job over that old idea from twenty-five years ago that turned out to be erroneous. Once he could see that his ears were fine, and he understood where his belief about them had originated, he had no trouble getting a haircut and saving his job.

Dean further discovered that being a twin had also influenced some of his views about women, marriage, and fidelity. "Being a twin almost compels you to have somebody on your hip, so I ended up being married—and divorced—four times."

To save face with himself, he had blamed the marriage failures on the women themselves.

One day at lunch with an AA friend I was complaining about my last wife's problems with intimacy. He stopped me cold. "Dean, you've been married four times. What's going on?" Since he's one of those people I listen to, he got me right in the gut. "Do you want to *do* something about it?" he asked me. When I replied with an "I don't know" and a shrug, he said, "*Who* should we ask?" That did it! For the first time I became willing to look at my part in all those marriages and infidelities. Besides, I was unhappy with my conduct. It made me feel so damned bad. Why bring these women into my life just to treat them badly? What was that all about? For somebody whose be-all and end-all in life was respectability, my actions certainly weren't cutting it.

Dean was able to trace the problem back to childhood, too. He realized that it all started with an embarrassment at the tender age of seven.

I'd been publicly humiliated by someone I'd considered an important woman, my second grade teacher in Billings, Montana. She'd only been trying to get me to shut up and sit down, but all I wanted to do was make her laugh, so she'd like me. She and I had totally different agendas, and she finally sat on me pretty good. I came out of that with the notion, "The important women will humiliate and embarrass you. There's no way to understand them or keep them happy. You can't trust them. They don't care. And if they don't care, I don't care!"

I took that away with me and poisoned the well at home. I was in love with my mother and father. I wanted to be a source of joy to them, but from age seven until my mother died when I was fourteen, I pretended I didn't love her, that I didn't care. I never broke. It takes a lot of daily effort and discipline to do that, but I did it. The funny thing is, my brother doesn't recall that incident. He was in the classroom that day, but he doesn't even remember it. He developed his own problems with women, but not that one. Anyway, what accompanied my effort not to trust, not to care, was a real need to get out of the house and the notion, "The woman I love is not at home."

Later on, each time I got involved with a new woman, I'd put that notion on the shelf for awhile, but eventually it would kick back in. It's a life sentence. And I'd end up cheating on her—even as recently as my second marriage in sobriety. Why? Because "The woman I love is not at home." I started a serious extramarital relationship with a woman I met in law school. But as soon as I got divorced—in other words, as soon as I could bring her "home"—I lost interest in her. That's when it became obvious to me that something was wrong!

Dean set about to remedy this old idea. He wrote out two descriptions: one of the kind of woman he wanted in his life and the other of the qualities he'd have to acquire to attract such a woman. Six months later he met C., a tall, beautiful, model-like, young Korean woman who was born in Washington, D.C., the daughter of a politically active national. C. is vice president of a corporation that conducts seminars, including the one Dean was participating in when he met her.

I fell in love with her the way I'd never fallen in love before. Later people told me, "You were gone, Dean, just gone!" I was forty-eight, the same age as my dad when he met and married the woman he was with for the rest of his life. I'll be with C. for the rest of my life. Of course, attached to this relationship is a tremendous responsibility on my part to let go of all my old ideas and games about women. No more "If you loved me, you'd know intuitively what I want" or "The woman I love is not at home" or " You can't trust the important women." C. once said to me, "You can have this relationship any way you want it." So true! You tend to want to take care of somebody like that.

Having the same AA sponsor for twenty-two years has taught Dean some valuable lessons about making relationships endure that he hopes to apply to other kinds of relationships, including his current one with C.

People talk about outgrowing one another, but I don't know if that's it. I think you only outgrow a relationship that's cast in concrete. Unless relationships are periodically updated, people will end up going their separate ways. You have to continually redefine the relationship and find a current purpose for it. You have to ask yourself, how can I keep this relationship useful in my life?

Dean doesn't for a minute believe that he's a finished product. He's acutely aware that it's "progress, not perfection."

"In twenty-two years, I've managed to give up a lot of my old ideas, but I know I'll probably discover something else tomorrow. The journey continues."

14

THE SLIP:
Hugh, Sober Thirty
Years/NinetyDays

It's not a "slip," it's a "drunk." I don't like pretty words. It's a human trait to gloss things over, but calling it a "slip" tends to condone it. I drank again. I wanted to drink again. I planned to drink again. And I did drink again.

Slips Don't "Just Happen"

Alcoholics Anonymous warns that alcoholism is "cunning, baffling, powerful—and patient." What this means is that no matter how long a man has been clean and sober, even if it's thirty years, he's still vulnerable to relapse. If he is not careful, that little alcoholic beast lying dormant within might wake up and strike again.

To guard against this, recovering alcoholics in AA have devised ways of reminding themselves of this ever-present danger. One way is by continuing to refer to themselves as "alcoholics" or "recovering alcoholics," no matter how long it's been since their last drink. In other words, once an alcoholic, *always* an alcoholic. Sometimes this makes outsiders uncomfortable: "Introducing yourself as an alcoholic seems so negative," they say.

215

"It's the past. Can't you focus on the present, on something positive? After all, you're not drinking anymore." But AAs understand that the fact that they're abstinent simply means they aren't drinking; it doesn't mean they're cured.

When an alcoholic drinks or an addict uses again after a period of conscious abstinence, it's called a "slip"—at least in AA jargon. Outsiders are more likely to refer to it as a "relapse." Even within AA, not everybody agrees on what the most appropriate word for it is. Many AAs think that neither word takes into account the alcoholic's responsibility in the matter, arguing that the words *slip* and *relapse* make it seem as if drinking again were random. But a slip—*or* a relapse—doesn't "just happen." There are reasons for it.

A slip doesn't always mean getting drunk, although it can mean that. A slip is the purposeful using of a mind-altering chemical (unless there's a legitimate medical reason for it) after a period of abstinence. A slip can be anything—from taking a Valium, to taking a prescribed medication without asking what's in it, to taking a hit off someone else's marijuana cigarette, to sticking your tongue in a glass of cooking sherry, or, as in the case of one woman I know, to holding scotch in your mouth "for a toothache" and then swallowing it. When this woman was asked why she swallowed the scotch, she said defensively: "Well, I didn't know what else to do with it!" *That's* a slip. On the other hand, it's not a slip if you order orange juice, take a gulp, and then discover there's vodka in it. Even if you've already swallowed it, it's not a slip. If you take a second gulp, however, it is. A slip is directly related to the thought, the conscious intention, behind it.

When a Drink Is Not Just a Drink

A slip is a big deal in Alcoholics Anonymous, especially when the slipper has had many years of sobriety. The news that an AA member has slipped is only less shocking than the news that he has died. The first thing most people want to know is "How much time did he have?" To outsiders, a drink is just a drink, but to an active AA member a drink is a life-changing happening with all kinds of consequences. First, the "slipper" loses his time. He has to start all over again with day one. Second, the slipper loses status. This "fall from grace" affects not only the slipper but also his family, who likely have been basking in some of his reflected glory, touting "my husband (father, son, and so on) has fifteen (or twenty) years of sobriety, you know." But now he has only three days, or two weeks. His peers, as well as the people he may have been sponsoring, suddenly have more time on the program than he does. He has shattered his credibility. But, you might ask, what about those fifteen or twenty years of learning? Are they wasted? Of course not; he was sober after all. Yet, while AAs may concede that he has indeed gathered a lot of wisdom over the years, he still hasn't learned the most important thing of all: how to *stay* sober.

When he gets back to AA—that is, *if* he gets back to AA—he'll have to raise his hand as a newcomer again for all to see. Then everybody on the block will know he's slipped, and he further loses face. Usually, as if it were calculated to put salt on the wound, some newcomer who has absolutely no idea that the slipper is a "retread," will walk up to him and treat him like he's still wet behind the ears: "Here's some of our literature, and here's my phone number. Call me any time and I'll explain our program to you." That kind is humbling, and it can either make a man out of him or kill him, like being in the Marines.

If this all seems harsh, consider its purpose: to save lives. Realizing the severe social consequences of drinking again, AAs tend to hang onto their sobriety more tightly. They become purists. They don't cheat or toy with trying "just one drink"—because if they do, that's a slip. It's not worth it.

On the plus side, once the slipper owns up to the slip, tells the truth about it, and comes back to the fold to accept the consequences, he's welcomed back into AA with open arms. In fact, he gets more hugs and pats on the back than he's probably had in years, and he's praised for being honest, for having the guts and courage to face the music.

Ironically, one man's slip may be another man's lifesaver or, again, as AA says, "Some must die so that others may live." When somebody with years of sobriety slips, it puts everybody on alert. If they've been getting a little sloppy about working their own program, it makes them shape up fast. At least for awhile. They reason—and rightly so—"If it can happen to him, it can happen to me." They begin questioning the slipper, not out of idle curiosity but because they want to know what mistakes he made so they can avoid them.

Phoenix Out of the Ashes

A slip can actually be therapeutic—if the recovering alcoholic survives it. The worst thing that can happen is that the slip retriggers the alcoholic's obsession to drink or use, and then he can't get sober again. The best thing that can happen is that the alcoholic drinks for only a short time, learns something important from his slip that improves his life, gets sober again, and stays sober. Of course, nobody should ever arrange to slip in order to achieve some end. That's a formula for disaster that usually results in a real "end"—death.

Although it's virtually impossible to pinpoint exactly why a specific individual slips, AA's fifty plus years of experience dealing with slippers shows us that there are five common reasons for relapsing. People slip because 1) they cut down on their meetings or stop going; 2) they don't get a sponsor; 3) they don't work the Twelve Steps; 4) they get arrogant and/or complacent; and 5) they don't deal with their feelings.

Our thirty-year/ninety-day man, Hugh, by his own admission, was guilty on all five counts.

HUGH

Rarely have we ever seen a person fail who has thoroughly followed our path . . .
—from the AA "Big Book"

Hugh is a trim, energetic, sharp-featured man of sixty-seven. He was born in Baltimore, where he spent the first twenty-three of his thirty years of sobriety. About eight years ago, he and his wife moved to California after she became ill, and they "had a few great years in the sun" before she died of cancer three years ago. He has two children, both of whom moved to California to be with him.

Hugh and his sister were the children of privilege. "I was born to wealthy parents. During my thirty years of sobriety, I made good money, invested well, and inherited well. I've never had any money problems." Hugh has been teaching computer programming and computer science since the 1950s and is currently dean of a business school. "I've continued to work, not because I have to, but because I want to. I need a reason to get out there every morning so I don't become a couch potato."

Hugh first experimented with drinking as a teenager—"I was always mature-looking for my age, so I could buy alcohol easily"— but he didn't get into it in earnest until college. He graduated from

Washington University in 1942 and was commissioned right into the Navy, where he spent the next twelve years.

> The Navy was a wonderful place at the time to further one's career as a boozer, and I more than earned that reputation. I even had the dubious honor of being transferred to a ship just because the captain needed somebody to sit and drink with. In the beginning, I had a real wooden leg. When we'd go to a party, people would say, "Hugh, are you driving us home again tonight?" And I'd say, "I sure as hell am. I'm too drunk to stay here and sing."

Hugh was a periodic alcoholic, as distinguished from a daily, or even a weekend, drinker. Periodics are much less common than "regular" alcoholics. They can drink like a normal person for a period of time, often months, and then suddenly something else clicks in and they're off on a bender. These drinkers are notorious for "lost weekends." Hugh recalls those times. "During my benders I'd get into all kinds of trouble. I'd usually paper the town with bad checks and break up eating establishments." When periodics get sober, they sometimes struggle with the question of whether they're really sober or just at an interim between drinking episodes. Only time tells them. By the end of Hugh's drinking, his episodes were getting closer together (as is often the case) and he was looking more like a garden-variety drunk every day.

In the 1950s, family members and health professionals weren't nearly as knowledgeable about alcoholism as they are today. Many of them were guilty of "enabling," unintentionally *helping* the alcoholic to prolong his drinking by protecting him from the negative consequences of his behavior. Hugh's wife, his father, and even his psychiatrist all enabled him unashamedly.

> When I'd go on a bender, my wife would track me down and take care of me. If I wrote out bad checks, my father would run down to the bank with instructions that under no circumstances

were they to return any of my checks. He'd say, "You will take the money out of my account to cover them," and they did. When I got depressed, my father took me to see a psychiatrist. When I told the psychiatrist about my drinking, he was quick to reassure me. "You don't have a drinking problem," he'd say. "Sure, you drink a little heavy, but I think your problem is cocktail lounges. Just drink at home, avoid those cocktail lounges, and you'll be fine." At the time, I was drinking so heavily that I couldn't even hold a job, but that didn't seem to strike anybody as relevant. The psychiatrist even called my wife in to tell her that "Hugh doesn't have a drinking problem, he just has to stay out of cocktail lounges. Make sure he has enough alcohol at home so he doesn't have to venture out to buy it."

Hugh's wife, much relieved that her husband wasn't an alcoholic after all, went off on a trip with the children to visit her sick mother in Rhode Island. Before she left, she made sure to fill the refrigerator with beer and stock the cabinets with plenty of bourbon and wine.

The last thing she said to me at the airport was, "Now remember what the doctor told you. Drink at home."

Well, hell, I got rid of what she'd bought in two days, and then I left the house. For ten days I was off God-knows-where on a big bender. I was supposed to drive up to Rhode Island to pick them up after ten days, but I never showed up. I'd vanished. Even *I* didn't know where I'd vanished to. My wife and the kids had to fly back, and my mother and sister picked them up at the airport. They arrived back at the house just two minutes before I walked in. I'd run out of money. "Well," my sister said, "the goddamned drunk is back!" My wife said, "I'm going to pack some clothes, and then we're leaving." My son was less than a year old then, and my daughter was only two.

I'll remember that scene if I live to be 100, seeing my wife and my children walking out the door with their suitcases, and I remember saying to myself, "Hugh, you're losing the only thing that has ever been important to you—your family. Something is wrong here!"

221

That's when Hugh had his moment of clarity.

I pleaded with my wife, "Help me. I need help." I meant it, and she knew it. She said, "Yes, I'll help you." But my mother and sister didn't buy it. "Don't pay attention to that goddamned drunk," my sister said, and my mother echoed, "He's my son, but he's still a drunken bum." But my wife said, "No, I love him and if he needs help I'm going to help him." Ten minutes later we called AA, which I'd heard of but knew nothing about. A few hours later, an AA man was sitting in our house, talking to me. That night I was at a meeting. I never took another drink after that— at least not for thirty years.

Hugh and his wife both jumped into the program (AA for him, Al-Anon for her) with enthusiasm. In the following highlights of Hugh's progress, you'll recognize many of the stages and phases he went through as typical.

On being a newcomer

During my first month, I went to a meeting every day and then three meetings a week for years and years. I tried to live within the Twelve Steps of AA to the best of my ability. There was much more stigma about being an alcoholic then; it meant you were an outcast. But I never had a problem with the word. After years of being called a "drunken s.o.b.," being called an alcoholic just lifted me up in the social strata. I joined the East Coast banquet circuit, and I'd speak whenever the clubs would celebrate different AA anniversaries [birthdays], including Bill's anniversary dinners in New York [Bill Wilson, better known as Bill W., the cofounder of Alcoholics Anonymous].

On relationships

Thanks to sobriety, my marriage became a true love story. We had a very happy marriage. I became a good father to my children, who fortunately were too young to remember ever seeing me drunk. And my sister and I, the one who had once said

"Don't pay attention to that goddamned drunk," became close. She ended up being proud of me.

On work

After a few years of sobriety, I went back to school, to a university to learn more about computers. I ended up teaching there, and later in prep schools. Those were the days when computers were humongous things that took up whole rooms and had 57,000 vacuum tubes, the average life of which was only fifteen minutes! They weren't nearly as powerful as the average little home computer we have today. But that was my niche. I loved it, and I was successful at it. I kept getting better and better jobs.

In summary

Those thirty years of sobriety were great. Everything happened as it should have happened. My worst days sober were far superior to my best days drinking.

So what went wrong? How, and why, did Hugh slip?

Hugh believes that his slip ultimately happened because, after the death of his wife and then of his sister, he failed to do what mental health professionals call "normal griefwork." Many things led up to the moment when he took that fatal drink. The stage could have been set when he and his wife moved to California, after twenty-three years of AA membership in Baltimore. Without recognizing it at the time, this move, although they both wanted it, involved many losses—old friends, old routines, their children, familiar AA meetings, a total AA support network built up over all those years.

In California AA, I just never seemed to develop any meaningful social contacts, so it wasn't that difficult to cut down on my meetings. I wasn't going there to see good friends anymore. For a long time it was okay. I didn't suffer any bad effects. But later it caught up with me.

Then, three years ago, Hugh suffered the terrible loss of his wife; three months later, his sister died. Instead of going into the bosom of AA for emotional support, Hugh stayed by himself.

I was now living alone, not going to AA much, and the old thinking crept back in. I began to tell myself, "What the hell do I need AA for? I've been sober thirty years. I can handle this thing on my own. In fact, I have a lot better things to do with my time." I handled my new loneliness by chasing women instead. I even got remarried but that lasted only ten months. Fortunately, my ex and I are friends now. I went to only one AA meeting after I celebrated my thirtieth AA birthday. With hindsight, I can see now that I was becoming complacent and angry. The next think I knew I was saying to myself, "You know, I was the one who said I was an alcoholic in the first place! Alcoholism is a disease of self-diagnosis after all." In other words, I was back to denying that I was even an alcoholic! I just kicked my admission that I was a drunk right out the door. Arrogant me! And of course, by doing that it was that much easier to start playing footsie with alcohol—you know, "I can try it. Why not? Besides, what's life got to offer me now?" At first it was just a beer or a highball, maybe a glass of wine. Then I said, "Hey, I'm good at it!" so I'd have more.

Well, I found out real fast that I'm a "real" alcoholic. Within six months, I was passing out every night and calling in sick to work every day. The only time I'd leave the house was to walk to the market to buy whiskey. Everything I'd ever heard about how alcoholism progresses in the body, even when you're not drinking, was true. I was much worse than where I'd left off thirty years ago. I went from being a guy who loved talking to people every day on the phone and had a monthly phone bill in the hundreds of dollars, to being a guy who said, "Leave me alone! Don't bother me!" if anybody called.

My kids weren't used to a drunken father and they were frantic. They couldn't sleep worrying about me. They'd constantly question me, "Why are you doing this to yourself and to us?" Then came the last night when I was such a stumbling idiot that my son had to help me into bed. I was seeing creepy-crawly things on the wall. That's when I said to him, "Call AA."

224

Sylvia: How did you feel drinking all that time? Did you feel any guilt?

Hugh: No. None. It was just taking a drink, that's all. I didn't feel any guilt until I went back to AA. Then I felt it. I was apprehensive maybe about how I'd be received. But when I got there and raised my hand and identified myself as an alcoholic who'd been sober for thirty years and had gone out drinking again—that I'd had my last drink just yesterday—people I'd never seen before embraced me and welcomed me, and for the first time in years I was able to feel that AA love and understanding I'd been denying myself for years. The weight of the world dropped off me. Since then, I haven't had a single desire for a drink, and now I have ninety days.

Although Hugh made it very clear that he didn't drink because his wife died or because of any other losses ("I'd be a blithering fool if I tried to blame those things"), he *does* admit that not dealing with his grief weakened him and made him more vulnerable to relapse.

> I'm not clever enough to figure out exactly why I drank, but three things weakened me for sure: one, I had stopped going to AA; two, I lost sight of the fact that I was an alcoholic; and, three, I didn't grieve when I should have. I kept a stiff upper lip. I thought by doing so I was protecting my children, who'd just lost their mother and their aunt. I thought I was being a big, tough guy. That, too, was arrogant of me—to think that I was above grieving! Never before had I been ashamed to shed a tear, even in public. But in this instance, at first I wouldn't, then I couldn't. I froze up, got stuck, and mucked around in a lot of self-pity. I remember thinking to myself, "Hugh, here you've been a goodie-goodie for thirty years, and look what happens—you've lost the people you love!" Well, the truth is, that's life. The minute we're born we're going to die. That's called reality.

But just because it's "reality" doesn't mean the "normal grief-work" doesn't have to be done. It *does*. What does it consist of?

Different cultures have different ideas about how to handle mourning and pain. Having funerals or wakes and encouraging such behaviors as crying and wailing (or, as is the Japanese custom, smiling so as not to burden others) all may help. Their central purpose is to accept the loss, deal with the pain, let go, say good-bye, and get back into life again. When this process is stifled, it can backfire. The denied grief, which is relegated to the unconscious, may sneak out years later in the form of depression, physical illness, and slips, as in the case of recovering alcoholics.

To remedy this, mental health professionals as well as AA sponsors may encourage people to find ways to reexperience the pain so it can be resolved. The grieving person can write a letter to the dead person to complete "unfinished business" and say those things that still need to be said. Another technique is visiting the grave and talking to the gravestone. Another is to put photos around to stimulate memories and blocked feelings, or even to watch sad movies to try to trigger tears.

So Hugh set about to do his own griefwork to deal with his own pain:

> Fortunately, I was able to do some of my griefwork within the first ten days of my new sobriety. It happened automatically. I was sitting in my living room one evening, and my mind wandered to my wife, and then to my sister, and finally to my mother who'd died at age ninety while I was back out there drinking again. The realization hit me that I'd had to contend with three deaths in two years. I found myself talking to each one of them, saying, "Look, you're not here now, so I've just got to let you go." And with that, I started to cry. And I cried and cried. I can't tell you how long this went on, but when I stopped I felt better. I felt cleansed. I looked in the mirror and for the first time in months I was able to say, "Hi, Hugh," instead of "Hi, asshole." And then I said, "You're not an old man yet, Hugh. You have a lot of life left in you, and it's a good life. So go out there and live."

226

Hugh was lucky. His slip "worked": it blew apart his defenses and forced him to deal with the pent-up feelings of grief that were suffocating him.

I'm glad now that I drank again. I think it made a better person of me. It certainly humbled me. When I was first back in the program and it took me three or four days just to get over my shakes, I was reduced to the lowest common denominator. I realized that I can never again pull away from the program. The reason for me to keep going to meetings is to be ever-reminded of who I am, an alcoholic. It was only when I stopped going to meetings that I forgot.

Back in the 1960s, when I was attending some question-and-answer AA meetings where I'd see Bill W., somebody once asked him, "If you were to change anything that was written in the Big Book, what would you change?" And Bill W., without hesitating a beat, said, "I'd change one word. In Chapter 5 where it now says 'Rarely have we seen a person fail who has thoroughly followed our path,' I would change *rarely* to *never*—'Never have we seen a person fail who has thoroughly followed our path.' "

I keep finding myself recalling Bill's words. They impress me even more today than they did then because now I know how right he was. All you have to do is look at the people sitting at meetings who have various lengths of sobriety and listen to their stories of what life was like before and what life is like now, and that's proof positive that AA works. They're not bullshitting you. They're not weaving a tale for your entertainment. They're sharing and purging their souls, because they hope that in so doing they'll be able to help somebody else avoid his mistakes.

Had I listened better—had I "thoroughly followed their path"—I don't think I would have felt compelled to drink again. After all, "Never have we seen a person fail who has thoroughly followed our path . . ."

I marvel at how great I feel—better physically than I have in fifteen years. Mentally, emotionally, and spiritually. I have a better outlook. I surrendered—and won! And at this point, I don't even care why I drank after thirty years of sobriety. All I care about is that I never, never do it again.

15

SECRETS OF A LONGER SOBRIETY:
Warren, Sober Thirty-five Years

I tell people, "Kick me in the shins if you ever catch me forgetting that I'm a very sick person with a disease called alcoholism!"

Never-Ending Commitment

By now it's probably clear that it takes the same level of commitment and the same actions to stay sober for years as it does to stay sober for days. It's a never-ending process.

Men like our last interviewee Hugh, who stopped doing the basics, who stopped going to meetings and working with others, who forgot why they joined AA in the first place, are usually doomed to drink and use again.

In this chapter, Warren, who has been sober for thirty-five years, shares with us some of the secrets of staying sober over the long haul, secrets that are open and available to everyone but that most alcoholics, for whatever reasons, flatly refuse to pay attention to.

Alcoholics Anonymous offer three basic "secrets of success": one, the secret of living one day at a time; two, the secret of going to meetings; and three, the secret of working with others. (There are more, but these are the fundamental ones.) By doing these things, the recovering alcoholic man will develop over time the most heroic characteristic of all—wisdom.

AA, like certain Oriental cultures, reveres the wisdom that comes of experience. Old-timers like Warren are admired because of their longevity, because of what they know. This is unusual in a youth-worshipping culture like ours that isn't accustomed to respecting its elders. Certainly, it helps make AA a nice place to grow old in!

But this reverence for wisdom can put a certain amount of pressure on the old-timer to pretend to be more wise than he actually is. Wisdom, obviously, must be tempered with humility. Even AA's cofounder, Bill W., who had thirty-six years of sobriety at the time of his death, felt this pressure to be "all-wise" as he dealt with people all over the world who flocked to see him to discuss their problems. Yet apparently no one was more aware of his own weakness and limitations than Bill himself, who once commented, "I feel much more comfortable if I'm in a position of being *less* wise."

The truly wise man learns not only from his own experiences but also from the experiences of others. For that reason, at the end of this chapter, Warren shares with us the story of *B.*, an alcoholic whose downfall was so classic it reads like Greek tragedy.

Disciple Status

AA's two cofounders are dead. Bill Wilson died in 1971; Dr. Bob Smith in 1950. Individuals who happened to know either of these men personally are now finding themselves in the unique position of being "disciples" of sorts, encouraged to share their memories of these two remarkable men with others. AAs are always fascinated to hear new details and fresh versions of the Bill and Bob stories they've read in the AA "Big Book" and in other AA literature.

Our interviewee, Warren, is one of the fortunate people who knew Bill W. personally. Some of Warren's recollections of Bill are included here, not only for their pertinence to our topic but also for their historical value.

WARREN

Don't think you're talking to somebody who knows it all, because I don't. I can't preach. All I can do is tell people how I feel and what I think I've learned. I don't wake up each day and say, "Gee, I've got it licked." But I do wake up each day with an appreciation for what sobriety has taught me and a desire to keep coming back to the source, to Alcoholics Anonymous, to learn more.

Warren, seventy-seven, a medium-height, high-energy man with silver-gray hair and a deep, booming voice, was born in Texas, the son of a Methodist minister. There was no alcoholism in the family, at least none that anyone talked about. His was the first "case" of it, and he was a late starter at that. Booze didn't give him any real problems until he was in his mid- to late twenties.

Warren worked as a musician, playing the saxophone and clarinet while working his way through college, and later made a name for himself working as a radio announcer, plus he played with many name bands. He is also a composer. He has been married for over half a century to *R.*, a former band singer and fellow recovering alcoholic, herself with thirty-four years of sobriety. Together they have three children, one of whom has been sober in AA for eleven years. Much of Warren's AA experience took place in New York, which explains his East Coast AA lingo. He and *R.* are now retired and live in Palm Desert, California.

I was an ambitious, fearless kid. My life plan was to become a
lawyer and then go on to become the governor of Texas. But it
was 1929, Depression times, and money was scarce. I knew that
if I was going to get an education, I was going to have to pay for
it, so I joined a dance band and played nights, studied in the
john, and went to school during the day. Sometimes I wouldn't
finish a job until four in the morning, and I'd have to be in a
political science class at eight. I nodded off in class a lot.

After three years of this, even though Warren was getting
good grades, one of his professors expressed concern. "You're
killing yourself this way." He suggested that Warren temporarily
drop out of school, work, save money, return to get his law
degree, and *then* go on to become the governor of Texas.

We were still in the middle of the Depression, and this professor
sent me to see a friend of his, who owned a newspaper and a
radio station. His friend sized me up quickly. "You've got too
good a voice to waste it working on my newspaper. How about
working at my radio station?" When I told him that I didn't
know anything about radio, he just laughed and said, "Who the
hell does! You'll learn!" I didn't know it then, but that was the
start of my radio career. In my mind, it was just a job until I could
go back to school, get my law degree, and become the governor
of Texas. It took me ten years to give up that dream.

The first radio job led to better ones—in Oklahoma City, in
Chicago. One day Warren was buttonholed by one of the engineers
who said, "Kid, I can tell you're not really serious about this radio
business. You're making a mistake, because someday radio is really
going to be a big business, and with your voice you'll do well.

The man got Warren's attention. He agreed to an audition for
an announcer spot at a major radio station in New York, and he
got the job. "I met all the top-named bands like Glenn Miller and
the Dorseys. I got to know all of them. What an adventure! I
loved every minute of it, and I kept making more and more
money." Drinking still hadn't become a problem.

When Warren was twenty-four, he met a band singer, *R.* "She had a big, wonderful voice. I was intrigued with her music—and with her. She was only twenty-three. She told me she was 'on the wagon.' We got married."

For *R.*, being on the wagon didn't last long. When she finally resumed drinking, Warren saw nothing wrong with it. He recalls those early days vividly.

Everybody in this crowd drank. That's just what you did to have fun. People thought nothing of it. They boasted about their hangovers. Looking back on it, I realize that the radio and advertising business was a sea of alcoholism, but none of us had any idea that alcoholism was a disease, or that *R.* had it, or that it was starting to happen to me. People simply didn't know such things. Alcoholics were skid row bums, not people like us.

Drinking didn't really create any problems for us in the beginning. We could still put alcohol aside for six months and not miss it. Later on, we couldn't even stay away from a drink for half an hour. One of us would end up saying, "Let's just drink socially." Oh, those fatal words!

I'd wake up with horrendous hangovers. But I'd never have any "hair of the dog" if I had to go on the air. I knew even a little alcohol could affect my speech, so I'd go on with one of those hangovers! Talk about willpower! Alcoholics have tremendous willpower. Of course, the minute I was off the air, I'd drink.

The more Warren drank, the more isolated and depressed he became.

You just didn't talk about things like that at the country club. I thought the only explanation for why I was drinking and destroying myself—and my family—was that I was losing my mind. I thought I was crazy and only pretending to be sane. I really suffered over this one, but I suffered in silence. I hadn't a soul on earth to talk to. It finally got so crazy that I thought I'd go mad if I didn't find somebody to tell about what was happening to me. I was suicidal with despair."

Warren finally made an appointment with an internist, Dr. Webb Marxer, a "tall, Germanic genius," and he unburdened his soul.

> I told him about my drinking, my "craziness," my fears. I didn't know that only weeks before, somebody had sent him a copy of the AA "Big Book" and Marxer had devoured it. At the time the level of ignorance about alcoholism among physicians was staggering. Had I been talking to any other physician, I'd probably have been institutionalized as insane, but this doctor was unique.

The two men ended up in a doctor-patient confrontation that wouldn't seem all that unusual today, but back in 1955 it was unheard of. When Warren told him, "I'm drinking too much," Marxer said, "Of course you are! You're an alcoholic!" Of course Warren, being an alcoholic, replied, "No, not me!" to which the doctor shot back, "Yes, *you*!" Warren resisted, but Marxer knew better.

> You're an idiot! You think you have to be in the gutter to be an alcoholic, but I treat people like you all the time—doctors, lawyers, nuns, priests, advertising people, writers, business executives, even ministers. And though you all have different patterns, you're all alike, and you're all crazy from drinking. It's drinking that makes you crazy. It's drinking that's killing you!"

Then he added, with great frustration, "And I can't do a damn thing about it!

But Marxer had a suggestion. "Four of my patients whose stories are just like yours joined a support group called Alcoholics Anonymous. Today they are the healthiest, least crazy patients I have. Why don't you give them a call?"

Warren called them. Within hours, two were at his house, talking to him, making what Warren was later to find out was a "twelve-step call." It's what kept *them* sober.

I was flabbergasted by the visit of these AAs. I kept saying to them, "My God, you felt crazy too?" "Yes, that's just part of the disease pattern," they kept telling me. "You need to go to a meeting." "What's a meeting?" They said, "We'll take you." On the way to the meeting, I said, "I'm in the public eye. What if I see somebody I know?" And they said, "Of course you'll see somebody you know! Just remember, they'll be there for the same reason you're there." That thought just hadn't occurred to me. At the meeting when I heard a man boom out, "Hi, I'm Joe, and I'm a drunken banker!" I squirmed in my seat. I wanted to say, "My God, don't say that, somebody might hear you!" But the more stories I heard, the more I began to identify, the more comfortable I felt, the less alone and crazy I felt.

Warren has been sober ever since.

As we discussed in earlier chapters, a married man who gets sober is usually encouraged by AA to stay put and not make any major decisions, like getting a divorce, in his first year of sobriety. But if his wife is also a practicing alcoholic, that changes things. In Warren's case, he saw R.'s drinking as a real threat to his own sobriety.

R. was vitriolic and suicidal. I'd come home from an AA meeting and get attacked with comments like "You're no damn good! You're running around to those AA meetings and you're never home. You're useless!" Warren's sponsor finally told him, "You're too vulnerable right now to put up with that. She'll drive you to drink. At least if you leave you'll have a chance of staying sober—and who knows, R. may even sober up herself. But if you drink again your whole family could go down the tubes."

To stay sober, Warren moved out.

He had a rough time. "To get through it, I'd say the serenity prayer up to fifty times a day." He also went to lots of AA meetings, and it was there that he met and got to know, Bill W.

Hearing Bill share about getting through some of his own dark days and depressions helped me to get through mine. The fact that I was having such a hard time made me feel so inadequate. But Bill would tell me, "There are no wise men in the beginning," and that would help me to hang in and press on, one more day.

When Warren was nine months sober he got a phone call. "Guess who I just saw at an AA meeting?" a friend said. It was *R.* A short time later, the family reunited.

R. was still full of anger, and I had real doubts that this marriage thing was do-able, but old-timers—in those days that meant anyone with over ten years of sobriety—kept telling me that I could certainly put up with *R.* for one day, one twenty-four-hour segment, at a time. And if we couldn't talk to each other, we could still go to meetings together. We discovered that we communicated better if we brought newcomers back to the house for coffee after the meetings, where we could all sit around and talk, talk, talk for hours. By the time they'd leave, we'd be too tired to fight and we'd go to bed.

That's what Warren and *R.* have been doing ever since. "I'm almost seventy-eight years old, and thirty-five years sober, and *R.* is seventy-seven and thirty-four years sober, and our kids are fifty-one, forty-nine, and forty-six. We even have four grandchildren!" Warren laughs. "Now when did all that happen?"

It happened, of course, "one day at a time," the concept that is one of the main secrets of long-term sobriety.

A day at a time is not just a jingle. It's a description of reality. At first it was a notion that was hard for me to understand. I'd been too influenced by all those business books that said, "Make a long-term plan, stick to it, and don't be deterred." Then I got to AA, and I had to learn how to be flexible and just take things— like my marriage, my work, and my kids—in daily units. One *unit* at a time. As some wise old-timers told me, it's okay to still make *plans* for your life, but only *execute* these plans one day at a time. That's the difference. At the end of the day, another day will start; and if I'm still around, I'll take that day, and whatever is in it, one unit at a time. It took a lot of practice before the one-day-at-a-time notion finally made sense to me to the point where it was helpful. When I got it, I found that there was tremendous freedom in it.

But as Warren points out, even the best philosophy won't work if it isn't backed up by actions. Faith without works is dead. And the best action to take is to go to meetings. Lots and lots of meetings. It's another open secret too many people ignore.

When people first get sober in AA they're all excited and enthusiastic, just as I was, and they say, "Good, maybe this means I can get out of whatever mess I was in." But then their life begins to improve, and they start taking things for granted. They say, "Well, I think I've got it now. I don't need do go to all those meetings. I'll just go once in awhile to touch bases." They jump right back into their prison of self-involvement, and they disappear from AA. We don't see them back at meetings until after they've had a slip. If I ask them, "What happened?" the answer I usually get is "I stopped going to meetings." If I ask them why, they say, "Because I thought I knew everything there was to know about this disease, and I didn't think I needed AA anymore."

For me, I know one thing for sure: If I don't show my face at meetings, if I'm not available to new people in case they want to ask me a question or two, then I'm a doomed man.

That is, of course, another open secret of long-term sobriety—working with others. Twelve-step work. It was what Bill W. discovered when he had his famous spiritual experience in Towns Hospital in New York, the experience that catapulted him into sobriety and resulted in starting Alcoholics Anonymous. Part of Bill W.'s revelation was an understanding that the action he needed to take to maintain his sobriety involved helping other suffering alcoholics.

> I heard Bill relate his whole recovery story three different times, and each time it was wonderful hearing him describe it so vividly. At first, I thought he was having a hallucination caused by a drug they'd given him in the hospital, and he likened it to a light bulb going off in his head. And then afterward he recalled having this instruction like thought—"Bill, when you get out of this hospital room, go immediately and find yourself another active alcoholic to talk to and tell him how you feel without trying to convert him. If you can do that, you *might* be able to lick this thing."
>
> After Bill got out of the hospital, that's exactly what he did. He had a friend set up a meeting between himself and another alcoholic, who happened to be the physician, Dr. Bob Smith. Dr. Bob had a bad hangover that day and didn't particularly feel like meeting anybody, but the friend begged him, "You've got to! Bill says he *has* to talk to another alcoholic." So Bob reluctantly agreed to meet Bill, and their "talk" turned into a five-hour conversation! And, ironically, Bob was under the impression that Bill was there to help *him*. "Oh, no," Bill explained, "I'm not here to stop you from drinking. I just needed to talk to somebody so *I* can stay sober." That's when Dr. Bob finally understood what this meeting was about. "Oh, I see," Dr. Bob said. "This is a very different kind of approach."

When AA calls itself "a selfish program," this is what they mean. Put more crudely, it's a "Save Your Own Ass" program. The recovering alcoholic doesn't have to understand it; all he has to do is carry it out by working with others. If he doesn't, he'll pay the price.

When he was only a few years sober, Warren learned this lesson well as the result of his experience sponsoring a man named B. The following story, in Warren's words, clearly illustrates what "working with others" is really all about.

THE STORY OF B. AN ALCOHOLIC TRAGEDY

This is such a classic story of the power of alcoholism that it still haunts me. It also helps me to remember who I am: An alcoholic. For many years, I sponsored a man named *B.* He was undoubtedly the man who had everything. He was brilliant, a graduate of Harvard Business School, and at the age of twenty-nine, he was already president of an ad agency, married, and making nearly $225,000—and this was in the early 1960s.

Well, he drank that ad agency right down the drain. He couldn't get a job. That's what forced him into AA. He got sober. I became his sponsor. After awhile, another agency took a chance on him. They hired him for one-fifth of what he'd been making before. He did well. He built himself up again. But I began to notice that the more involved he got with his work, the less involved he was with AA. I warned him, "*B.*, unless you go to meetings to remind yourself that you're an alcoholic, you'll forget; and if you forget, you'll drink; and if you drink, you're doomed." And *B.* said, "Oh, no, not me."

After a while *B.* attracted the attention of one of the biggest ad agencies in New York. They said, "This guy's been staying sober. Let's bring him on board." They did. They gave him a lot of money. All he had to do was stay sober, keep on doing what he was doing, and eventually he would have become president of this agency and CEO. They even had a "watchdog" there to keep an eye on him, an AA old-timer who told *B.*, "Don't you ever try to pull any shit with me because I'm an alcoholic, too, and you can't con a con." And the agency took a strong stand as well, warning *B.* that "if you ever drink again, don't even bother to come into the office. We'll settle everything up and send you your severance check and personal effects."

One-and-a-half years later, *B.* drank again. He got into a big scrap with the police in Old Greenwich, Connecticut, and it hit the papers. The next day the ad agency, as it had warned, sent a limousine out to his home with his severance check and his personal effects.

After that, *B.* came limping back to AA. Before long, he had developed a pattern: he'd come back to AA, sober up, get another job, leave AA, drink, get fired, come back, sober up, get hired somewhere else, stop going to meetings, drink again, lose that job, come back. At one point he was working as an assistant to a man who used to be one of his office boys—and he couldn't even hold that job. Somewhere along the line he lost his wives. I personally put him in three different hospitals.

The last time I saw *B.* was when I went to visit him in a mental hospital in Connecticut. He wasn't even allowed to wear his watch for fear he'd cut himself with the crystal. The hospital was a collection of dirty, old brick buildings stretched across seventy or eighty acres with a little stream meandering through the place. When I looked up at the buildings, there were iron bars with faces peering through them, like gargoyles. My heart nearly stopped, and I thought, "God, could these all be alcoholics whose families have stuck them away in here because nobody knows what's wrong with them?" That's what happened to alcoholics in those days.

They let me take *B.* for a walk. "God, it makes me want to weep," I said to him as we walked across the grounds, those gargoyles watching us through the windows. "They're like animals." We sat down on the grass. I didn't want to preach to him, or scold him. That's not the AA way. So I said, "That could be me up there behind those bars if it wasn't for AA. *B.*, that's why I've stuck with AA. I believe if I don't stay in AA, eventually that *will* be me up there." He was silent. I went on. "I look at you, *B.*, in here, and I wonder why it is that you never seemed to be able to buy this AA thing." And he said, "Yeah, Warren, you're right. I used to look at you sober AA guys and I never understood how you could ever have any fun again." Dumbfounded, I said, "After what we've just seen up there, those grotesques staring out from behind those bars, those poor alcoholics put away like they're animals, and you talk about having *fun* again? Do you know what you just said?" Then I got up. My final words were "*B.*, you are making my day very uncomfortable," and with that I left for the railway station and returned to New York.

About a month later I heard that B. committed suicide by

hanging himself from a tree. For weeks I walked around with a lot of guilt. What did I *not* do for *B.* that I could have done? What did I *not* get through to him? I was angry at him, too, because he hadn't bought this AA thing.

Finally I called Bill W. and asked him for fifteen minutes of his time. When he agreed, I went over to his office and told him the story. "I feel so badly. I feel that maybe I didn't make *B.* a priority." Then Bill looked at me, gave me that big laugh of his, and said, "Let me ask you something, Warren. Did this bird's drinking ever make you want to start drinking again yourself?" And I said, "Hell no, that's the *last* thing in the world I want to do!" And Bill smiled and said, "Then this AA thing kind of works, doesn't it?"

That's when I finally realized what Dr. Bob had realized so many years ago after his five-hour talk with Bill W. I understood that because I'd tried to help *B.*, *I* was still sober. *I* was still alive! Bill went on: "When you carry the message and the guy doesn't want it, all you can do is pray for him, and then go find somebody who *does* want the message." I walked out of Bill's office that day with a huge boulder off my back.

Working with others has been a mainstay of Warren's sobriety every since.

Originally, it was never part of my life plan to think about somebody else. What I've learned in AA is that it's an absolute must to stay in touch with other newly recovering people. Today I'm concerned with their problems, not just my own, and what I see all around me are examples of the program working—even in the worst of circumstances. I see so many heroic people, and when I hear about their problems and how they work through them, it inspires me.

I never could have forecast what has happened to me in my life. Periodically, I have moments of despondency about all the things I could have done, or should have done, but when I think back over the years and look at the good things that have happened, at the gifts I've received, the feeling disappears. If not for AA, I might have committed suicide. If not for AA, I'd have ended my career. If not for AA, I'd probably have done more awful things to my children and my wife. Today I have freedom. I don't have to pretend anymore, about anything, to anybody. I know who I am.

I also know that if I don't keep it simple and do the basics, if I don't continue to make my amends and try to be a better person, wherever I am, and if I don't pass on these secrets about staying sober over the long haul to others, then I'll lose it all.

Come to think of it, a funny thing happened to me on the way to becoming the governor of Texas. . . .

16

KEEPING IT SIMPLE:
Phil, Sober Forty-one Years;
Ray, Sober Forty-three Years

At AA meetings you hear people talking about all kinds of problems, like relationships, but they're complicating things. Alcohol is the problem. If they'd just follow the AA program, they'd see that it's all nothing to get drunk over. —*Phil*

I wouldn't take ten minutes to look back to see why I became an alcoholic. Intellectualizing this thing is a waste of time. The cause of alcoholism is alcohol. Period. It has nothing to do with anything else. And to recover from alcoholism, you have to stop drinking alcohol. If you're not drinking alcohol, then the disease of alcoholism doesn't enter into your life. It couldn't be more simple. —*Ray*

To most recovering alcoholics, especially the younger ones, forty years without taking a drink or any other mind-altering chemical is almost incomprehensible. Some have *fathers* who weren't even born yet when these old-timers decided to sober up! Newcomers don't understand how these older members can even remember what it was like to get drunk, but the old-timers will tell you they can remember very well. Even a whiff of booze brings it all flooding back to them.

Whenever a forty-plusser stands up at an AA podium to celebrate another AA birthday or anniversary, there's usually an audible gasp in the room, a sense of awe. If he did nothing more than just sit around looking wise, he'd still be valued by the group. But, of course, if that's all he did he'd probably drink again.

Old-timers, as we've seen, have much to offer. Perhaps one of their most valuable gifts is the constant reminder to "Keep It Simple." Ironically, it's the same reminder that Dr. Bob, AA's quieter cofounder, often had to give Bill W.

According to our own old-timers (Hugh and Warren from earlier chapters and Phil and Ray in this one), all of whom knew Bill Wilson personally, Dr. Bob and Bill balanced each other out like partners in a healthy marriage: Wilson was the idea man, the one with the vision; Dr. Bob, the sensible one, was the one who was able to keep Bill grounded when he started flying too high on the wings of his passionate enthusiasm and occasional grandiosity. For example, when Bill wanted to open a string of alcoholism treatment hospitals "all across the land," Bob was the one who gently restrained him by commenting, "That's a good idea, Bill, but let's remember to keep this thing simple." And Bill would listen to him.

Today, old-timers are helping to balance out the many potentially disruptive influences in AA by giving newcomers the same advice. The newcomers would be wise to listen.

PHIL

There aren't many of us old-timers left out here, so pay attention: Work the steps, don't drink, and don't die, and you'll be fine.

Phil, seventy-seven, is a solid, large-boned, and prominently featured man of nearly six-and-a-half feet tall. He and his three younger brothers were born in Virginia and later moved to New

York. Phil is unaware of any other alcoholism in his family. "But for me, drinking came as easily as shining my shoes. I loved to drink. I could drink anytime—even when I first woke up. Sometimes it did me good, sometimes it did me dirty."

Phil has been married three times and has two sons. His third marriage is still intact. By age sixteen, Phil had already had his first drunk-driving arrest, for which he spent a night in a drunk tank. "That's when I learned never to take the lower bunk!" At the same time, Phil also had his mind made up that he was going to become an actor. "I just had a feeling for acting, and I stubbornly refused to get sidetracked." He took tap-dancing lessons and ended up as the youngest chorus boy at the Brooklyn Paramount.

Unfortunately, his drinking was getting rapidly out of control. Having developed a pattern of drinking *at* people, Phil would often get into an "I'll-show-them" mood and lash out. Usually, however, *he* was the one who ended up getting hurt. On the evening of Pearl Harbor when World War II was declared, Phil got drunk, told off his stage manager, gave notice—and found himself in the army for five years, two-and-a-half of which were spent smoking "ganja weed" in India, China, and Burma.

After his discharge—"honorable" despite the ganja weed—Phil came back to the states, resumed his show business career, and managed to do fairly well. Eventually it brought him to Hollywood. One night he accompanied a friend to an actors-only AA meeting. "But I didn't for a minute believe that I had a problem, nor did I believe those guys were sober. I just thought they were a little loose in their loafers and should probably be seeing psychiatrists."

Phil went out on the road again, and his addiction progressed further. He began having some really low moments. For example, he'd married, and as a direct result of his drinking, his wife nearly died in childbirth. While she was in a hospital awaiting a life-saving operation, Phil was drunk in a bar. When he finally showed up, he passed out on a couch in the waiting room. In the middle of the night he was awakened and told to "sign this." It was the consent form for his wife's operation.

> After I saw my wife and son, I went out and got drunk again. I was gone for five days. When I showed up, the doctor chewed me out. "Where the hell were you? You were supposed to take your wife and son home days ago!" "I was celebrating," I said, to which he replied, "You celebrate too damn much!" But my wife wasn't surprised. "Oh, you were out with your drunk friends, eh?" was all she said. Yet she had almost died because of *me*.

Phil finally hit bottom a short time later while appearing in a play in Louisville, Kentucky, during Derby week. He emerged from a blackout one night to learn that he'd had another of his "I'll-show-him" fights, this time with a fellow actor right on stage! That was his moment of clarity, when he finally realized he was in trouble and needed help.

He remembered the meeting of Alcoholics Anonymous he'd attended in California, and thinking that it was the only meeting of its kind in the country, he hung on until he could get back there. He *did* get back there, and he's been sober ever since.

Phil's singleness of focus, his stubborn refusal to get sidetracked, and his ability to "keep it simple" probably had a lot to do with how he managed to sail through those early years of sobriety without problems. Just as he'd made up his mind to become an actor at age sixteen, once Phil resolved to become sober, that was it. So it never bothered him in the beginning that others around him were drinking. "I'd just say, 'I'll have some coffee or cola.' " Nor did it bother him if he ran into people he knew at AA meetings. "Everybody and his brother knew I was a drunk, so why the hell shouldn't they know I'm sober?"

Phil believes that learning the basics is what makes AA work.

When I got sober the old-timers were rough on us. "Do it our way or no way," they'd say. My sponsor often told me to "sit down, shut up, and listen." When I'd ask him why I couldn't talk, he'd say, "Because you don't *know* anything, that's why!" The only thing I was allowed to do was make twelve-step calls. AA says, "If you go talk to another drunk, *you'll* stay sober." They taught us what we had to do to survive. I didn't want to do those things, but I figured there must be a reason why I had to. When I was five years sober, the reason came to me: If I *hadn't* done those things, I'd have been dead by now. Instead, I was sober five years.

Many of these new kids come sailing into AA, fresh out of chemical dependency treatment centers, with their $20,000 AA "Big Books" under their arms—which they've never read, of course—and they think they're a new breed. They assume that, because they mostly used cocaine or dropped pills, their status is different and they don't have to do the basics the rest of us alcoholics were taught to do, that they can just skip all that stuff and play it by ear, and it's all going to work out okay. Well, that's probably why only about eight out of a hundred of them stay sober.

They complicate things. By introducing themselves as "addict/alcoholic" or "cross-addicted" or some such name, they become totally confused. They forget that alcohol is a drug too. It was the first drug we knew about, the original drug. I ask them, "Why can't you say you're an alcoholic, period, instead of using all those hyphens and slashes?" And they say, "Because we took pills." Hell, I don't know any alcoholic who didn't take pills! There weren't many pure alcoholics even back in Bill W.'s day. He took pills, Dr. Bob took pills, they *all* took pills. I took pills before these kids were born. I had cocaine when I was eleven; it was called Coca-Cola! But I don't go around saying I'm a "cross-addicted cocaine/alcoholic." Alcoholism doesn't recognize the new breed from the old breed. If you're an alcoholic, you're an alcoholic. Next question?

Phil isn't for kicking these people out of AA meetings, however. Over the course of his forty-one years of exposure to the AA philosophy, he's learned to trust the AA process.

> The people who come into AA for the wrong reasons, who are just playing games, won't last. They'll work their way out. Eventually they'll fall on their faces, so we might as well give them the right to be wrong and find out for themselves.

By doing the basics and by keeping it simple, Phil has been able to stay sober despite career ups and downs, and even despite seven cancer operations since 1979. Possibly the biggest blow in his sobriety was the death of his lifelong friend, Eddie.

> He and I were friends since we were kids, long before we both ended up in AA, and I didn't think I could live without him. I was in the hospital myself when I received the phone call, and I sat straight up in bed and said, "God, why Eddie? I could have given you the names of five other guys you could have taken instead!" That's how badly it affected me.

But Phil stayed sober and continued to "do the Twelve Steps," especially the twelfth step—working with others.

> Back in the old days when they told me I'd stay sober if I went to talk to another drunk, I believed them. I don't do twelve-step work because I'm a saint; I do it because I'm an alcoholic, and it keeps me alive. I do the basics. So my advice to newcomers is this: Don't complicate things. If you're an alcoholic, go to meetings, sit down, shut up, and listen. It might just save your life.

RAY

Without us, you newcomers don't have a chance!

Ray, seventy-three, is a tall man with gray-white hair and a businessman look. He has spent most of his forty-three years of sobriety working as a salesman. He and his sister were born in Nebraska. The family later moved to Colorado. His father was a successful mortician who retired at age forty-eight. Like Phil, Ray was the only drinker in his family. He started drinking at age twelve, by fourteen he'd crossed over the invisible line into alcoholism, and by thirty he was in AA. He has been married three times—once while drinking and twice in sobriety. He has three sons by his first marriage. For the past thirteen years Ray has been married to a woman he met in AA who has thirty-one years of sobriety. They live in Los Angeles.

Ray is a man full of contradictions. Although he came from an affluent family, he rode the rails and ended up on skid row three different times, in Kansas City and in San Francisco. He was an altar boy yet remained an agnostic for more than six years into his sobriety. In trouble with alcohol and the law early in life, he was sent to military school (from which he graduated) rather than reform school. When he finally decided to go to a meeting of Alcoholics Anonymous, he was sitting in, of all places, a *bar*.

Ray was an angry, violent drunk. Although AA has taught him a few tricks ("Now I just walk away!"), he admits that even with forty-three years of sobriety he still has an ongoing problem controlling his anger.

"I killed two men in violent drunken arguments, and another time I killed three men when I drove a car off a cliff in the Colorado mountains. In that accident I also paralyzed my good friend and put him in a wheelchair for life."

The only way Ray was able to live with himself after these tragedies was to "rationalize away" his responsibility in the matters.

> It was always everybody else's fault. It was the county's fault that I drove the car off the cliff, because the railing on the curve at the end of the hill had been knocked down and the county hadn't replaced it. It was cold and icy and I skidded, and it was all "their fault." That kind of reasoning allowed me to survive. But, of course, I knew better. Having been raised in Colorado, I knew

perfectly well that it wasn't normal to be coming off the mountain that fast at that time of year. I shouldn't have been driving at all.

Sylvia: Were you badly injured in that accident?

Ray: Not *badly* injured, just injured. We dropped 2,000 feet in my car, but for some reason I wasn't seriously hurt. And later on I killed somebody else, though I didn't do it deliberately. It was in a basketball game. At that time I was considered one of the top basketball players in the state and this guy was outplaying me. I didn't like it. So I hit him hard to knock him through an open window, and he fell down one floor on his head and was killed. Of course everybody, including myself, was able to say it was an accident. Even his parents said it was an accident. But I knew that I shouldn't have done that.

By age twenty-five, Ray's drinking was so bad that he tried to stop but couldn't—The obsession had him by the throat. "I went to a drying-out place, but forty-five minutes after I was discharged I was back in a bar. I wasted a lot of good drinking money on that treatment!" Ray couldn't even keep a job.

> I'd take umbrage at something and be gone. My attitude was, "There's another job across the street so to hell with you!" And where people were concerned, it was the same thing: "There's always another pebble on the beach, so if you don't like me then I don't like you, and I don't care. I can go someplace else." That's why I bummed around the country on freight trains.

But being a hobo and a skid row bum is exhausting work. By thirty, Ray finally hit bottom. He was sitting in a bar when a friend cajoled him into going to an AA meeting, and he went. He liked it. He committed to it. And he has never wavered. At this first meeting, a black man named Jim all but appointed himself as Ray's sponsor.

He was a guy I never would have gone out with for a drink, yet here in AA I was letting him tell me what to do. He really laid things on the line. I talked to that man every day for the next eight years until he died—sober.

In those early days, old-timers were hard on newcomers. If you still had a car or even a watch, they'd tell you that you weren't ready to get sober. The old curmudgeons still think like that. Younger members treat newcomers with kid gloves. They say, "Newcomers are the lifeblood of the program." But back in the old days, old-timers would say, "*We're* the important people around here, so do what we say." As a result, we didn't seem to have this revolving door phenomenon that you see today, where people are in and out of AA constantly. I was astounded the first time I ever saw a man drunk at an AA meeting. He had a bottle in his hip pocket, and he fell off his chair and broke the bottle, leaking that whiskey smell all over the room. It was fantastic! But I felt sorry for him. I thought they weren't going to let him back in because he drank!

I had to go to meetings seven days a week, and in those days there weren't that many meetings, so you'd go a long way to find one—a different place every night. We'd all drive together and have a meeting going to the meeting, and then we'd have another meeting coming home from the meeting.

Around the time of Ray's first AA birthday, his parents came to California to disinherit him and take his wife back to Colorado with them. But after seeing how much AA had changed him, they returned to Colorado without carrying out their mission.

Unfortunately, Ray's first wife was one of those women who couldn't seem to adjust to her man's sobriety. She tried to sabotage it with remarks like "For Christ's sake, Ray, we were better off when you were drunk. At least *then* I got to see you. At least *then* we had sex!" They divorced.

His second marriage—to an extremely jealous wife—lasted only forty-five days.

I discovered that as bad as the disease of alcoholism is, jealousy is worse. I never cheated on my wife, but she'd be waiting by the door every night when I came home with the same broken record. The first thing she'd say was, "Who did you sleep with today? I called the office and you were out." And I'd say, "Don't do this to me. I'm a salesman. Ninety percent of the time I'm out." But she'd persist, "No, I know you were sleeping with somebody." I finally had to walk out on that one.

His third marriage is still intact.

Sylvia: Did you ever meet Bill W. or Dr. Bob?

Ray: Bill W. many times, and he deserves every accolade he gets for the program of Alcoholics Anonymous. But my biggest regret is that I never met Dr. Bob, because to me *he* is the backbone of Alcoholics Anonymous—the one who was able to keep Bill's feet on the ground, who was able to keep it simple. If Bill had been allowed to go at his own rate, we wouldn't have this program today. He would have upset it. He had quite an ego, which he himself was painfully aware of, and sooner or later it would have gotten in his way.

Sylvia: How did that ego show up?

Ray: In wanting attention. When Bill was out in California visiting his mother, he used to drop in on AA meetings and clubhouses unannounced. Once he and a friend dropped by the old "6300 Club." Bill walked into the cardroom where some guys were playing cards. There was this big picture of him on the wall, and Bill went and stood right under his picture, but none of the guys in the room paid any attention to him. Finally, one of them realized that this was Bill Wilson, and he said to the group, "Hey, guys, this is Bill." One of the guys looked up from the card table and nonchalantly said, "Oh, hi, Bill. What's the bid?" Well, Bill was absolutely enraged. He turned around and said, "Let's get the hell out of here!" Another time my friend Al took Bill to visit an AA guy in the hospital, and the guy said to Bill, "You know, your face is familiar, but I can't put a name to it." Again, Bill turned to Al and said, "Let's go!" and walked out.

But it was a whole different experience talking to Bill one to one. I was often included in lunches he had here in L.A. with friends, and when you were sitting across the table from him, when he didn't have to be "on," he was a marvelous man to talk to, full of information and witticisms. And he also made a conscious effort to avoid "forcing" his personal opinions on AA as a whole. We'd try to pin him down anyhow. I'd say, "Bill, I want an answer to this question, and I want your opinion," and he'd say, "Well, Ray, you know, if you look at it this way . . . and then again, if you look at it that way, and cha-cha-cha." Then I'd accuse him of being a fence sitter. I'd say, "Is that why the New York office won't make a definite statement about anything?" He'd just grin and usually commented, "Yeah, settling fights isn't their function, or mine. That's up to you people here to decide for yourselves." He just wouldn't get caught up in it, and he was right. It's when he started making his grandiose plans that he got into trouble. That's when Dr. Bob would step in and say, "Remember, Bill, let's keep this thing simple."

Ray, like Phil, has concerns about AA's future.

Ray: Today I don't worry about things—not death, not illness, not financial setbacks. Today the only thing I worry about is the continuation of Alcoholics Anonymous. Bill W. once said that if AA gets destroyed, it will destroy itself from within, and sometimes I'm afraid maybe that's what's happening.

Sylvia: What did he mean by that?

Ray: He meant that AA will be destroyed if people don't abide by its simple principles, like the principle of focusing on only one issue, alcoholism; the principle of anonymity; and the principle of twelve-step work, of one drunk talking to another.

I think the problem started originally when the New York office decided to let other self-help groups use AA's Twelve Steps and adapt them to their own purposes. Suddenly the powerfulness of AA seemed watered down, and it became more and more bastardized by these newer groups like Narcotics Anonymous, Overeaters Anonymous, Gamblers Anonymous, and all the other spin-offs since then, like Pills Anonymous, Sexual Addicts Anonymous, Emotional Health Anonymous. Next it will be Masturbators Anonymous. I wouldn't be surprised if there already *is* a Masturbators Anonymous!

The next mistake was to let the cocaine, heroin, crack, and PCP addicts into AA meetings and let them start *talking*. Now they're overrunning the halls. The alcoholics are beginning to feel pushed out of their very own meetings. In some parts of the country, AA meetings have become so bastardized that you can't even *find* a meeting for true alcoholics. I don't deny the addicts the right to come to AA, but unless they are willing to publicly identify themselves as "alcoholics," I do deny them the right to *talk*. Both Bill W. and Dr. Bob warned us early in the program that we cannot be all things to all men, yet it seems like that's what we're trying to do. I'm afraid that it won't work, that it'll destroy us. There are other places now for these people to go and be with their peers. But AA was established for the alcoholic who has the disease of alcoholism, and that's how it should stay. I'm beginning to hear more and more people, like myself, who are beating a drum for keeping AA for the alcoholics. We have to start telling the addict, "Look, no offense, but this meeting is for alcoholics only. If you want to stay and listen, fine. But if you want to talk, do so at your own anonymous group." That's the only thing we can do to protect our organization in the years to come.

Another of Ray's major complaints has to do with twelve-step work.

Ray: Today, nobody takes the time to teach the newcomer, to oversee his progress, and to make sure he is reading the "Big Book" and working the Twelve Steps. They're just letting the newcomer come in and wing it, as if he could get it all by osmosis. And if the newcomer doesn't get what he needs to survive, he'll drink and die. I didn't like the twelve-step work when I got here, but now I know it's critical. I have a minimum of ten to twelve calls a day from people who want to talk. I can remember a time before I got to AA when *nobody* wanted to talk to me.

Sylvia: What about all the recent anonymity breaking in the media?

Ray: I decry that! It's ironic that in the beginning nobody would own up to being an alcoholic because of the stigma. I can remember when I first started doing AA twelve-step work by going into prisons to speak. Not only was I strip-searched, but I heard the guard get up on the phone to the upper compound and say, "The wino's on his way up. Tie everything down!" And on the way out, I was strip-searched again and heard a similar comment, "The wino's leaving. Check to make sure nothing's missing." But today membership in AA is socially acceptable; it's a claim to fame, it's trendy. Times have indeed changed! Going to an AA meeting is now a social event. But making a social event out of Alcoholics Anonymous is a bit like making a social event out of chemotherapy. Pretty soon you forget that the purpose of the treatment is to save your life!

Sylvia: What about anonymity for celebrities in AA?

Ray: AA is full of celebrities and the tradition of anonymity is intended to protect them, too, not just the rest of us drunks. AA members are not supposed to blab about who they've seen at meetings, but many do. It's as if they think anonymity is out of style. They just don't seem to get the spiritual reasons for it. They're too caught up in this damn "Let it all hang out" business, and they don't understand that there are times when silence is golden! This has really become a problem in Los Angeles because of all the famous faces in the program. But these prominent people would like to go to a meeting in peace without having somebody ask them for an autograph. That's not what they're there for. They're there to save their lives!

It's understandable why men like Phil and Ray feel so passionately about the survival of AA: they owe their lives to AA.

> I'm a very fortunate guy to have been a part of this thing. Because of AA, today I live without fear, without resentments, without hate, without secrets. I remember sharing once at an AA meeting about the first time I ever saw a nude woman lying on the embalming table in my father's mortuary—about how I touched her breasts. If I hadn't been in AA, I *never* would have told anybody about that, ever. But the wisdom in AA is that if you can share your secrets with somebody else, you will *both* be freed.
>
> Without AA I never would have looked at my shortcomings, and I never would have gotten honest with myself about who I am. It ultimately showed me how to take responsibility for my own actions.

Alcoholics Anonymous says that, after alcohol itself, the Number one killer of alcoholics is resentment. Why? Because a festering resentment will inevitably lead the alcoholic back to drinking again to kill the pain. To deal with resentment, the alcoholic needs to learn forgiveness, the most spiritual lesson of all. Ray learned about forgiveness, not as the result of dealing with his resentment toward somebody else, but as the result of witnessing how somebody dealt with their own resentment against him. Teachers are everywhere.

One year when I went back to Colorado to visit my parents, my mother said to me, "Please go and see *H.*" *H.* was the friend I'd put in a wheelchair for life when I drove drunk off that cliff. I didn't want to go see *H.*, but I knew I had to. To this day, it was the hardest thing I've ever done. I drove around the block until my conscience said, "Do it!" I knocked on the door. *H.*'s mother answered and I introduced myself. Then, in a very cold voice, she said, "I know who you are." When I walked into the living room, *H.* was sitting there in his wheelchair. I said, "*H.*, you know I've put off coming to see you. I just couldn't bring myself to do it."

And he said, "I know, Ray. Don't worry about it. Your dad has been filling me in about the work you've been doing through AA, your work with the prisons and the hospitals. I want to tell you something. The first two years I was living in this chair, all I could think of was how I wanted to get even with you, what I could do that would be worse than what you've done to me. I deeply resented you, and I wanted to maim you so badly you couldn't even sit in a chair. Thinking about that was an all-absorbing activity for me.

"But then one day a couple asked me to look after their children at the playground and keep an eye on them. I decided to do it. And after a short period of time, when I'd go out in the morning here would come all these kids to help me down the ramp, and they'd bring me their puppies and their kitties, and we'd play. Then they'd wheel me back home.

"After that, the coach in the high school asked me to do the same thing with the basketball team, and I've been supervising them for over twenty years. These boys are like my own sons; they bring me their problems and I become totally immersed in them. I want to thank *you* for that, because if you hadn't put me in this chair, I'd never have had that opportunity. I really thank you."

257

By the time *H.* had finished talking, we were both crying. When his mother came back into the room, he said to her, "Everything's fine between Ray and me now, Mother." A few years later when he died, his mother wrote me a lovely letter saying what a good life he'd had.

Without AA, I would never have known that. I'd have said, "Well, the poor son of a bitch, he's crippled, so what? It's not my fault. It's the county's fault. After all, the railing on the curve at the bottom of the hill had been knocked down and the county hadn't replaced it. . . . "

Alcoholics Anonymous has been the same program for over fifty-five years. It's a simple program for complicated people, and it works! The fact that the world is full of AAs is *proof* that Alcoholic Anonymous works. And that's all I need to know.

EPILOGUE
Sobriety 2000

Without heroes we're all plain people and don't know how far we can go.   —*Bernard Malamud*

The twenty-one recovering alcoholic men interviewed in this book started out looking more like antiheroes than heroes. But they became heroes along the way. In the process, they took us on some "mighty adventures," as one of them put it, and proved that one hero's example can inspire us all.

If their stories tell us anything, it's that no story ever ends. Sobriety isn't one event; it's an on-going experience with both good times and bad times along the way. It's life. There is always more to learn and more to do. No doubt these men will be learning and doing until they finally end up at that great big AA meeting in the sky. Three of the twenty-one, as we've learned, are already there.

The journeys of these men offer the rest of us hope. They prove that people *can* change, change dramatically, and *stay* changed—something that hasn't received enough attention. When these men first dragged themselves into AA, all they were looking for was an end to the pain. They wanted to get sober, stay sober, and die sober. (After all, it's not very "heroic" to die drunk.) This motivation wasn't self-improvement, it was survival. The fact that they made it is remarkable. The fact that they learned the art of living along the way is even more remarkable. It proves that anybody can become a hero if he is willing to do what it takes.

AA's Survivability

The men interviewed here feel they owe their lives to Alcoholics Anonymous, so it's understandable that they are worried about AA's future.

Once upon a time, AA members feared that the organization wouldn't survive because it was too small and too unknown. Today, members fear that it won't survive because it is too big and too popular. Old-timers cringe when they see AA's honored traditions (like the tradition that members remain anonymous at a public level) broken, especially by movie stars and sports figures who hit bottom publicly, go into treatment publicly, admit to AA membership publicly, and sometimes slip—publicly.

AA members also worry that all the twelve-step spin-offs will result in watered-down programs with only minimal effectiveness. Some also worry that the influx of drug addicts (drugs other than alcohol, that is) will have a negative impact.

Bill Wilson, AA's cofounder, was once asked if he ever felt afraid that AA was going to fall on its face.

> Many times! Especially when there was in-fighting. But after a few years it dawned on me that dissidence is the mother's milk of AA. Somebody doesn't like the way an AA meeting is being run, so they go off and start their own meeting. Then you've got two meetings instead of one. At first when this sort of thing happened I thought, oh-oh, there it goes—they're going to wreck this thing, tear it apart. But now I know that AA survives on cooperative disagreement. That's what makes it grow.

Sponsor Jack has had personal experience with this phenomenon:

It's like cell-division. An AA Men's Stag meeting that I started at my house with only eight guys, is now up to fifty guys on a small night, eighty guys on a big night. Another meeting that I started ten years ago is now six different meetings.

So Sponsor Jack isn't worried about AA's future.

By now it's clear to me that AA has taken on a life of its own and no one can destroy it. You simply cannot affect that which cannot be affected. Even if AA became outlawed in the United States, somebody, somewhere, would start a meeting and we'd have AA again. AA is, in a word, unstoppable.

AA As a Family, Tribe, or Herd

This unstoppable force, Alcoholics Anonymous, is more than a sum of its parts. It's an emotional place. Many describe it as the functional (as opposed to the *dys*functional) family they never had. Others say that being an AA member is like having their own "tribe" so that no matter where on earth they travel, AA is there to welcome them. In his book *The Craving Brain*, author Ron Ruden, M.D., describes AA as a "herd." He cites animal studies which offer evidence of the healing power of the herd. In a herd of oxen, for example, if one ox gets separated from the rest, he becomes acutely anxious. When he finds his herd again, he'll plow right into the middle of it until he's surrounded by his own kind. Only then will he begin to relax. Many people view AA exactly the same way.

Sobriety 2000

Here are some of the elements that are already impacting, and will continue to impact, the addiction field:

261

Increased AA flexibility

As more people walk, wander, stumble, or are sent into Alcoholics Anonymous, the organization finds itself in the position of having to bend to accommodate diversity. Sponsor Jack is convinced that flexibility is the answer.

> We have an obligation to tailor AA to the kinds of people who are flocking into it these days—drug addicts as well as pure alcoholics; people who are younger (the age-level of recovery is continuing to fall); people who still have all their toys; people from detox hospitals and treatment centers; insurance company rejects; employees who've been caught in Employee Assistance Program (EAP) traps, or caught in workplace drug screen traps; people who've been sentenced to AA by the courts; reluctant people; people with dual addictions (e.g., alcoholism and sex addiction); people who have a dual diagnosis (e.g., alcoholism and a bipolar disorder); people who are on medication; more women and more teens than ever. All kinds of people in all kinds of circumstances.

Alternatives to AA

New addiction assessment tools (along with the old standbys, like the well-known Johns Hopkins University *20 Question Test for Alcoholism*), and new treatment alternatives, give both the addicted man and the addiction professional more choices than ever. Treatment wise, even for those who don't want to venture beyond twelve-step groups, there are, to date, some 135 spin-offs to cover all the addictions: Alcoholics Anonymous, Cocaine Anonymous, Narcotics Anonymous, Marijuana Anonymous, Pills Anonymous, Overeaters Anonymous, Gamblers Anonymous, Debtors Anonymous, Adult Children of Alcoholics, Codependents Anonymous, Sex Addicts Anonymous, Emotional Health Anonymous, and the list goes on. "Recovering people need to be able to identify with others of their own ilk, even if it means going to five 12-step groups for five different addictions," author Ruden states. "If you're hungry *and* thirsty, and then you drink water, it still won't take your hunger away."

New attitudes

Men in recovery after 2000 are likely to show up with a new set of attitudes. There's an upside and a downside to this. The fact that a man comes into AA younger, richer, healthier, and less burdened with shame and guilt over his addiction (because he believes in the *disease theory*, and in the *genetic* and *biochemical* aspects of his condition) is good. Less denial and resistance can mean a faster recovery. The downside is that as a result, AA has less leverage over him. The addicted man thinks he still has options. He thinks if he doesn't like something in AA, he can go elsewhere for treatment, or simply come back to AA another time when he's in a better mood—or when AA has changed its ways. He may not be "willing to go to any lengths" to get sober, may not be desperate enough to do "whatever it takes—no matter what" not to drink or use again. As so many who have gone before have found out the hard way, this attitude can kill them.

Lessening of the "right to drink" mentality

Alcoholics have long been able to trade on a shared attitude in this culture that somehow they have an unchallengeable "right" to drink, no matter what it does to other people. Society's attitude is changing on this one. Groups like *Mothers Against Drunk Driving* and individuals, weary of being victims, have helped see to that. Today's talk is of the rights of the community, not just the rights of the individual. Laws against drunk-driving are getting harsher. This is even having an influence on normal drinkers who are beginning to watch their own intake for fear of getting nabbed on the highway.

The Internet

This phenomenon will continue to keep bringing a wealth of information on addiction to those who need it. There will no doubt be even more on-line twelve-step meetings taking place in real time, and more chat rooms, allowing people in recovery to communicate with each other all over the world, and in other languages. Who knows what the impact of new technology, such as TV phones, will be. One only has to use one's imagination to think of the possibilities.

Genetic research

Ongoing research on brain chemistry and genetic involvement in addiction may soon challenge what we *think* we know about the causes and treatment of addiction—and make it all irrelevant.

Pharmaceutical research

That "pill" for addiction may happen yet.

What Every Hero Should Know About Character

By the time a man has been sober a few years, he begins to figure out that staying off the sauce and dope is just *part* of it. The other part is becoming a hero, a man of character. There's a practical reason for this: If he keeps misbehaving, even if he remains sober, he won't be able to live with himself. His conscience will bother him, and then there's a good chance he'll drink or use again.

The other thing he figures out is that it's not easy being a hero—at least at first. Within AA it's easy. He gets unwavering support for becoming more honest, more responsible, more self-disciplined, for keeping his promises and commitments, for showing a willingness to work hard, for respecting the rights of others, for listening, for not jeopardizing important relationships with bad behavior, for not letting people down, for confronting situations that need confronting, for having integrity, for being faithful and loyal. And primarily, for not caving in to his impulses (if he still has them) to drink or use—no matter what.

The problem is, while AA supports these virtues, the outside world often does not. Or so it seems initially. When the sober man starts to step out into the Big World again, expecting a pat on the back for seeing the light, he finds that nice guys are still finishing last, and bad guys are still getting ahead, and nobody seems to care that he has cleaned up his act. He tries to act like a prince and sees others getting away with murder. He tells the truth about his alcoholism on an insurance application, and then gets turned down for coverage! Where's the justice in that? It doesn't seem fair. He feels his efforts are unappreciated. He's tempted to throw up his hands. His sponsor or therapist or AA buddy tells him it doesn't matter what other people are doing, if he wants to stay clean and sober he's still got to keep acting like a hero.

Fortunately, the man who gets sober today may find a lessening of this jarring clash of value systems (AA's vs. The Big World's). As pointed out earlier, the word "character" has finally started creeping back into our language after having been effectively filtered out of it for years, so hopefully AA members will find the Big World more *simpatico* in the future, more supportive of his attempts at virtue. It sure would be nice if, outside the AA world, the vocabulary of character didn't seem like a foreign language.

Why the culture is starting to worry about character again is anybody's guess. Maybe it's just because it's time for the pendulum to swing back again. Maybe it's because crime and other social ills have been giving us visions of a *Mad Max* society on the horizon of the new millennium, complete with anarchy and chaos, and that's scary. Maybe some of the 1990's news stories have made us aware of what we've been missing. Or maybe it's just nostalgia for the picture we have of "the good old days" when a man's word was his bond; when business deals were sealed by a handshake.

The Perks of Character

Many, many years ago a drunken used car salesman from Laguna Beach, California, found AA and sobered up. After he'd been around the program for awhile and saw what it was all about, he made a bet with himself: He bet that he could make more money by being honest with his customers than he ever had by lying to them. When he retired in his early seventies, he was a millionaire many times over. Having "character" paid off.

It may not *seem* as if people are paying attention to the man who has integrity, but the truth is, if you have it people will spot it. And when they have a job that requires a man who has all the traits that go along with that word, they'll think of you. Any man, inside AA and outside of AA, who struggles to live an honest life, gets rewarded in the end. He may not end up a millionaire, like that used car salesman, but chances are he can now live in his own skin and that feels good. It's true what they say: Virtue *is* its own reward.

And obviously, the contrary is also true. When a person is dishonest, disloyal, undependable, out for himself, that also shows.

The guy you wouldn't feel safe with in a foxhole is probably the guy with character problems, and you're picking up on it. Just think of the people you know. Can't you sense who has character and who's just trying to get away with something? Which friends shade the truth? Which ones never do what they say they're going to do? Which ones are "flakes"? Which ones falsify their expense accounts? Cheat on their taxes? Cheat on their women? Expose confidences? Backstab? People *think* they can con other people and get away with it, but nobody really gets away with anything. Without even realizing it, they're always giving out subtle cues and waving red flags that tell you they can't be trusted. Other people know (not always consciously) that they're being lied to. In most business relationships, when you get caught in a lie, the business relationship is basically over.

AA, then, teaches a man how to get sober, stay sober, and cope with life. That's a good deal.

For those interested in pursuing this hero-training theme further, I've included Appendix C, *How To Upgrade Your Character.*

The Secret of Success Is . . .

When AA says that alcoholism is *cunning, baffling, powerful,* and *patient*, that's a warning. It means that sobriety is tricky and slips are common. But if you make it—especially if you make it to "hero" status—the rewards are immeasurable. That should be clear from the twenty-one stories in this book.

It takes persistence (another virtue) to make it and stay there. It takes turning away from the nay-sayers who warn you that your chances are slim to none. It takes ignoring the fact that some people are getting away with things you can't get away with any longer.

If the twenty-one men in this book didn't think it was worth it to hang in there, they wouldn't have done it. They are fully aware that eternal vigilance is required, that no matter how "long-term" they are, they're never out of danger. The obsession to drink or use may have gone away, but chances are it didn't go far. It's always hovering in the wings, ready to pounce on those who let down their guard even for a moment.

AA members *train* for this moment. Their training consists of going to twelve-step meetings year after year even when they don't feel like it (how you feel is considered irrelevant), and even if they hate AA (liking AA isn't a requirement). The deal is simple: Just go there, sit down, and listen. Everything else will take care of itself. If you slip, try again. That's it. That, and learning some of the clichés and using them as life-preservers: Live "one day at a time" (which means don't project down the road, just do the task at hand); "work" the twelve steps of recovery (learn all those great coping tools); "do service" (mentor or sponsor others), which has a paradox built in: "You can't keep it (meaning the perks of sobriety) unless you're willing to give it away."

"The *real* secret of long-term sobriety," says one old-timer, quoting a famous line, "is that you just *outlast 'em*!"

APPENDIX A

The Generic Addiction Quiz

"**P**eople slip into all kinds of patterns of behavior that can eventually become destructive and counterproductive," says addiction specialist Jokichi Takamine, M.D. "Whether something's an actual addiction depends on how far you carry it, and whether or not you eventually lose control."

But how do you know when you're carrying a habit too far? When should you start to worry that you're drinking too much, eating too much, having sex too much, spending too much, gambling too much?

If you're worried that you may be losing control, this 15-question quiz will help you decide.

Pick an activity or substance that's causing you concern and answer the questions below by checking Yes or No. Retake the quiz for each activity or substance you're involved with—once for alcohol and once for cocaine, for example. Your score on each one may differ.

1. Is somebody in your life complaining about whatever you're doing or using?

Yes / No

When people closest to you start telling you there's a problem, they are not "on your case," they're telling you the truth.

2. Do you think or obsess about doing or using during times when you're not?
Yes / No
If you're thinking about your next drink or line or meal ahead of time, you may have a problem.

3. Has your using or doing increased over the last year or two?
Yes / No
For many, increased tolerance is a major symptom of addiction. First you need a six-pack, then a twelve-pack to get the same results. It's progressive.

4. Does what you're doing or using negatively impact your work, school, love, sex, family, social, health, financial, legal, creative or spiritual life?
Yes / No
If it's having a negative impact on any major area of your life, maybe you've crossed over the line into addiction.

5. Do you ever find yourself doing or using more than you intended?
Yes / No
What distinguishes an addict from someone who just likes to do something is lack of choice. If you can't stop, then you no longer have a choice.

6. Do your peers influence your doing or using?
Yes / No
If so, you may not be doing what you really want but what your addiction wants.

7. When it comes to what you're doing or using, has "want" become "need"?

Yes / No

When wanting the activity or substance gradually and insidiously starts becoming a coping mechanism rather than merely a pleasurable activity, that spells trouble.

8. Do you ever blame anybody or anything else for the extent of your doing or using?

Yes/ No

Addicted types usually make excuses or blame others. They'll say, "It's my job; it's the pressure; it's the boss; it's the wife; it's the kids—it's not my fault."

9. Could you comfortably go without what you're doing or using for a month?

Yes / No

One of the classic tests of addiction is to abstain for a week or a month and see what happens. If you're truly addicted, you'll have physical and/or psychological withdrawal symptoms and you may start doing it again before the time is up.

10. Has your reputation with your family, friends, and associates been tainted by what you're doing or using?

Yes / No

Somebody who's overdoing an activity or substance will usually attract the attention of those around him. They'll get a "reputation." What do you imagine your reputation is?

11. Have you ever noticed your mood changing when you're doing or using, or even just anticipating it?

Yes / No

271

Activities like sex, gambling, thrill-seeking sports, spending, and exercise can elevate brain dopamine levels and make us feel high. So can substances like food, drugs, chocolate, nicotine, and alcohol. When we're addicted, our mood usually improves noticeably when we do or use these things.

12. Do you ever cover up, minimize, or tell lies concerning something you're doing or using?

Yes / No

Denying there's a problem is another classic symptom of addiction. It could mean that on some level you agree that what you're doing is wrong and may be out of your control.

13. Do you ever make promises to stop what you're doing or using, only to break them later?

Yes / No

Breaking promises is also typical addictive behavior; it could mean you're hooked.

14. Do you ever feel guilt or shame about what you're doing or using?

Yes / No

Sometimes we feel guilty for good reason.

15. Did you ever stop what you're doing or using, only to slip back?

Yes / No

That should show you two things: that you have a problem, or else you wouldn't have tried to stop; and that you're addicted, because you couldn't stay stopped.

Answers: If you answered Yes to three or more of the questions above, you may be addicted to the activity or substance you had in mind when taking the test. If so, begin dealing with the problem by educating yourself, going to a twelve-step meeting, or seeing a doctor or psychotherapist who specializes in addiction—and take it from there.

APPENDIX B

Seven Steps to Trigger
a Spontaneous Remission

Once you get this far, even if you haven't turned the corner yet, you're in a much better position to experience the most fascinating (and least talked about) phenomenon in the addiction recovery field—*a spontaneous remission*. Following are seven actions you can initiate to trigger such a state.

1) **People Actions:** Put your body where they're talking about your primary problem. If your primary problem is alcoholism, then a twelve-step meeting is one obvious choice. Go be with other alcoholics who want to stop drinking. Talk to them. Press the flesh. You're not in this alone. People *can* motivate and inspire others. It's been happening since the beginning of time. If AA's not your ticket (for now at least), then go to an addiction lecture, take a workshop, anyplace where there are other people focused on the same subject—addiction. It's a myth that you have to have a good attitude or "really want to change." Spontaneous remissions can happen to cynics with lousy attitudes. What changes your attitude is the spontaneous remission itself. A good attitude isn't a requirement for a spontaneous remission, it's a result. Spontaneous remissions can happen to people who've never even heard of them. When the timing is right, that silver dollar you drop into the slot machine is going to deliver a jackpot no matter what your belief system is or what you're feeling at the time.

2) **Physical Actions:** "The feet are the wheels of thought," wrote a famous mathematician. Sometimes the only way to get free of our chains is to get physical: Run, jog, play squash, swim, paint the house, wash the dog, simonize the car, even pace back and forth—just like you see people doing in movies just before they say *Eureka!* It is difficult to jog and get bogged down in deep thoughts at the same time. This is good because mind-chattering is what keeps your real wisdom (your intuition) buried in your subconscious. When you get physical and eliminate the mind-chattering, your real wisdom has a chance to pop into consciousness. And sometimes what it says is: "Time to stop drinking, buddy! Now!"

3) **Intellectual Actions:** Are you an information junkie? If so, this may be the way to go. Read everything about addiction that you can get your little alcoholic hands on. Cram, as if about to take an exam. Articles, pamphlets, books, radio, and TV shows. Surf the net. There is more information on the Internet than you could possibly download in a lifetime. Every new fact you absorb is like another silver dollar in your slot machine. Any one of them could trigger a spontaneous remission. You'd be amazed how many people have been "triggered" into sobriety by learning that alcoholism is a disease and not a moral issue. This fact alone has freed a lot of guilt-ridden souls, and let them see their illness differently so that they were willing to turn themselves in for help. Facts have the power to break through denial. The Internet is a great place to get "facts." Anything you ever wanted to know about addiction but were afraid to ask can be found on-line. You can even "attend" AA meetings on-line in "real time"(meaning it's going on live, right now. What you type into your keyboard is read by as

many as fifty other people at the same "meeting" and they can respond right back). While on-line AA meetings might not be as good as eyeballing another recovering alcoholic, it can be a savior for alcoholics who are housebound or don't live in big cities and can't get to meetings.

4) **Quiet Actions:** If you don't like people, don't want to get physical, and hate to read, then try something more on the quiet side, like meditation. It's just another way to turn off the mind-chatter and let that "still, small voice within" be heard, and when you hear it, it will probably tell you to quit drinking. Ancient Chinese wisdom has an expression for it: *"If you are still, it speaks. If you speak, it is still."* In the East, meditation has been the preferred method of hunting down transformational experiences for thousands of years. Aside from learning how to meditate (and there are books and tapes to teach you how), there's prayer, self-hypnosis, silent chanting, rhythmic breathing, float tanks, daydreaming, guided imagery with tapes, gazing into a fire, or sitting in a hot tub staring at steaming bubbles.

5) **Nutritional Actions:** You are what you eat, or drink, or ingest, or snort. That's why mood–altering chemicals can hurt you. They get inside. But there are people who have gotten sober just by changing their diet. What kind of diet you pick, or what you decide to add (vitamins? herbs?) or eliminate (sugar? carbs?) is up to you. Maybe changing even one thing can tip the scales just enough so that a spontaneous remission is triggered.

6) **Contrary Actions:** *"What we resist persists,"* it says in the *Sermon on the Mount.* Sometimes you can fight addiction too

hard. Simply piling on more and more AA meetings, or checking into yet another treatment center, won't increase your chances of getting sober. And the discouragement factor can set in and make it worse. People get frozen, stuck. That's when it might be a good idea to cut loose, do something paradoxical that might seem to have nothing to do with your goal of sobriety. Instead of stepping up your AA meetings, go take guitar lessons, or ski, or see a bunch of new movies, or visit a new place as far away from home as possible. New places are great perspective makers. You can't count on this to work, and maybe you'll end up drinking or using more than ever, but it's worth a try.

7) **Hitting Bottom:** This is not supposed to be a joke. It's a truism that rarely fails: When the pain of drinking or drugging gets bad enough, you'll either die from it—or change. *No pain no gain.* Some people seem to be able to take a ridiculous amount of pain, loss, humiliation, and sorrow. Too bad for them, because they're the ones who may be just too tough for their own good, who may not cave in to sobriety and survive. Hopefully, your breaking point will come before it's too late. Sometimes the only advice you can give a man who thinks he's tried everything is to tell him to keep on drinking or taking those lousy chemicals. Sure, it could kill him, but what you're counting on is that *this* time out he'll hurt so bad that he'll have a spontaneous remission just to make the pain stop. "Hitting bottom," then, is a legitimate way to court a healing. It's just not much fun.

APPENDIX C

How to Upgrade Your Character

Alcoholics Anonymous teaches men how to get sober, stay sober, and become heroes in the process—men of character. Once a man gets a whiff of what having "character" feels like, he usually likes it and he wants to learn more about it. Here are some hints and tips on how to upgrade your character that are consistent with AA's teachings:

- Basically, character means doing the right thing, so whenever something happens and you don't know how to handle it, ask yourself: "What's the *right* thing to do?"— and do that. It's that simple.
- Get your house in order (literally and figuratively). Clean up your messes. Pay your debts. Repair past damage and get it behind you.
- Find meaningful work.
- Educate yourself about what character is. Read books and magazine articles about the qualities that make up a "hero." Talk about it. Think about it.
- Apprise your own character, determine what's lacking, and set specific goals to change your behavior. Start with short-range goals and work up. Examine your progress each day.
- Seek role-models and teachers and mentors for support.
- Make truth a discipline. Don't toy with it, and don't shade it. Go one day without telling any lies, then two days, then a week, and so forth. Bust yourself for lying.

- When you've practiced not lying, then start telling the truth. However, this doesn't mean using truth as a weapon to hurt people. Learn the difference. Be clear about your motives before uttering what you assume is "truth." There *are* times for silence or even for a "white lie," but don't abuse this fact.
- Get clear about your life goals, then make sure your actions match them.
- Keep your promises and commitments.
- Learn how to evaluate the character of others, to get better at distinguishing the good guys from the bad guys. Get good at spotting red flags others wave at you. As Grandma would say, "Burned once, shame on them. Burned twice, shame on you."
- Guard your reputation. It's your only one.
- Before you act, think the action through to its logical conclusion. Philosopher William James said, "The moral act is to think." Better to take a short-term loss and not lie, steal, or con—because in the long run it's better for you, and better for society.
- Make a commitment to be helpful to others. Do volunteer work, mentor, or sponsor others. In AA it's called *twelve-step work*.
- Don't lose heart. Sure, there are lots of scumbags out there who seem to be feeling no pain and are getting away with murder, but keep the long-view in mind. All you need to do is look at history to see that what goes around comes around.
- To *feel* good, *do* good. That's how self-esteem is created.

INDEX